HARD LYING

THE STORY OF THE "V&W" CLASS DESTROYERS AND THE MEN WHO SAILED IN THEM

by

Cliff Fairweather

HARD LYING

ISBN 0 9529440 4 9

Typeset, printed and bound in Great Britain by Avalon Associates

Published by
Avalon Associates
23 Dunmore Road
Chelmsford
Essex CM2 6RY
United Kingdom

1

"HARD LYING"

THE STORY OF THE "V&W" CLASS DESTROYERS

AND THE MEN WHO SAILED IN THEM.

* * * * * *

This book is not particularly about the statistics of the ships, but of the experiences of the men who sailed in them, related to me over a period of ten years, in mainly their own words, you may find some of the stories similar because those telling them served on the same ship. Most of them will now be well into their eighties, and nineties, some will have already 'crossed the bar'. To all of them I am very grateful.

Having never previously attempted such a task I apologise for any shortcomings. I sincerely hope that I have not infringed any copyright laws, wherever possible the stories are as related to me, therefore the phraseology, punctuation and spelling are those that were used by the authors.

A number of Royal Naval Officers were discussing the virtues of the various classes of destroyers, when one mentioned the old V&W class. One officer then said "Oh yes the old V&Ws, but they did not do much did they?".

I will leave the reader to judge whether this officer was correct in his assessment.

Chapter 1

Ship, boat, rust buckets, call them what you will, but over a period of almost twenty years they were the pride of the British Fleet. They were fast and sturdy, and proved to be very good seagoing vessels. From 1917 when the first took to the waters to beyond WW2, they served in every part of the world, from China and the Far East to North Russia and the Arctic, from Newfoundland to the Mediterranean, they served with great distinction in all theatres of war.
Between the wars, most men serving in the Royal Navy, at some time during their career became part of the crew of a V&W destroyer. So this is the story of these old rust buckets (a name acquired in the latter years of their lives) and the men and boys (although the boys soon became men) who served in them. If you were fortunate enough to have served on one, other members of the service treated you with respect.
These destroyers evolved from the need of a fast torpedo carrying destroyer, as well as having the armament to engage an enemy on the surface and in the air. They were also capable of laying mines in enemy waters besides being armed with depth charges, and as one of these ships is called "Versatile" so was the whole class. In their early days they were the pride of the British fleet, a terrier and a bull dog all wrapped up in one sturdy frame. Their weight was approximately.1100 tons they measured 300 feet in length and 30 feet at the beam, their draft being 11 feet and with 27.000 horse power, which produced a speed of 30 to 35 knots, which made them, at that time the fastest destroyer afloat.

* * * * * *

The first two were built in 1916 and were given the names "Malcolm" and "Montrose" but as it was required to maintain the alphabetical system they were then changed to Valkyrie and Valorous. These two prototypes were built by Denny's of Dumbarton and proved to be the ideal answer to the Admiralty's requirements. They were armed with four 4-inch guns and four 21 inch torpedo tubes and were by far the heaviest armed destroyers at that time.
Soon other shipyards were engaged in the production of these vessels. Cammell Laird's were very soon in production, their first to be launched was the "Valentine", which came off the slipway in March 1917. John Thornycroft & Son produced the "Viceroy" and "Viscount" to their own design which had six 4-inch guns. Another feature of the Thornycrofts was that their funnels were slightly different, being flatter in shape, unlike the "Woodbine" funnel forward and a shorter fatter (cigar) funnel amidships,

which was the distinguishing feature of this class. Other shipyards joined in as the Admiralty placed their orders, J. S. White built the "Vectis" and "Vortigern" and so it went on, most of the shipyards in the country were at some stage engaged in the building of them. Until, after the initial seven leaders, 26 with their name beginning with "V" followed by 32 "W's" were all completed and launched. In addition the orders for 37 others were cancelled! Had they all been completed and launched it would have made quite an amada!

* * * * * *

1917

It was not to be long before they would see action, and indeed sustain casualties. The first of these was the **Valkyrie** who was mined whilst escorting a convoy in the North sea on 22nd December 1917 although the damage was extensive she managed to make port and was eventually repaired which meant almost a complete rebuild. The **Warwick**, was also struck by a mine, again the damage was severe and she bore the scar for the rest of her days. It was months before she was able to resume service. It was then the turn of the **Vehement** another mine victim, unlike the previous two, she did not survive, the terrific explosion which occurred left her with nothing forward of the funnels, however what remained of her remained afloat and the efforts of other destroyers to sink the remains by gunfire failed, only depth charges set shallow and dropped only a few feet away sent her to the bottom. The fact that these ships had survived such damage shows without doubt the strength of the their construction Besides those mentioned two of the leaders had also been lost. Throughout the first world war only one of the V&Ws could claim a "kill." On the 27th July 1918 the **Vanessa** depth charged and sunk the U-boat 107 after it had been spotted by a trawler.

* * * * * *

One of those ships, (my ship) that was to be worked hard was the **Westcott,** she was on active service during most of her life until she was finally scrapped in 1946. The following stories give a good indication of this:-

Chapter 2

Sub-Lieutenant Henry McCall went on board the **Westcott** for the first time on April 1st at Dumbarton where she was being fitted out, on completion of which the advance crew joined, she then carried out her first trials during which she recorded 35 knots over the measured mile. After inspection and the acceptance trials, she set out for the Forth. Her first trip took just thirty hours at an average speed of 25 knots. McCall wrote at the time, "The ship herself is a wonderful craft, absolutely "IT" in the destroyer line, with a compliment of 115. A fine ship and it is up to us to make her a fine fighting unit" **Westcott** was to be involved in a number of incidents in the coming months.

During the six weeks up to 8th June as part of a striking force, the ship crossed the North Sea many times, having clocked up 400 hours sailing time and run 5-6000 miles. She then carried out exercises with the British Fleet before escorting the Furious who's planes bombed the Zeppelin sheds.

On the 24th October McCall wrote "We went out for a three day trip and got it properly in the neck. It was the first bad trip that we have had in this ship and it shook everybody up a lot. They were all fairly new to the sea except for the older hands, and absolutely new to rough weather in destroyers. The wardroom staff were incapacitated to a man. Taking up screening stations on the battle cruisers we got properly knocked about. The fore gun shield was flattened out over the gun, the plating of upper works for'd bent in, ammunition racks torn out, the mast nearly carried away owing to a shroud parting."

On 9th November the war ended and **Westcott** started a boiler clean. "Sir David Beatty, C in C made a signal ordering the main brace to be spliced according to a time honoured tradition, which everyone did with right good will." This was the second time most of us celebrated the event, as we had a trial run a few days earlier when a false buzz came through. But oftener the better! How the false buzz came through no one knows, but it was very authentic.

Celebrations for nine of the V&Ws (**Valkyrie, Veralum, Veralum, Vendetta, Wakeful, Wessex, Windsor, Wolfhound, and Woolston**) was very short lived, for they were dispatched to the Baltic to show the flag against the Bolshevik regime. At that time the Baltic was strewn with mines laid by the Russians and Germans and it was not to be long before casualties would occur. One of our cruisers, the Cassandra struck a mine and started to sink, two of the V&Ws (**Vendetta and Westminster**) immediately went to her assistance and in total darkness and freezing temperatures took her crew off.

On 21 November. Westcott sailed with the Grand Fleet to attend the surrender of the German Fleet, and Lt McCall wrote: "At 8am the German big ships loomed up out of the mist. The visibility was poor, somewhat similar to Jutland. First came five battle cruisers, then followed nine battle ships and next the light cruisers. Last of all, in one line came fifty destroyers. We proceeded to get them organised into a cruising formation and surrounded them on all sides, 120 of us. The whole fleet proceeded in and anchored east of Inchkeith, the destroyers in Aberlady Bay. That in itself was quite a feat, 173 destroyers, and the whole lot came to anchor in beautiful formation. Thus was the German Fleet, that was built to defeat the British Navy, and so the British nation, led into our ports like a flock of lambs without one effort to contest us after four and a half years of war, during which time it had hardly dared to show itself even in the extreme limits of the North Sea." The last order to the German Fleet from Admiral Beatty: "The German flag will be hauled down at sunset today Thursday, and will not be hoisted again without permission."

A demoralised fighting force is a depressing thing to see. The moral of the German Navy was the first to go and led to the rapid collapse of the rest of the country.

On 1st December 1918 Lt McCall took over command of HMS **Westcott** while the captain was temporarily elsewhere and on 28th the captain having rejoined, the ship went to Scapa Flow to keep watch and ward on the Huns for three weeks. There he wrote "The Huns are now at anchor, guarded by our battle squadron and half a flotilla. We were guard destroyer on New Year's night."

In March 1919 the ship took mails to Hamburg, and on the 11th May he wrote "The C Class Cruiser (Coventry) had a commission on board examining all the ships in the port, and the Commander said the ship (**Westcott**) is the best looking destroyer he had ever seen."

Chapter 3

THE BALTIC

The Bolshevik conflict of 1918-1919 brought them into action again, where the 13th flotilla was deployed, and once more, casualties would occur but not without first showing their metal. On boxing Day 1918,
one of the large Russian destroyers began bombarding Tallinn where the British ships were at anchor. Many of the British officers were ashore attending a banquet given in their honour by the Estonian officials. **Wakeful** however soon raised steam and set out to investigate. At the sight of the British destroyer bearing down on her, firing her guns, the Russian immediately turned and fled at high speed, sending a signal saying "All is lost. I am being chased by the British." In her haste the Russian vessel ran over a shoal damaging her propellers and rudder. The Russian crew must have been very inexperienced for they caused much damage to the ship and she slowly began to sink. The **Vendetta** who had come up in support, sent a party of seamen to board the stricken vessel and remove anything of value. One of the items removed was the ships bell, this was duly installed on the **Vendetta** where it remained until the end of her days. On examining the Russian ship, the **Vendetta'**s engine room artificer examining the situation in the engine room concluded that it could be kept afloat simply by closing the sea-cocks and pumping out, this was done and she was towed back to Tallinn to great victory celebrations.

Chapter 4

1919

In January 1919 the 2nd flotilla took over from the 13th who returned to Rosyth. Soon the 2nd flotilla was strengthened by the 1st flotilla.
Whilst this was going on an unusual incident occurred. Early June, Midshipman Brian De-Courcey-Ireland aboard the **Westcott** recorded the following incident.
Westcott, had been for some weeks in Hamburg. A country in defeat is a depressing spectacle, when orders were received to make the crossing to Harwich in daylight hours at thirty knots, for large areas of the German Bight were still waiting to be swept of mines. The danger from moored or floating mines were less for a destroyer travelling at high speed. It meant however that they must anchor off the island of Heligoland for the night. They were glad to be away from Hamburg, It was a calm evening as they hove to in ten fathoms, clear of the southern arm of the outer breakwater. The harbour was empty of shipping. The little town nestling at the head and the foot of red sandstone cliffs appeared to be deserted. The ships company wondered whether any of the great eleven and twelve inch batteries were still manned and how many eyes ashore were watching them. Sentries were posted forward and aft. When the light began to fail the ship was darkened.
At about 21.30 hrs the quarter sentry reported the faint sound of motor boat engine somewhere off the stern. We stood to. It was quite dark now. The Captain was debating whether to carry out a sweep with the searchlight, when a cautious hail came over the water.
"Warship, ahoy. Permission to come alongside? We have a petition."
Please." the voice was urgent.
"Do not show a light."
Permission was given. A minute later an open boat crept out of the night, drawing alongside the ships quarter. Lowering a Jacob's ladder, four men climbed up the side. Their leader climbing over the guard rail, saluted and addressing the officer of the watch in English he said "My name is Nickels. I am chairman of the Elders of Heligoland. With me are representatives of the Islanders. May I speak to the Captain please?"
Leading them down below, they explained their mission. They were very unhappy under German rule. For centuries they had governed themselves. Then for eighty years, had belonged to England. It was against their wishes that in 1890 they had been sold to Germany, in exchange for concessions in East Africa. The years that followed had been of increasing oppression as

their isolated rock had been turned into a fortress, culminating in that fateful day in July 1914, when they were turned out of their homes at six hours notice, and interned on the mainland. They were only allowed back a few months before our visit. They had found many of their houses looted or still occupied by the German garrison. In great secrecy they had drawn up their petition

waiting patiently for a British Warship to call. At last, to their joy, they had seen us and, under cover of darkness, brought off their document. It was written in English and in their Frisian dialect. With touching faith it was addressed to:

THE SUPREME COUNCIL OF THE ALLIES NOW SITTING AT VERSAILLES TO DECIDE THE FATE OF NATIONS:

As the Captain took it from the Chairman, a dawning of recognition came to his face, but all were completely unprepared for his question.

"What was your last ship Nickels?"

The reply rang out proudly "Master at Arms of the Glory, Sir, 1907 I remember now, Sir, you were one of the midshipmen."

That was one of those moments that will live forever in ones memory. There is not space to tell his full story here. Suffice to say that he joined the Royal Navy as a boy in 1887, when Heligoland was under British rule. He served for over twenty-two years and, when he took his pension and retired to his native home, he found he was under German rule. What followed was the all too familiar pattern of Prussian bullying arrogance. Through it all shone the courage of this man, whose loyalty and faith never faltered, and who led the Islanders in their fight for freedom.

The petition?.

When they left the Officers read it. The poignancy of the concluding paragraph will be remembered forever.

"We Heligolanders, in our little Island in the middle of the sea, far from the worlds commotion, form the very smallest nation that has for centuries retained its independence and local customs. We seek neither wealth nor ostentation, but desire only to live our lives in peace and contentment as our Fore Fathers did before us."

Alas, their prayer was not answered. Did some statesman, wise to the problems that assent might raise, pause before he ruled reluctantly against? Or was it pushed indifferently aside by a mind hardened by politics, blind to the trust of simple men? Just another little Island. Another inconvenience of history to be buried and forgotten.

Chapter 5

Westcott, at full speed made her way back to Harwich. She then made her way to Scapa with the **Wolsey** to take up duties guarding the German Fleet. She remained at immediate notice for steam at a buoy in Gutter Sound from where they could view most of the seventy surrendered ships. It was about noon on the 21st June 1919. Most of the officers were in the wardroom having a drink before lunch, when suddenly the senior Sub Lieutenant Tony Coombe who was officer of the watch shouted down to the wardroom that one of the German ships was sinking. "Don't talk such tripe" said Captain Charlie Peploe. "But there is" came the excited reply. They all to a man dashed up on deck to find that every German ships had hoisted their flag and appeared to be sinking, all around they were lowering their boats and Jacobs ladders. The German seamen were abandoning their ships en mass. **Westcott** ordered the Germans to get back on board, when they ignored the command she opened fire with her Lewis gun spattering the ships side just before the gangway, they scampered back, others were donning life jackets and jumping over the side.

There was complete chaos all around. **Westcott** went to as many ships as possible parting their cables so that they might drift ashore. They then turned their attention to the battleship Hindenberg who seemed to be rather slow in carrying out the scuttling Captain of the **Westcott** Lt Cdr Peploe ordered the first Lieutenant, Henry McCall, Lt, Brian DeCourcy-Ireland an Engineer Officer and a party of ratings to board her and as the **Westcott** tried to push her to shallow waters they closed as many watertight doors and scuttles as they could. Working in the dark and in an unfamiliar ship the task proved difficult and the great ship began to sink so they eventually had to abandon their task, but the upper superstructure remained above the water line. The survivors were soon rounded up and interned.

HMS Westcott on convoy escort duty. North Atlantic 1941

HMS Westcott with the Home Fleet 1918

Photograph by courtesy of the I.W.M

Chapter 6

Then it was back to the Baltic where the 2nd and 3rd flotilla's were engaged mainly in bombarding the Bolsheviks military and forts ashore, and once again **Westcott** was to see action, as the following pages will show, although not all were of a violent nature.
Brian De Courcey Ireland recalls:-
We were ordered to join our flotilla (2nd destroyer flotilla) based at Byorko Sound in Finland at the extreme end of the Eastern Arm of the Baltic, on the way we were to call in at Libau in the state of Latvia to report on the situation there.
Somewhere perhaps in some dusty file is the copy of a brief, "letter of proceedings:"
"Sir, I have the honour to report."
The little Baltic port lay still and almost deserted in the autumn sunlight. The long breakwater of concrete blocks protecting it from the sea was intact, as was the stone pier reaching out from the shore; but in the harbour, the rusting upper works of two steamers and the masts of two wooden schooners, protruding above the water, told their story. On the pier a line of cranes, their jibs leaning drunkenly at odd angles, and the rotting roofless warehouses, completed the picture.
The town had fared no better; along the front facing the harbour the houses bore tragic witness to the havoc of war. Some were heaps of rubble or burnt out shells; others had been patched with salvaged material in an attempt to provide some sort of shelter from the coming winter. The road was potholed and rutted, cluttered with mounds of half cleared debris and the wreck of abandoned vehicles. A few people picked their way through the litter, their features grey and drawn, and adding to the air of despair and death that hung over the place like some dreadful miasma.
We felt our way cautiously in through the entrance at dawn, and secured alongside the pier. After an interval, a small group of men had appeared, and contact was established. They had brought an interpreter who spoke remarkably good English, and soon he was explaining the situation. He spoke in a flat voice, devoid of expression, drained of emotion, the voice of a man who had seen so much and been through such terrible experiences, that no hope or spark or feeling was left.
"When they first came in there was some resistance, but there was little we could do. Nearly all the men were away fighting, and we had few weapons. But those that could, sold their lives dearly. For the first two days after the fighting stopped they did little, and we began to hope. Then came the order.

All the women between the ages of 15 and 40 were ordered to parade on this pier. The houses were searched, and those found hiding or trying to escape were dragged here and shot. The German soldiers then formed a line, and two by two the women were taken into that hut and raped. Their particulars were all written in a book; oh yes, the Germans are always thorough. Afterwards the women had to report, and if a child was born it was taken from the mother at six weeks, and sent to Germany to become a German. Twice this happened during the occupation."

The terrible recital went on. A woman in ragged skirt and black shawl drawn close about her face, drifted aimlessly by, her lined face and vacant stare haunting in its tragic setting.

The interpreter paused. "That was one," he said. "Two children she had."

"How old" I asked.

"About eighteen" he replied.

I began to feel sick with the horror of it, and behind one of the sailors exclaimed, "Oh my Gawd". Maddox was cleaning the shield of "Y" gun on the quarter deck. As the gun layer of "Y" gun he held himself responsible for the cleanliness and proper working order of the gun and gun mounting. And woe betide anyone who laid a hand on it without his permission; not that anyone was particularly anxious to be on the receiving end of Maddox's opinion of his ability, efficiency, or ancestry.

As I passed:- "Any chance sir, of having a go at the swine what did that," he asked nodding shore wards.

I looked at him in some surprise. Maddox was not given to opening any conversation, by nature he kept himself to himself, and seldom spoke unless riled.

"A slight hope," I replied. "They say ashore that the Huns are advancing up the coast again. Why, do you feel strongly about it?"

"I got what you might call a special interest," he answered and relapsed into silence. I know he would not be drawn any further.

It was a few days later when the Captain spoke to the ship's company.

"I need not remind you," he said, "of what we saw and heard at Libau, few of us will ever forget it. The German army, force, call it what you will, has been located camped on the shore road twenty miles of our present position. This force consist of an estimated 4,000 men under the command of a Prussian officer. It is not in any sense a regular formation, but lives off the country, and is reported to be preparing to move northwards again. An ultimatum was delivered to the Commander of this force. He was to commence evacuation of this area within 48 hours and to return with his force to German territory. It was made clear to him that unless he struck camp and was seen to be

moving south by the time set, punitive action would be taken against him by H.M ships."
The Captain paused. "I understand that the German Commander replied, "You will not dare, I will blow your little ships out of the water, I will go where I like."
A ripple of amusement stirred the intent faces of the sailors.
The Captain continued. "The time limit set has now expired. The third subdivision has been detailed to carry out the punitive action. We are now proceeding to a position close inshore. When the enemy has been located, fire will be opened and continued for fifteen minutes. I want to make it quite clear to you all that this is a punitive action, and I expect rigid fire discipline and self control. There may be opposition, the rest of the flotilla will remain in support to seaward. We shall close up at action stations in two hours time. Dismiss the ship's company please First Lieutenant."
The low shore line, with its flat sand dunes was clearly visible now. The gun's crews were standing alert and tense round their mountings. The Layers and trainers had their eyes glued to their telescopes and the range finder crew were calling out the ranges as we closed in. A puff of smoke came from near a sand dune, followed by another, and a couple of shots from a field gun came ricocheting across the water and passed between us and our consort.
"Open Fire!" Ordered the Captain.
The ship shuddered and shook to the crash of the 4.7's. I fired two salvo's to get the range, and then changed into "Independent," with the foremost gun concentrating on the field gun battery. The crews were working like demons, sticking rigidly to their drill. Even without glasses I could see the terrible carnage on shore. The field guns were silenced under a hail of fire, tents and vehicles were burning, ammunition boxes exploding. Men were running blindly in every direction, a few even plunged into the sea. Our consort was plastering the road, shifting fire to and fro. There was no escape, they were trapped.
"Cease fire."
Our ears were singing with the crash of the guns, the smell of blistering paint and cordite were in our nostrils, the canvas screen round the bridge rail hung in tatters. The gun crews stood panting with exertion, sweat streaking from their faces. Some of the loading numbers had stripped to the waist, and as they begun the task of sponging out and stacking the empty cartridge cases, their bodies glistened in the sun. I made my way from gun to gun, receiving reports from each in turn.
When I reached the Quarter Deck the crew of "Y" gun were still sponging out. Able seaman Maddox was squinting carefully up the barrel from the

breech end. “One more with the clean rag lads,” he said “and she’ll do.” He looked up. “49 rounds, Sir,” he reported, “and I ‘ad good targets for them all.” That’s three more than anyone else,” I said. He grunted with satisfaction, and gazed at the receding shore.
“I’ve waited four years for this,” he said quietly, “and when the War was over I never thought as ‘ow I’d get another chance.” He turned and looked at me, his eyes burning. “I ‘ad a kid brother,” he said, cabin boy in the merchant service, just turned fifteen. ‘Is ship was torpedoed by a U.boat. They got away in the boats, but the bastards surfaced and fired on them. ‘E was hit in the face and died slowly before they was picked up two days later. It broke our Mother up.” He jerked his head to the shore. “I paid some of that off today,” he said.
I went up forward again to my cabin on the break of the foc’sle to file the reports. It was a bit of a shambles, the blast from “A” gun had broken the bookshelf off the bulkhead and the water jug had been shaken out of its rack and the contents upset. I began to clear up, and as I picked up a book of verse written by a soldier in France, I remembered the verse that had been written by a Tommy who had seen his mates killed by a sniper when reading a letter from home:-

There’s some as fights for freedom,
And there’s some as fights for fun.
But me my lad I fights for bleedin’ ‘ate
You may blame the war and blast it,
But I ‘opes it won’t be done.
Till I’ve got the bloomin’ blood price for my mate.

Is that where it ends, I wondered. I heaped the books on my bunk and went outside. We were up with the flotilla again, and as we swung round into station astern of the leader, the signalman was hauling down a flag signal and restowing the flags in their locker.
“What are the signals.” I asked.
“From us,” he replied “Operation completed.” And from the Leader “General to Flotilla. **Westcott** take up station in the van. She will lead the Flotilla on the return to Byorko.” Said the Leading Signalman. They manned ship and cheered us as we passed up the line.

❧

Chapter 7

We then proceeded on our way to Byorko Sound in Finland.
As we steamed past the point, on which was a small lighthouse, the sound opened up, and soon we could see into the anchorage and the two lines of destroyers at the far end. The Leading Signalman started making our pendant number with his signal lamp, and in a few moments the Leaders lamp was answering.
"Ask for an anchor berth," ordered the Captain, and to the Officer of the Watch, "Send down and tell the first Lieutenant, and warn the engine room that we shall be anchoring in half an hour." A few moments later I heard the Bosun's Mate pipe, "Special Sea Duty men close up, cable party muster on the foc'sle." And so it went on, all the normal routine for entering harbour.
The Leading Signalman came forward with the reply to our request for an anchor berth, written on a pad. He seemed slightly embarrassed, and read it out nervously.
"Anchor in position five cables, 268 degrees from Niki Point, end of B line. Behave yourselves and eyes down for Leika."
"What did you say?" Asked the Captain. The Leading Signalman repeated the message.
"Someone on the signal deck trying to be funny?" demanded the Captain suspiciously.
"No sir, truly sir," replied the unfortunate man, "I got a repeat to make sure."
"Oh well," said the Captain, "Captain D like his little joke. I suppose we'll learn what he means soon enough."
It took us two days to realise that there was something most unusual connected with our anchor berth. On the afternoon of the second day we were working ordinary part of ship routine. I happened to be on deck more than I would normally have been. Gradually it dawned on me that a large number of men appeared to have discovered some work that required to be done on the port side of the ship, the side facing the shore only a few cables distant. I next observed the Quarter Master on watch gazing through the trainers telescope of "Y" gun which was trained on the shore.
"What the blazers are you doing?" I asked. The quarter Master emerged somewhat sheepishly, and murmured something about practising.
I let it go at that and turned my own gaze shore ward. Immediately opposite the ship was a sandy beach, studded with a few large boulders. Sitting with her back against a rock reading a book, was an elderly woman, clad in black, holding a parasol, while running up and down near the waters edge was a girl. Nothing exceptional about that except for one thing, the girl, or to be more accurate, young woman, was as naked as the day she was born!

Smugly I went down to the Captain's cabin and knocked at the door. "I beg your pardon Sir," I said, "but I have discovered who Leika is, she is a young woman."
"And what is so remarkable about that?" Replied the Captain. "Have you never seen a young woman before?"
"Oh yes Sir, of course Sir" I said. But this one has not got any clothes on."
The Captain leaped to his feet. "And what precisely is she doing without any clothed on, if it is not a rude question?" He demanded.
"I think she is swimming off to the ship, Sir."
The situation on deck was rapidly assuming crisis proportions, for it was indeed true. Leika was in fact swimming vigorously towards the ship, and obviously aiming for the accommodation ladder on the port quarter. Reaching the platform at the bottom of the ladder, she hoisted herself gracefully up on to it, and sat there like some beautiful mermaid. Wringing out her long hair, she coiled it skilfully on top of her head, and after a friendly wave called out cheerfully, "I speak little Inglish."
I should perhaps explain here that, contrary to the beliefs of the younger generation, it was quite normal etiquette in the Baltic seas in those early days of the twentieth century for people of both sexes to bathe without costumes, it would in fact have been considered prudish to wear them. Leika was thus only following the custom of her country, and it would never occur to her that it would cause embarrassment. In truth, as a well brought up lady, she would undoubtedly have been distressed had she realised the effect of her appearance upon the British sailor.
Our First Lieutenant was a resourceful and forceful Scot, and before Leika had reached the ladder he had taken steps. The Midshipman had been despatched to find a towel, and armed with this was instructed to go down the ladder, and wrap it round the most exposed contours of the uninvited guest.
Carrying the towel, only too conscious of the number of eyes upon him and the sotto voce advice being freely given, the Midshipman advanced, his face scarlet with embarrassment. Leika stood up, accepted the towel with a polite smile, spread it carefully over the platform, sat down again on one side, and patting the spare section, invited the Midshipman to occupy it. "What is your name called?" She enquired conversationally.
"When you have quite finished your tete a tete," said the First Lieutenant acidly, from his position on the quarter deck, "perhaps you will be good enough to carry out your instructions. If she won't put the towel round her, tell her to go."
"But she doesn't want to go," pleaded the Midshipman.
"Then push her in," replied the First Lieutenant.

The Midshipman stood up reluctantly. “You must go,” he said desperately, “Go swim ashore.”
“Pardon,” said Leika puzzled.
“Go,” said the Midshipman. “Swim.”
Leika stood up. “You swim?” She asked.
“Yes” said the Midshipman, “I mean no.” He gave her shoulder a nervous and half hearted push.
A mischievous look came into Leika’s face.
“Go,” she said, “swim,” and gave the Midshipman a hefty and most unmaidenlike push.
The unfortunate Midshipman caught completely unawares, lost his balance, and clutching wildly at thin air, hit the water with a resounding splash, A hearty but hastily suppressed cheer from the sailors forward, greeted his act.
Leika dived in neatly, retrieved the Midshipman’s cap, which was floating away, perched it jauntily on her head, waved gaily, and in response to frantic calls from the elderly lady in black, swam swiftly back to the beach. “And a fine mess you made of that,” said the First Lieutenant unkindly, as the wretched Midshipman clambered out of the water and stood dripping on the Quarter D. “Now you can take off all your clothes before you go below and cover anymore of the ship with sea water. You may use my towel,” he added generously.
“Permission to go ashore and recover my cap,” asked the Midshipman, with commendable spirit, and disappeared below wrapped in the towel, and with what dignity he could muster.
“Yes I see your point,” said Captain D. We will give you another berth, I think perhaps we will leave B3 berth vacant.”
In the interest of good order and Naval discipline.” Said our Captain.
“Quite,” said Captain D. “By the way, I saw your Midshipman ashore this afternoon, looking very smart. No doubt he was paying a social call. Oh well, we were all young once.”

Chapter 8

Russian submarines were becoming a menace, and their destroyers carried out the occasional sortie but were no match for the V&Ws and made a hasty retreat whenever the British destroyers gave chase and on occasions the **Versatile, Vivacious, Walker** and **Walrus** were involved in exchange of fire, it was also necessary for the V&Ws to carry out depth charge attacks on the menacing submarines when they came across them. However the Bolshevik submarine Pantera torpedoed the **Vittoria** on the night of the 31st August.

Having been a dog trainer and handler for the past forty years, I've learnt that dogs have a perception of foreboding that we humans do not possess. The following is just another example of this:-

September 4th 1919. Officially she did not exist, but unofficially "Lummy" was as much a member of the Ships Company of HMS **Veralum** as any Officer or rating on board. Her great jaw and lumbering gait - she was a bulldog, and was a familiar sight to most of the destroyers crews in the 2nd flotilla. She slept in a specially made and low slung hammock in the galley flat, she had a fine repertoire of tricks, a somewhat regrettable taste for beer and a passion for football. Sporting a jersey knitted in the ships colours, white shorts and a uniform cap, she attended all the ships matches. To the other crews of the "chummy" ships which formed the 4th sub division she was an old friend. It was natural therefore that when we rejoined the Flotilla in Byorko Sound that the Wardroom of the **Veralum** should come over by boat to give us the gen, and bring "Lummy" with them.

The situation was a strange and unreal one. Based on a not too neutral Finland, we were supposed to be giving moral and physical support to a White Russian army under a General Yudenitch advancing on

Petrograd through Estonia. The difficulty was that we seldom knew of the whereabouts, or the identity of our "allies". Admittedly if we steamed close to the fort of Krasnaya Gorka the Reds would open up with their 12inch guns. If we bombarded the shore further to the west, as we were sometimes invited to do, the chance were that we might hit a red shirt, a white shirt, or even a green shirt, the latter being a mysterious body of men who were apparently fighting everybody. Actually the chance of hitting anything but a number of trees in the seemingly limitless pine forest, were extremely remote. Apart from the Russian Fleet at Kronstat, the main hazards other than Krasnaya Gorka, were the unreliability of our charts, the suspected presence of minefields, and the activities of a lone Russian aviator, known to all as Reckless Rupert, who would occasionally fly over and drop a few bombs on the anchorage. Thus when the two Wardrooms got together there was much to talk about.

It was when **Veralum's** boat came for them after supper, that the trouble started. Lummy refused to go down the gangway, and when they tried to carry her down she turned savage, broke away, and retreating under the torpedo tubes, defied all attempts to dislodge her. Eventually it was decided to leave her alone, and as **Veralum** was due to go out on patrol the next morning we agreed to look after her until they returned.

In the morning the dog emerged, and behaved normally. She went for a run ashore with the Canteen Manager, who was buying eggs, and returned in good spirits. But she was off her food, and as the day wore on became morose, lying for long periods with her head resting on her front paws. She remained on deck all evening, and was lying in the
same position when we came up for some air after supper. She seemed to be listening or waiting.

It was I remember, a calm warm night, very dark, and the scent from the pine forest along the shore line very strong. We were discussing what Lummy could be sickening for, when a flash of light momentarily lit up the horizon to seaward. In the pause that followed we all turned instinctively, and the dog raised her head. A moment later an expanding arc of yellow shot skywards, and in the midst of it the debris of a great explosion.

One reacts automatically on these occasions. Before the sound had reached us across the water, the First Lieutenant and the Quarter Master were racing forward, the Chief Engineer making for the Engine Room hatch and I was scrambling down the ladder to the Captain's cabin to report.

When I made my way up to the bridges a few moments later the cable party were already on the foc'sle shortening in the cable, and the Leading Signalman reading out the signals as they were made by the Leaders shaded lantern.

D2 General. Following from **Walpole**. Immediate, **Veralum** mined or torpedoed, position 175 Niki Point 2 miles. After magazine blew up, ship sank in two minutes. Am searching survivors.

D2 general. Raise steam with all despatch and report when ready to proceed, cover **Walpole**. 2nd Division will take up patrol line 155 Niki Point. 1st Division remain at instant notice. Acknowledge.

A dark shape slid by, heading for the entrance, the stand by destroyer. We waited impatiently for the engine room to report ready. The parts of ship were closing watertight doors, and securing for sea, the gun crews were clearing away their mountings.

I worked my way along the upper deck, check as best I could in the dark that all was secure. Just abaft the break of the foc'sle I bumped into a little procession. It was headed by the mess decks Petty Officer, with Lummy next, and the ships butcher bringing up the rear. They were coaxing the dog along and above the roar of the engine room fans I could hear snatches, "come on old girl, got to get below, action stations, doing all we can." As they reached the blackout screen leading into the mess decks the dog stopped and looked up into their faces. Then she moved slowly on through the gap in the screen, and was lost to sight. The mess deck Petty Officer wiped his face, and said something. I didn't hear what it was. I made my way back to the bridge.

Chapter 9

With the help of the British Navy and in particular the V&W destroyers the troubles in the Baltic was now nearing its end and in December 1919 they returned to their depots in the UK Where they were to be reorganised into eight flotilla's comprising of eight destroyers in each with one leader. Some underwent refits with armament being altered, triple torpedo tubes replaced the twin tubes that were originally installed plus other modifications., however conditions on the mess decks remained very basic.

PEACE

Whilst all this was going on the British ship yards were continuing to build the V&Ws, in fact the last V&W to be completed and launched, the **Worcester** was not completed until October 1919 and launched 1922. WW 1 having come to an end and the need for those in the process of being built or laid down diminished, therefore all the orders for the remaining 37 were cancelled.

Chapter 10

1920

It was not long before some of the V&Ws would be back in the Baltic, on a courtesy visit to the Scandinavian countries and the other Baltic ports, this would be the role for many of them, "Showing the Flag" in many different ports in the United Kingdom and other destinations plus exercising with the Atlantic Fleet. Some had a brief spell in the Mediterranean during the occupation of Constantinople.
10th November 1920 HMS **Verdun** had the honour of bringing the coffin of the "Unknown Soldier" back to Britain from France. The whole idea of the "Unknown Warrior" was originated by the Rev; David Railton, who came across a grave with a plain white cross with the inscription "An unknown warrior of the Black Watch". He made the suggestion that an unknown soldier should be buried among the most illustrious dead of the country in Westminster Abbey. The then Prime Minister Lloyd George and HM King George V gave their consent.
Six unknown soldiers that were impossible to identify were exhumed. Each body was covered with the Union Flag and placed in a hut, then at midnight on November 8th - 9th a high ranking officer was blindfolded, entered the hut and touched one of the bodies. Thus the "Unknown Warrior" was selected.
The body was placed in a coffin. The remaining bodies were removed and reburied.
The following morning a service was held in the hut. An ambulance arrived and the body was taken under escort to Boulogne, there the body which was in a rough wooden shell was placed in a plain Oak coffin which had been designed and constructed by the British Undertakers Society and had been made from an Oak tree that had stood in the gardens of Hampton Court Palace, it was made secure by wrought iron bands and a crusader sword was placed on top. The sword was from the personal collection of King George V Lt Commander C Thompson and his officers stood on the deck of H.M.S. Verdun with the ships flag flying at half mast. The Verdun had been chosen for this task as a special tribute to the French for their gallant stand at the battle of Verdun, for the motto of H.M.S. Verdun and the town of Verdun is "Ils ne Passeront Pas" (they shall not pass).
Six barrels of earth from the Ypres salient were put on board to be placed in the tomb at Westminster Abbey.

THE WARRIOR'S PILGRIMAGE
ARMISTICE DAY-1920

The Destroyer "Verdun" Coming Alongside the Admiralty P.er at Dover with the Unknown Warrior Aboard

The "Verdun" passed into Dover Harbour at a little after three o'clock on the afternoon of November 10, and as she entered a Field-Marshal's salute of nineteen guns was fired in honour of the precious burden on the destroyer's deck. The vessel moved up towards the Admiralty Pier alone—the escort remaining outside the harbour—and slowly moved alongside, where her arrival was awaited with the greatest expectancy

The Double Column of Bluejackets Following the Procession as it Left the Cenotaph

The double column of bluejackets made a striking display as they passed the Cenotaph, reuniting behind the coffin for the march to the Abbey. These bluejackets had, in fact, joined the procession at Victoria Station, and marched from there to the Cenotaph behind the gun-carriage. The men moved off from the Cenotaph in perfect alignment, marching three abreast past the monument until the two columns reunited, when they marched six abreast

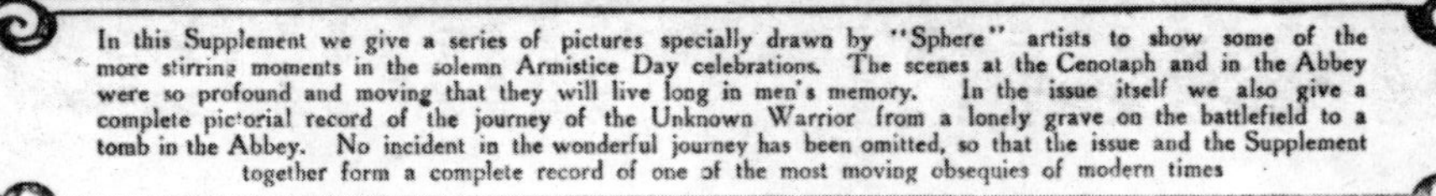

In this Supplement we give a series of pictures specially drawn by "Sphere" artists to show some of the more stirring moments in the solemn Armistice Day celebrations. The scenes at the Cenotaph and in the Abbey were so profound and moving that they will live long in men's memory. In the issue itself we also give a complete pictorial record of the journey of the Unknown Warrior from a lonely grave on the battlefield to a tomb in the Abbey. No incident in the wonderful journey has been omitted, so that the issue and the Supplement together form a complete record of one of the most moving obsequies of modern times

Six destroyers of the Third Flotilla of the Atlantic Fleet waited in mid channel to escort H.M.S. Verdun to Dover.
The ships lowered their Union Flags and Ensigns to half mast. On approaching H.M.S Vendetta flashed the signal "Who are you?" And received the reply "Verdun and escort with the Unknown Warrior" As she arrived in Dover just after three o'clock, and leaving the rest of the escort she made her way slowly to Admiralty Pier, as she berthed, a nineteen gun salute was fired, a band played "Land of Hope and Glory". The coffin was then borne down the gang plank as H.M.S Verdun sounded the "Still" and colours were lowered as the coffin made its way to the Marine Railway Station where the coffin was placed in a railway luggage van to be transported to platform 8 at Victoria Railway Station where it arrived on the evening of the 10th November. With the exception of the wreaths and soil the van remained padlocked.
At 9.15 am on the 11th November the coffin was placed on a gun carriage for the final journey to the Cenotaph where the King was waiting. When the gun carriage came to a halt the King saluted and stepping forward paced a wreath of red roses and bay leaves on to the coffin with a hand written card which read :-

In proud memory of those warriors who died in the Great War
Unknown, and yet well known, as dying and behold they lived.

At 11am Big Ben Struck and on the last note the Union Flags were unveiled the new permanent Cenotaph and a two minute silence began after which the procession made its way to Westminster Abbey. As the procession reached the Abbey the music stopped, the coffin was then borne between 100 holders of the Victoria Cross. The King took up his place at the head of the grave and the service commenced and the coffin was lowered into the grave. The king then sprinkled some of the earth over the coffin, it was then partly filled with Flanders soil, thus making a part of the Abbey a foreign field.
At the end of the week the grave was sealed and covered with a large slab of Tournai Marble bearing the inscription:-

A British Warrior
Who fell
In the Great War
1914 - 1918
FOR KING
AND COUNTRY
Greater Love hath No Man
Than This

Chapter 11

August 1921 they were again back in the Baltic, the 2nd destroyer flotilla embarked upon a cruise visiting all the Scandinavian countries. So on August 31st 9am P.O. George W. Smith aboard the **Vanquisher,** wrote:

We met up with, **Venetia** and **Viceroy** and left Plymouth Sound to rendezvous with **Spencer**, **Victus** and **Winchelsea** off the Isle of Wight. They then proceeded to Deal where they anchored to await the arrival of **Viscount, Violent** and **Wolfhound** and the 2nd light Cruiser Squadron. They took up cruising stations and proceeded to Brunsbuttel, Heligoland was sighted through s slight haze, a loud explosion was heard, it was thought to be caused by the blowing up of one of the forts in accordance with the terms of the armistice. They formed into line ahead prior to negotiating the locks of the Kiel canal.
After being raised ten feet and taking aboard a German pilot, they began their journey through the canal which was lit up with electric light standards placed at about every 200 yards, a number of British as well as foreign steamers passed loaded with Pine, on reaching the end of the canal they once again went into the locks, this time to be lowered four feet to the level of the Baltic. Several obsolete German Battleships and Cruisers were at anchor off Kiel.
The squadron formed up and proceeded en route to Dantzig, during the night the destroyers made a successful practice night attack on the Cruisers.
Sunday September 4th they arrived at Dantzig and were ordered to secure alongside the Torpedo Harbour in the Naval Dockyard which had not been used since the signing of the Peace Treaty, consequently it was overgrown with grass and presented a forlorn appearance. With two others I went ashore to have a look around the place. At the gates of the dockyard we were met by the usual crowd of money changers offering German Marks for one pound notes, the exchange rate being 320 Marks to the pound.
Dantzig appeared to be in a thriving condition, well set out and clean but there was a peculiar smell of burning pine trees. We went into one of the cafe's where I got into conversation with a German who spoke very good English, he had served aboard British Merchant ships and had at one time lived in Barrow. He had been interned on the Isle of Man during the war. After leaving him we made our way back through the back streets to the main road, whilst we were passing through one of the narrow lanes, someone in one of the houses on the opposite side threw a stone at us, happily it missed us otherwise I would have been out for the count. We did not stay to argue

but carried on. No more back streets for us. The merchandise was very cheap so the majority visited the main stores and bought curios etc.
After two days we left Dantzig for our next port of call, Memel, which was a distance of 60 miles and as it was an overnight trip, we once again took the opportunity of making a night torpedo attack on the light Cruisers commencing at 10pm and finishing at about midnight.
Thick fog developed so we had to reduce speed and when eventually arriving at Memel we anchored about two miles from the coast with the exception of the Flagship and Spenser and Wolfhound who proceeded alongside the jetty. Shooting and horse riding was provided for the officers and there was a football match against the French Chasseurs. I did not go ashore and by all accounts I did not miss much, for it was a miserable place, and there was nothing to purchase.
Thankfully we were not to be there long and we set sail for Libau and after yet another overnight trip we arrived in Libau at 6am on the Saturday 10th September, there was a strong wind blowing, because of this we had to anchor in the commercial harbour, it was 10pm by the time we were tied up alongside the jetty. Immediately we were surrounded by hordes of women and children begging for bread and clothes, we witnessed some awful sights as most of the people were half starved. A policeman in a nondescript rig and carrying a rifle and sword was patrolling up and down the jetty trying to keep the women and children on the move. He hit one old woman and nearly got murdered for his pains by some of our lads, after that he kept a respectable distance and later was withdrawn altogether. We gave away to some young lads, old sailor suits etc.
Four of us went ashore to view the sights. We had to cross the river by a small ferry. None of us had Latvian Roubles so someone suggested that we give a cigarette each for the ferry crossing, when we reached the other side we were agreeably surprised when the man took the cigarettes with a smile all over his face and repeated thank you's, we thought that a good start, anyhow we exchanged some pound notes for roubles receiving 1,300 roubles in exchange.
Libau is noted for its Amber necklaces, but after visiting several shops we were disappointed for those offered to us were of poor quality, and had flaws, those that were reasonable were very costly so we gave up. As the streets were all cobbled and full of ruts, we decided to take a Drosky. We found a young Latvian lad who could speak a little English and after a little bargaining it was agreed that we pay 100 roubles each, the Drosky driver would take us round the town. It was more like a switch back and were glad when it came to an end as the sights were very disappointing. However we had to pay 200 roubles each before we could get clear because the arguing

was drawing the attention of a crowd and there was a possibility of bringing the traffic to a standstill, so we paid up and tried to look pleasant. We then searched for a cafe' where we could partake of the succulent hop, that too proved disappointing for it tasted like onion water kept over night, but it had plenty of froth on the top, but one bottle was enough. The bill of fare said that the price was 40 roubles a bottle but when we came to pay it was 55 roubles a bottle it was explained that the extra was made up of 5 roubles for tax, 5 roubles for the waiter and 5 roubles for the proprietor, so we had been had again, but it was equalised out by two of us walking out without paying, after that little lot we just bought a few postcards and returned on board in time for tea.

When we arrived on board the amber merchant was there with some decent specimens, so I bought a necklace for 1.100 roubles.

The following day the General of the Latvians paid his official visit followed by the band, "Some band"!! The General looked more like an old farmer than a distinguished soldier. I suppose he was distinguished according to the marks of respect paid to him by the whole population. He was probably got rid of a few weeks later, that sort of thing does not bother the Latvians. During the afternoon the Lettish band arrived in full force to play a few selections as we slipped the jetty and gave us a farewell tune as we steamed past the entrance. I can't say that I enjoyed Libau.

Riga, the chief Russian sea port in the Baltic, exporting large quantities of timber and hides etc: On our way here the cruiser Cordelia had a man go overboard, the first intimation of this was when we heard the cries of help from the man in the water. We switched on our searchlight and fortunately the rays fell directly on him. We stopped engines, a boat was lowered to pick him up, he was very fortunate to survive for the water was beginning to get very cold at that time of year. As we neared the mouth of the river Diva a flight of aircraft flew over to escort us up the wide river to Riga which is about ten miles from the entrance. The aircraft performed the usual stunts just to impress us, but after five years of war we were used to this sort of thing, but we admired and appreciated the compliment paid to us. The first view of Riga is very impressive, the town seems to be one mass of gilded domed churches. It is one of the most magnificent cities that I have visited. It is very well laid out with broad avenues flanked with trees on either side, the roads are divided, one section for carriages another for bicycles. The buses are large and imposing. The people seemed well clad and the shops were full with eatables with black and white bread and plenty of confectionery. It was hard to believe that the Bosheviks had only recently been evicted from Riga. A football match had been arranged between the Destroyers and the Union Club, also the Light Cruisers and the YMCA. The Destroyers won 1-0 but

the Light Cruisers lost 2-1. They played a very good game and both matches were well worth watching. After the match we explored the place and fell in with a Lettish Soldier who could speak a few words of English. He gave us an invitation to his home which we accepted with some misgivings as to whether we were doing the correct thing. As there was three of us we chanced it. He took us to a large house opposite the Opera House and introduced us to his Mother and Father, Aunt, four Brothers and two Sisters. They could all speak a little English. There was a decent spread of boiled fish with a kind of Irish stew mixed with it, cold beef and boiled potatoes, fruit tea, coffee, black and white bread on the table and we were invited to dinner but it was 8pm and we assured them that we were not hungry, I plumped for a glass of coffee and an apple, I did not like to tackle the other stuff. Another Brother arrived who could speak perfect English. He said that he had been in England for several years, but at the outbreak of war he had returned to Russia. After the revolution he had been taken prisoner by the Bolsheviks and was twice stood up against a wall to be shot, but was reprieved each time through influence, he informed us that they were Russian Jews and big merchants in pre war days so perhaps that accounted for it. We had a pleasant sociable evening, smoking long Russian cigarettes and drinking glasses of coffee. We eventually left at 11pm escorted by two of the sons back to the Custom House in the pitch darkness, there were no lights. We left Riga at 4pm on Thursday September 25th bound for Revel.
On Saturday at 8pm a floating mine was sighted at the entrance to Revel. The Fleet was stopped whilst Violent was ordered to sink it. It proved to be a large 500lb mine with horns, as it did not have a rusty appearance it was probably laid during the last twelve months. During this operation Petty Officer Mitchell of the Flagship Curacoa was caught in one of the paravane wires and dragged over the side, his body was cut in two and passed between the lines partly submerged and before it could be picked up, sank, despite searching for half an hour it was not found, so Ensigns were half masted and the funeral service was held over the spot where he sank. The Fleet then got under weigh and proceeded to Revel.
On arrival off the entrance we were met by a squadron of seaplanes which manoeuvred very well considering the very high winds and rough state of the sea.
The Fleet formed in line abreast in three columns, the third division of destroyers leading followed by the four light cruisers at two and half cables apart with the fourth division of destroyers bringing up the rear.
As we rounded the point to the harbour, Revel presented a very pleasing appearance with its large domed churches showing up against a clear sky and back ground. We were given to understand that we were to go alongside the

jetty, so steam was kept raised ready. It was ten o'clock on the Sunday morning when the destroyers were ordered to proceed to the outer arm of the jetty, Vanquisher leading the way. It was rather a ticklish piece of work as the ships had to be manoeuvred through a small gap which didn't allow much room for turning as the channel was very narrow with mud banks either side and owing to the strong winds it was anything but an easy job. We made two attempts before successfully negotiating the turn, eventually we secured alongside a small steamer, the other boats coming in as the others cleared the entrance.

The President of Foreign Ministers invited all the Captains to lunch with him, while a concert was arranged at the Town Hall for the men. An hours entertainment was arranged, but assistance in the way of turns from the men of the Fleet was asked for, it finished up with three and half hours entertainment.

I did not go ashore here, but from reports I received the outside appearance was far superior to the interior, the streets were very narrow and dirty, the homes in bad need of repair etc:

At 6am on the Monday we left for Helsingfors the capital of Finland, which was about 64 miles across the Gulf. which we reached about five hours later even though it had been a rough passage.

The entrance of Helsingfors is surrounded by numerous small islands, so it was necessary to have Finnish pilots Our pilot could not speak English or French, but as he could speak Russian, one of our Petty Officers who had spent two or three years in Russia could speak some Russian and so did the interpreting. All the destroyers proceeded to the inner harbour while the Light Cruisers went to the other side of the Island.

It is one of the prettiest little seaports that I have been to. The streets were well laid out. The main street especially was very pretty with extensive gardens running through the centre. The people were very civil and obliging.

As the rate of exchange was 230 marks to the pound we found things very cheap. I purchased quite a lot of glassware, scent and other things. The Franco Restaurant that I went to put on a very good spread for 12 marks, which was equivalent to one shilling. The orchestra played while we had lunch which consisted of steak, onions, potatoes and cabbage with cheese Black and white bread with pats of butter, all for a bob.

I had a thorough good walk round, it seemed hard to believe that Helsingfors is ice bound for four months of the year.

We stayed for three days, I think we all enjoyed the visit and would have liked to have stayed longer, but we had to adhere to our original programme, so we left at 2pm on Thursday for our next port of call, Stockholm, Sweden.

On leaving Helsingfors we ran into some rough weather crossing the Baltic. We were tossing and rolling all night long, ploughing through heavy seas being tossed about like corks, but as it was only a one night trip we didn't mind too much By 5am we were well under the shelter of the Aland Islands and picked up pilots off the Island of Upsala for our 60 mile trip up the Fjords to Stockholm.
The scenery was magnificent, even though it was toward the end of the summer season the bungalows were gaily decorated. We passed a Swedish Naval Base and Garrison about twenty miles before we reached Stockholm, the Swedish sailors standing to attention as we passed quite close to the shore at this point.
We arrived off Stockholm at noon and proceeded directly to the jetty to land Lt Donnell who was taken to hospital seriously ill. The remainder of the Fleet anchored close to the oiler that had been sent out from England to fill us up with oil fuel, as we had by this time run short of oil. After oiling, all ships proceeded independently and anchored in pairs off Stockholm.
The football team was due to play against the Swedish Navy at their stadium, we lost 4-3 The city is built like Venice, on a group of islands. I believe it is called the Venice of the Baltic. The Royal Palace was quite close to our anchorage, but the King and Queen were away. Balls and Concerts were arranged for the officers as usual. Things were very expensive here. The rate of exchange being 16.80 as against 18.44 pre war. It cost 1 Krona to open your mouth, and two to shut it, not reckoning the cost to fill it! Three of us went into a cafe' and ordered steak, vegetables and stout. The piece of steak was about half the size of the palm of the hand, with two potatoes, a spoonful of onions with a glass of stout the price was 21/- the three. Next move, exit the three of us.
Everyone here seemed to own a bicycle. What I saw of the place, I thought very nice, but owing to the lack of funds and as the banks were closed, so if you wanted to change any money, at the cafe' they diddled you, offering 13/- instead of the 17/- at the banks so we abstained. Life didn't begin until 11.30pm when it was time for us to return on board. I did not bother going ashore again.
A stoker on Curacoa fell over board and drowned before he could be picked up. He was buried the next day with full honours, the Swedish Army and Navy lining the route.
The ships were open to visitors on Sunday, we had crowds come aboard, but due to the lack of knowledge of their language very few of us offered to take them round, for it proved a difficult task trying to explain things to them and reply to the large number of questions being asked.

I was not sorry to leave Stockholm, I couldn't say why, except that I was disappointed with the place. We left at 9am on Tuesday 27th bound for Copenhagen a distance of about 500 miles and as it was planned to carry out a night exercise we did not expect to arrive until Thursday morning. The weather was till rather rough.
We arrived at 8am on Thursday September 29th. The destroyers proceeded up harbour with the Flag Ship, whilst the other three cruisers remained outside.
The next day the King arrived in his yacht accompanied by three destroyers. As soon as the King arrived the ships were dressed and manned as the yacht made way to her mooring just abreast of us. The King did not remain long, making his way ashore in his steam boat and then to the Palace. He was due back at 2pm to inspect the Flagship and did so as Hon' British Admiral for which he received a 17 gun salute, the forts returning the same.
All Captains were commanded to dine with him at 7pm on Saturday October 1st. Invitations were received for the officers to visit the porcelain factory. The Danes were a very kind likeable people and our men made many friends, consequently we had many visitors come aboard. The town itself is planned on a large scale as regards the width of the roads in the form of avenues with a special track for the bicycles, which are very cheap here, everyone seemed to own one. The Langalene Gardens that run parallel to the river, posses some very fine monuments. We had a very pleasant four day stay here and was sorry to leave, which we did at 9.30pm.on the 3rd October, heading for Gothengburg in a nasty gale. We arrived at Gothenburg at 5.30 the following morning, tugs and pilots came out to receive us.
An invitation was received for 500 men each night to visit the cinema ashore. They also showed the squadron entering harbour.
Although the main streets were very imposing I found nothing here tempting or exciting. The Swedish Petty Officers made a visit of inspection and the ships were open to visitors in the afternoon.
The local newspapers were full of the significance of the British Fleets visit, but as part of the German Fleet had been here some months earlier, and had the same sort of stuff served out to them, we took it all as a part of a great game (Diplomacy)
Once again the rate of exchange was against us, which made things very dear. Again we played Gothenburg at football and lost 10-1, so we did not have much to be proud of.
We left Gothenburg on Friday 7th October for the last port of call of the cruise, Christiana, again it was rough weather, it seems to have followed us around.

We arrived of Christiana at about 7.30 the following morning, but as we had about 40 miles to go up the fjords we did not arrive off the town until 11am. After we arrived we were ordered to man ship as HM the Queen of Norway was going to pass the Fleet on her way to England on board SS Bessheim. The steamer passed at about 12.15. A salute was fired.
Invitations were received from the Anglo-Norse Society to attend a concert in the Opera House in Carljohans Gade, at which the King of Norway was expected to be present. I went to the concert which was a tip top one, but the King did not put in an appearance.
I also had a trip up the mountains to a place called Hollamskolen which was about 40 minute on the electric railway. It was a spectacular view of Christiana and the surrounding Fjords. The people were so friendly and fraternised a lot with us sailors. It was rather surprising to find the number of people who could speak English. HM the King gave a Command Dinner for all Captains and paid an official visit to the flagship.
We had a very nice time here, prices were good, and I think most of us would have liked to have spent longer here, but as we had to adhere to our programme we left at 4pm on Thursday 13th October for our home ports. The Light Cruisers going to Invergordon and the destroyers to the destroyer base at Port Edgar.
We had one of the roughest trips across the North Sea that I think that I have ever experienced in a destroyer, so we were thankful when May Island hove in sight at about 11am on Saturday 15th October, we eventually reached our base at about 2pm very pleased to get it over with.

Chapter 12
1922

Saw some of them being deployed in various ports around Ireland in an effort to stop illegal arms entering the country whilst others were despatched to the Mediterranean. Whilst operating in the Mediterranean or other warmer climes the seamen on the old V&Ws were often reduced to hard tack, for there was no refrigeration aboard, the meat was kept in meat cages on deck exposed to all the elements. Each man would receive a daily ration of bread meat and potatoes, and usually it would be for four days, it was reckoned that they would not be more than four days at sea before returning to the depot ship or going alongside at some port and thereby able to replenish stores, if they should happen to be away for more than four days, the staple diet would be reduced to bully beef and ships biscuits. On occasions when other commodities were available, the "Cook of the Mess" would purchase what he thought necessary for the days meals each man contributing from their allowance. This was called mess catering, and if the "Cook of the Mess" was able to provide a decent meal without using all the allowance, at the end of each month or voyage, the surplus would be divided between those in the mess. The cook of the mess who could do this soon became very popular. It was normal for each watch in each mess would appoint a cook of the day or take it in turns to prepare the meal and take it to the galley for the chef to cook.

THE MEDITERRANEAN

With the exception of exercising with the Atlantic or Mediterranean Fleets occasionally, and taking part in the annual spring cruises there was little for the V&Ws to do except to pay good will visits to different ports throughout the United Kingdomand other ports on the continent. The 3rd Flotilla was engaged in protecting the Greeks from the Turks in their withdrawal from the Smyrna, this Flotilla became desperately short of food and victuals having left their depot in haste and unable to stock up with the necessities. This situation brought about the need for an independent canteen, and eventually they all had canteens run by the NAAFI others spent much time in pens or docks being refitted with more advanced armament and the fitting of depth charge release rails and ASDIC domes to their hulls. As time went on, International agreements were made that the number of ships and tonnage should be reduced to an acceptable level, this entailed many of the V&Ws being paid off and put into reserve, this of course meant that no more V&Ws were to be built although it would not be too long before they would be called into action and many more years before the last of them would disappear.

Chapter 13

THE CHINA STATION
1926

There had not been any British destroyers in the Far East until 1926, but due to the civil war that was raging in China, it was felt necessary to send British ships to protect those British people and businessmen who were living there, so the 3rd Flotilla who had been joined by a new leader, the Keppel, the most up to date and largest destroyer at that time, and which had been operating in the Mediterranean was sent there. The conditions in the Far East did not bring good fortune for the ships or the men who sailed in them, for they had to remain on board, at times for many months and in that climate and conditions it was to say the least very wearing on the crews. After two years the ships and their crews were beginning to show the signs of wear and tear. So in the spring of 1928 the third was relieved by the eighth flotilla which had been held in reserve. The need for a constant presence of the British Navy to protect life and property, it was decided to establish a permanent "China Station" flotilla so the 3rd flotilla battled through the monsoons to Colombo Ceylon (now known as Sri Lanka) and then on to Aden a trip of 2.000 miles. On arrival the tired and battered vessels were all running very short of fuel. They were all in need of maintenance and repair.

MANCHESTER
1929

One of the goodwill or courtesy visits was when in June 1929, the 6th destroyer flotilla, with **Campbell** as leader accompanied by **Wakeful Wessex, Wolfhound** and **Westcott** navigated the Manchester canal, through the Asthma Locks to the excitement of the people of Manchester and the surrounding district, who lined the banks of the canal to welcome the ships before arriving at Tramroad Wharf, where they remained for seven days, enabling the crews to enjoy some shore leave and the civilian population enjoyed visiting the destroyers.

BACK TO THE MED'

1931

April fool's day 1931. **Wryneck** was with the Mediterranean Fleet on passage to the French Riviera, carrying out exercises before visiting French ports on that coast.

Rear Admiral Destroyers leading the Fleet with his flotilla's suddenly ran into dense fog, which he reported to H.M.S. Glorious some miles astern of him, aware that she had most of her planes airborne. Glorious immediately altered course to fly on her planes, but she too was soon immersed in the thick fog as well. Dilemma?

With the safety of the planes paramount, Glorious maintained her speed contrary to the rules of the sea which required ships to reduce speed for safety in these conditions. (remember there was no Radar in 1931). Alas she came into collision head on with the S.S. Florida, a modern oil fuel burning French liner carrying 600 passengers.

Everything came to a halt. The passengers were transferred to Glorious, including those injured, some had died. The cruiser Sussex was ordered to join Glorious and her attendant destroyer **Wryneck**.

Those planes still airborne were told to fly to Malaga. Four ditched for lack of fuel, but the crews were recovered without loss of life, although one R.A.F pilot had a broken arm. (A carrier carried R.A.F personnel in those days.

The Florida was taken in tow for Malaga, escorted by Sussex and **Wryneck**, while Glorious returned to Gibraltar. Sussex was ordered to remain at Malaga to provide a funeral party. I was a Midshipman at the time in the cruiser Shropshire, and theses scanty details were taken from my journal, made up from hearsay. We were not visibly in touch. Who towed Florida?. My guess is tugs from Malaga. I believe the case went to an International Court of arbitration for settlement of costs. This sort of calamity was new and unusual. An act of God - perhaps? Certainly the Captain of Glorious did not suffer. He was Kennedy Purvis who became an Admiral and continued to serve in the higher ranks of the service.

Many of the old V&Ws were now being retired into maintenance reserve at Chatham, Devonport and Rosyth. Although there was a maintenance crew left aboard, there was far too much work to be done necessary to maintain the ships in sea worthy condition, alas the financial expenditure was inadequate to provide the necessary tools and equipment for the maintenance crews to keep the ships in pristine condition, soon they became weather worn and began to deteriorate, those that were at Devonport were transferred to Rosyth, soon to be followed by those at Chatham and they fell further into disrepair and it was not to be long before the first, the **Valhalla** was sold for scrap in December 1931. Unfortunately more were to go the same way. Even though the V&Ws were still the most modern destroyers in the Royal Navy. In the 1930 London Treaty it was laid down that a destroyers age should not exceed that of fifteen years. This meant that by 1932 over half of those built would have to be scrapped. Little did the powers that be at the time could visualise that they would all be sorely needed in just seven years hence. In fact some of them would still be in extensive use 20 years later, serving the Royal Navy and the country well.

1932

However the Australian Navy were in need of upgrading their destroyer flotillas and after negotiations with the Admiralty, in 1932 five of the V&Ws, **Stuart, Vampire, Vendetta, Voyager** and **Waterhen** were transferred to the Australian Navy, they were to prove themselves in the forthcoming war.

1934

In January of that year Rear Admiral Cunningham as Rear Admiral destroyers was at Malta and under his command was the 1st destroyer flotilla of the V&Ws which was led by Earl Mountbatten in **Wishart** were carrying our manoeuvres and curtesy visits to the many ports in the Mediterranean
I joined the Defender, destination, Singapore, there we did a swop with the **Wren**. I soon came to learn what life was like aboard a 'boat'.
We eventually set sail for Malta and it was there that we had the 'misfortune' of landing up on the rocks off Malta's Tigne point. It was reported that our skipper Lt' Cmdr Robson shouted 'Whoa' but the ship took no B****y notice! While repairs were being carried out we swapped over to the **Worcester**. On returning to the **Wren** I stayed with her until 'paying off' time came which was sometime in 1936. Life in 'boats' was not my cup of tea, so I volunteered for the Fleet Air Arm.

Norman Hollis

Chapter 14
1935

"SWAIN"

I was born on the 14th January 1912, and being too young for the 1914-18 war, my Uncle represented me, as I found out later. He was serving on the Hampshire when it was sunk and carrying Lord Kitchener on board. So when I reached the age of 15 I decided I would like to join and lo' and behold I found myself along with thousands of others at H.M.S. Ganges in May 1927. After a gruelling twelve months there I was delayed in going to sea for I caught Diphtheria, but eventually I was drafted to H.M.S. Benbow, a battleship and training ship for boys. It was called the "White Lady" of the Med' being kept so clean, as she was a coal burner this was quite difficult, but with sand and holy stones the decks always looked smashing.
There were four divisions with six classes in each division, we soon found out how and who kept it white, with holy stones in each hand rubbing sand into the decks. The boys were only allowed to wear shoes or boots at Divisions or on a couple of hours leave on a Saturday or Sunday. By the time we left Benbow our feet were well marked by the sand.
After serving on the Battleships Repulse,Valiant and then the Cyclops a submarine depot ship.I was drafted to **Valorous** early in 1935 as Leading Seaman S/T we were then sent o Malta to join the 19th Flotilla, there we remained until April 1936 when we returned to depot. I then Joined **Westcott** who was at Devonport being converted to attend on Subs. We left 'Guzz' (Gosport) in November 1936 in company with 'Thracian' and sailed into a stinkng force nine gale, by the time we reached Gibraltar we were in a fine old state, we were carrying a number of spare crew for other ships, most of them had been violently sick in the galley flat for most of the voyage, and as coal for the galley was kept there, most of them were covered in coal dust. The journey continued to Malta and through the Suez Canal and eventually arriving at Hong Kong where we were attached to the 2nd submarine flotilla and the depot ship Medway.
Whilst in Hong Kong harbour we were hit by a typhoon, at the time I was coxswain of a picket boat from the Medway and had to take a party of sick people ashore, that was quite a trip, but we made it.
When the Japs invaded China our ambassador Huggeson Knotchbull was on holiday with his family on the island of Teaiho. **Westcott** was detailed as guard ship to the Ambassador, eventually transporting the whole family to a cruiser for the voyage to Shanghai.

April 1939 saw the end of the commission and we returned home and during my leave I was married.
I then joined Harvester as Chief Bosuns Mate, we were involved in the evacuation of Dunlirk after which it was the North Atlantic until June 1940, then it was a period of barracks and schooling until the 7th March 1941 when again I was drafted to my old ship **Westcott** laying at Liverpool where she was undergoing repairs after a collision. With HMS Bluebell. On completion we were detailed for Atlantic convoys again. On one of which we had a film crew on board to film depth charge explosions for a film that was being made. We were then detailed to join the Home Fleet in the search for the Bismarck and Prinz Eugen. Another incident happened when we came under air attack, we assisted a merchant ship that was on fire and took the injured off, then we took them back to the U.K.
Between these convoys **Westcott** was fitted with the new 'Hedgehog', a brand new anti submarine weapon. The scientist and manufacturers were aboard for the test firing, during which there was a nasty accident when one of the seaman lost his hand.
We were then sent to Gib' to take part in the 'club runs' to Malta. It was then that we were involved with the troop carrying ship, Llangibby Castle and the sinking of the U. 581. For my part in this action I was awarded the D.S.M. This story is related elsewhere. Then it was the 'Big One' We were senior officer for the screen of the Carrier 'Eagle' and stationed on her starboard side. As I was 2nd Officer of the forenoon watch, I was relieved at 1230 and had just finished dinner when we felt two explosions and on looking round saw that the Eagle had caught it and was sinking fast, tipping all its aircraft into the sea. In a very short space of time she had gone, quite a number were saved, but sadly most of her crew were lost, including two of our signal department who had been transferred just before sailing. The remaining part of the convoy we escorted the Liverpool and Nigeria back to Gibraltar as they too had been badly damaged. I found out that a number of my old shipmates had been killed.
We eventually got back home and I was paid off as the **Westcott** went in for a big refit.

Jim Mills D.S.M.

* *

ON PASSAGE TO HONG KONG
BY J.A. JOLLIFFE
D/MX. 52106

During the 1930s unemployment was a great problem, good jobs were scarce. I was fortunate in having a job, but with strings attached. Located 60 miles away from home in Plymouth, it offered little in the way of prospects. A case of waiting for 'dead mans shoes'. Financially it was hopeless, after paying for digs and the fare home at the weekends, I was broke. Eventually with the consent of my parents I resigned to return to Plymouth to seek work locally.

After several unsuccessful interviews, my moral was at a low ebb. A family friend suggested that I might consider joining the Navy as a writer, it offered job security, and of course at the end there was a pension to be had. In those days a job with a pension was looked upon with envy.

From enquiries I learnt that entry into the Writes branch of the R.N. was by open competition held twice yearly, with an intake of about thirty. With my future uncertain, I decided to go ahead and try to join up.

Following my success at the 1935 examination, I was granted my choice of Port Division - Devonport, and joined H.M.S Drake in November as a new entry. Training was a combination of square bashing and technical instruction and was completed without incident. I was rated Write and assigned to H.M.S. Drake as a supernumerary.

A few months later with my official number hardly dry, I received a draft chit to join H.M.S. Medway on the China station with passage as far as Singapore on the V&W class destroyer **Westcott.**

Initially it was an unsettling experience, particularly bearing in mind the distance involved and the period away would be at least two and a half years. Air mail had not yet started, a letter would take about six weeks to reach Hong Kong.

The formalities of a foreign draft completed the days began to slip by and it wasn't long before, that on a cold blustery November morning with my kit-bag and hammock I reported on board H.M.S. **Westcott.** My first impression was unforgettable, a mixture of super heated steam, hot metal and the sounds of auxiliary machinery. My adventure was about to begin!

Most of the forenoon was occupied in settling in, stowing away my gear etc;

The seaman's mess would be my home for the duration of the voyage, located in the fore part of the ship, by any standards it was spartan. In the centre of the mess was a steam engine used to drive the capstan, when the contraption was in use the whole mess was enveloped in steam.

Time is running out. Tomorrow we leave these shores bound for the Far East and it's many mysteries. Time for last farewells. The ships company offered theirs some days earlier, being Chatham Division they had very few connections with the West country.
Weather conditions throughout the night deteriorated, by daybreak the wind had reached gale force and was still rising. Many vessels were running for shelter. A grim prospect for us.
With final preparations complete, securing lines were cast off, the ship severed her link with the Devon shore heading into Plymouth Sound, passing the mile long breakwater with it's familiar lighthouse before entering the English Channel, to encounter more severe weather, in fact, a 'No Go' area for an elderly destroyer of just 1100 tons. Suddenly it happened, the ship turned about and headed back to Plymouth, eventually making secure to the duty destroyer buoy off Drakes Island. There we remained throughout the day, come late afternoon there was a 'buzz', shore leave? Needless to say it never materialised, for me as a 'sprog' it was a disappointment, especially living in the locality. There was still a great deal to learn about the Navy, particularly to take 'buzzes' with a pinch of salt.
This voyage could be described as my introduction to Blue Water, I was quite unprepared for such an experience that lay ahead. Racing 14ft dinghies in Plymouth Sound offered little by way of preparation for such a lengthy ocean passage
At about 11pm there occurred much activity, the ship was being made ready for sea despite the weather, which showed no sign of improvement. It seemed that the Commanding Officer, a Lieutenant Commander R.N. Was faced with a thorny problem, and the ball was squarely in his court. He could either wait for an improvement in the weather which would entail falling behind with his schedule as a result. How could he possibly maintain a schedule under these conditions? He decided to slip and proceed. Leaving the shelter of Plymouth the motion of the ship became increasingly violent, it was evident that we were in for a trying night with the sound of the wind and the terrible pounding from the seas, it was unnerving to put it mildly. Then suddenly it happened, I collapsed being seasick violently and repeatedly. I really did not care whether we did a vertical take off or plunged straight to the bottom. I was not the only one, but the other victims seemed to be at a lesser degree than I, but they were destroyer men and used to this sort of situation. I take my hat of to them, one and all.
Had I been left to my own devices I may well have been swept over the side. It was the Coxswain who put things right, patching me up and twenty four hours later I was up and almost ready to make myself useful. Never again

was I to suffer from sea sickness despite going on to serve in a variety of ships, from Aircraft carriers to Frigates.
Almost a week later we came alongside at Gibraltar where our stay was extended to repair the storm damage. This would be a lengthy itinerary which would offer countless opportunities for exploration of the 'Rock'.
My first impression was its size, relatively small with an area of about two and a half miles on the south coast of Spain, commanding the North side of the Atlantic entrance to the Mediterranean sea. Important strategically. The main town at the North western corner appeared to consist of a main street occupied by a number of bars, there seemed to be three types, some had an orchestra, others were a type of 'Bistro' bar, a drink that was popular at the time was 'Coffee Royal'. This visit offered the perfect beginning to a foreign commission,
The easy stages in transit into a working ship broke one in gradually. At journey's end one felt less of being a fresh arrival on a foreign station. With repair complete it was time to press on to Malta, our next port of call, it was an uneventful leg of the journey although useful in providing opportunities to increase the efficiency of the ships company.
Upon arrival at Malta we did not rate very highly in the pecking order, instead of the convenience of going alongside, it meant tying up to one of the many buoys. When shore leave was granted it meant going ashore in what can only be described as a cross between a gondola and a canoe called Dhaiso? The capital city, Valetta had much on offer to interest new arrivals. The other principal centre being Sleima. Familia sights and sounds recalled are the milk vendor with his flock of goats, his cry "Aleep,eggs, bread". The "Egyptian Queen" and the "Lucky Wheel".
Leaving Malta in our wake we are now bound for Port Said. Since clearing Malta it has become warmer, the sun reflecting off the surface of Mediterranean with the sparkle of a million diamonds. The rig of the day was changed to tropical in keeping with this type of weather.
From now on more time must be allowed for washing clothes during dog watches. The routine is simple, get hold of a spare bucket and a bar of 'Pussers' soap and you are on your way. I soon became a dab hand at it.
The time I spent in a seaman's mess as a junior rating was priceless. I was taught how to prepare a meal for the mess, take it to the galley, and fetch it when it was cooked. To keep the living space clean and tidy, and above all, to show consideration to others. These lessons I have never forgot and they stood me in good stead throughout my life.
The stay at Port Said was a short one. I could not fail to be impressed by the statue in memory of Ferdinand de Lessops the builder of the 101 mile long Suez Canal which was opened in 1869 linking the Mediterranean and the

Red Seas through which we were to make our way shortly. Also worthy of mention were the twin columns of the 1914-1918 War Memorial. The following incident remains undimmed in my minds eye, but as the years pass I can see the funny side of it. The ship was secured close inshore, it was during the early part of the forenoon. A party of official types came on board. It turned out that they were local Port Health Officials who had come to carry out medical inspection of the ship's company. All junior ratings were summoned to fall in on the quarter deck, step up to the official, dropping your shorts and allowing the said official, with the aid of a large and powerful torch to carry out the inspection in full view of the interested locals on shore.

Entering the Red Sea, change was evident, Western influence gave way to the Eastern, particularly among the craft at sea, mostly sailing vessels. The weather varied from cloudy to bright sunshine with rough seas, nothing that I could not cope with. It was now that my request to take a turn at the wheel was granted. I was elated, it isn't everyone that could say that they had taken the wheel of a Royal Naval Destroyer, especially a young writer.

Passing through Hells Gates we crossed the Arabian Sea to arrive at our next destination, Karachi, where much in the way of hospitality was received. One incident still unforgotten was the street entertainer with his act "Snake fight Mongoose 4 anna's.

Then it was on to Penang where Christmas was celebrated, the mess in common with the others was decorated with bunting and the menu supplemented. A present from the Captain, an unexpected one, two bottles of beer for each one of us. A generous act, particularly as apart from the rum issue the Royal Navy was dry as far as the lower deck was concerned.

Arrival at Singapore and soon a parting of the ways. **Westcott** would stay and take over from H.M.S. Bruce who was shortly due to return to the U.K. Whilst I was to make ready for the final stage of my voyage.

In January 1937 construction of the new Royal Naval Base together with a vast dry dock was going along on apace. In the mean time, local R.N. Affairs were conducted from H.M.S. Terror, a monitor armed with two 15" calibre guns, nearby was a medium sized floating dock. It was real Boy's Own stuff.

It was to H.M.S. Terror I made my way, explained that I had not been paid since Mid October. Whilst interim payments were made to the **Westcotts** ships company, no such arrangements had been made for personnel on passage. Had it not been for a postal order from my Mother received en route, I would have been up the creek completely.

I was made welcome in 'Terror', given a substantial advance of pay and told to avail myself of their Chinese laundry which transformed my No 6's.

It was six days later that I reached Hong Kong, disembarked from H.M.T Lancashire and joined H.M.S. Medway at last. The beginning of what was to be a happy commission of 2 ½ years in a splendid ship during which time I would visit many places of interest throughout the Far East.
Many of the old V&Ws were now being put into reserve, others had been earmarked for alterations and modifications to convert them into the "Wair" type of destroyer.
During the summer of !935 H.M.S. **Wishart** which was still under the command of Commander Lord Louis Mountbatten was in the Mediterranean and whilst paying a visit to Cannes welcomed his friend H.R.H the Prince of Wales accompanied by Mrs Wallis Simpson aboard.
After taking my leave which was due after three years abroad, I went to 'Vernon' to qualify S.T. After which I was drafted to Valorous as Ldg; Sea; S.T. We were soon sent to Malta to join up with the 19th destroyer flotilla and remained until April 1936 I was then returned to depot until September. I was then drafted to **Westcott** who was at Devonport and being altered to attend on submarines, picking up their torpedoes after practice firing. Leaving Guzz (Gosport) in November 1936 in company with 'Thracian' we sailed into s stinking force 9 gale and by the time we reached Gibraltar we were in a fine old state as we had aboard a number of spare crew taking passage to other ships, they had been violently sick in the galley flat for most of the trip, and as the coal for the galley was kept there, it was in a fine old state, so were the seamen who were covered in coal as the galley flat was always flooded in rough weather.
After a few days in Gib' cleaning up and drying out the messdecks etc; we carried on our journey to Malta and the Far East. During the journey we managed to play any team that we could find at hockey or football at every port that we called at, so by the time we reached Hong Kong we had very good teams at both, and quite a good water polo team.
Back to work which consisted of chasing after and picking up the 'tin fish' that had been fired by the sub's.
While we were out there in 1937-38 we managed to get hit by a typhoon whilst in Hong Kong harbour. At the time I was Coxswain of the picket boat from the 'Medway' and had to take a party of sick people ashore, quite a trip.
Earlier in 1937 when the Japs invaded China, our Ambassador, Huggeson Knotchbull was on holiday with his family on the island of Petaiho. Westcott was detailed as guard ship to the ambassador and eventually we had to transport the family from the island to a Cruiser for the trip back to Shanghai.
After quite a few incidents of Jap bombing and clearing up hundreds of Chinese from the cables each morning, we eventually came to the end of the commission and came home in April 1939.

HMS Witch crossing the line 1927

HMS Witch versus HMS Whitshead
Comical dress water polo match 1928

HMS Wishart at Cannes in the summer of 1935.
Commander Mountbatten welcoming
The Prince of Wales and Mrs Wallace Simpson aboard

1936

February:- General Sir Charles Bonham-Carter was appointed Governor of Malta, and was transported there in the liner Strathmore escorted by the destroyers **Wishart** and **Wren.** The curtesy visits were becoming less. They were no longer welcome in the Italian ports, and the fear that Malta would be an early target for the enemy, anti invasion exercises were carried out. In addition to this the Spanish civil war broke out which put an extra burden on the destroyers carrying out the evacuating of British citizens and refugees.

After Osborne and Dartmouth. Philip Saumarez joined the cruiser Hawkins on the China station as a Midshipman. He was one of the relief party that was sent ashore after the Shanghai earthquake in 1923. Four years later he joined the submarine service and served in L16, H32 and Oberon. He then turned to destroyers and served in Boadicea during the Spanish civil war. His first Command was the V&W destroyer **Wolfhound** which in December escorted Fury when she took the Duke of Windsor across the Channel after the Abdication.

* * * * * *

1936. The Admiralty sent the old liner Majestic to the scrap yard, but on realising their error, and before the breakers began their work, they halted the scrapping of the Majestic and as the Admiralty had been paid the scrap price for her, they had to replace the Majestic with equal tonnage, they achieved this by sending six of the old V&Ws to their demise,. The six were;- Valkyrie, Vectis, Venturous,, Violent, Shakespeare and Spenser. So the poor old V&Ws were reduced in number, something that was to be regretted in the not too distant future. However the rundown of the Royal Navy was halted in 1938, but alas it was too late, now there was a desperate shortage of destroyers. Soon other types of destroyers were to be hastily built to meet the need for escort vessels. The old V&Ws were also being brought up to date with various modifications and improvements. Heavier armament, Radar, Oerlikon guns, four barrelled pom-poms, all these modifications were transferring them into a force to be reckoned with. Unfortunate for one, the **Walrus,** this was to prove fatal. In 1938 on being towed to Chatham from Rosyth to undergo her refit she broke her tow and ran aground, the damage was so great that after removing all that was salvageable her hull was scrapped.

Chapter 15

1937

Tales from the defaulters table by Jack Stokes:-

The first time I had to respond to the order 'Off Caps' as a defaulter, was as a newly promoted Ordinary Seaman in about March 1937 when the charge was:- Ordinary Seaman Stokes did remain absent over leave fifteen minutes namely from 2300 to 2315 hundred hours
Result;- Scale One day's pay and one day's leave.
Appearance number two;- Able Seaman Stokes, slack in obeying the order, 'Hands fall in' at 0600. Result::- One days Number sixteen.
This was on H.M.S. Galates and I had just passed for leading seaman although only eighteen years. I was a Chatham rating on board a Devonport ship and as a consequence, took a lot of 'stick' about the indecencies of a Chatham rating compared with one from (Guz). My Captain of the top was a wonderful seaman who taught me an awful lot and badgered me with seamanship questions, apparently to prove what an ignorant sailor this Chatham rating was.
On the day I passed for leading seaman he jocularly (or so I thought) said " Think you're good now do you? I'll have you lifting you bonnet before the week is out" Sure enough a few days later, I and an ordinary seaman called Jones were lined on the quarter deck after 'scrub decks' and charged. We had been the last two to fall in, but were no means late. When I denied being 'slack in obeying' P.O. Cloete reiterated that we had turned up late, and were habitual late comers. I was flabbergasted, it could not be more untrue. However when the Officer of the Day ordered "One day's number sixteens I thought "What the hell". Two hours extra work will not worry me. So at 1700, I and the other seaman fell in, we were the only two and guess who was the duty P.O.? - P.O. Cloete. "Right down below, draw rifle and bayonet." I thereon protested. "We're 16 punishment not 8" P.O. Cloete reminded me what No 16 meant, two hours work or one hours drill and one hours work. So drill it was in the hot Gibraltar sun. He then proceeded to really put us through it, no rest, plenty of frog hopping with the rifle held above the heads eventually my companion collapsed, but I was determined for the honour of Chatham to carry on. At last came the order "Halt, Ground Arms". Hurrah I thought, he is giving me a spell, but no such luck. "On the ridge ropes, Go!, raise lower, raise lower etc; However the hour did come to an end and I welcomed the order to return

my rifle to the rack, and reported back to the P.O. For details of my one hours work, to my amazement he said, "Shove off, and well done!" I realised then that it was put up job to ensure that I did not get too swelled headed at passing for Leading Seaman at such a tender age.
My next appearance at the table was as Leading Seaman on the Veteran, and Captain of 'A' gun. At quarters 'clean guns' I found the piaba was not in its storage rack on a fixed screen just abaft the gun. I therefore reported this to the G.I. Consequence, "Report to the bridge. Off caps." I was charged with its loss. To both the Officer of the Day and the First Lieutenant. I replied "Nothing to say Sir." When the charge was read out when I faced the Captain, I simply said, "I did not lose it Sir, I only reported its loss." Without further ado, the Captain (Jackie Broome of PQ17 fame) said "Case dismissed."
My last appearance as a defaulter was in 1948 or 49 as a P.O.G.I serving as an instructor at H.M.S. Royal Arthur. My co-defendant was John Goulder (now Commander J Goulder D.S.O. RN Rtd). The facts leading to the charge were that John and I suspected that the President of the P.O's mess was working some fiddle with the rum. This P.O.was currently under close arrest and we decided to break into his cabin, find the rum and ditch it, neither of us had any interest in rum. Whilst we were searching the cabin, having got in via the window, the door opened and in walked the occupant, accompanied by an R.P.O. They were both flabbergasted. We were very promptly out of the window and away. Shortly afterwards we were piped to report to the main gate and as we expected it was a case of "Off caps." I cannot remember the exact charge no doubt something like 'Did improperly enter' We said "Nothing to say" when questioned by the Officer of the Day. As expected, the O.O.D. Ordered "Commanders Report. Later." Later the Master at Arms sent for both of us and asked us to tell him what this was all about. We decided to tell him exactly what our plan had been. He listened and then said "I'm not sure I got this right, you did say that if you found any rum you were going to hand it in?" We started to protest and say "No we were going" When he interrupted us and loudly said. "You were going to hand it in." We got the message and agreed that was what we intended. "That's your story and you stick to it." At the Commanders table we said "Nothing to say Sir." But when we saw the Captain we told our story and taking full advantage of the advice given to us by the M.A.A, The Captains verdict, "A very worthy scheme, badly executed." Admonished (This has been altered from the old 'Caution').
The last experience I will recount was from the other side of the table. As the Q.D divisional officer in a destroyer in 1957 I came off shore one Monday morning to find that one of the A.B's had the day before, been charged with

direct disobedience of orders, obviously a very serious charge. He refused to go to church when detailed, being of the opinion that going to church was voluntary. He put in a request to make a complaint, but, the O.O.D. After consulting the First Lieut. dismissed it saying that he had no grounds for complaint. When he appeared before the First Lt I advised him to reply "Nothing to say" and to stick to that, whatever asked. That night I studied at some length the relevant Q.R's and A.I's (Queens Regulations and Admiralty Instructions) about attending divine service and stating of complaints. I first questioned the O.O.D. "Are you aware of the provision of Q.R's and A.I's regarding stating of complaints?" To my delight he said "Yes vaguely" I then asked "Why in accordance with the rule, he had not made any attempt to contact me, as I was on board and the rule clearly states that "A rating must be assisted in all stages of his complaint by his divisional officer." He admitted that he was not aware of this. I then questioned him further as to whether he made any attempt to point out to the rating that Q.R's and A.I's clearly gave authority for a Captain to order a man to go to church under special circumstances. This church parade was a ceremonial parade in Portugal. Of course he didn't. I then questioned the First Lt in the same way and got much the same responses. I then put it to the Captain, that the Able seaman was only on this charge because the case had been wrongly dealt with by the O.O.D. Who had also been wrongly advised by the 1st Lt. I also pointed out, that had I been informed and able to advise the A.B, on the provision of the relevant Q.R and A.I's the A.B. would have accepted the order and gone to church. By this time the Captain was getting exasperated and interrupted the proceedings with "Right, change the charge to slack in obeying" I answered this by saying, "Could I respectfully point out that the two ratings have already been dealt with under that charge and got one day's number 16. The Captain then slammed his fist down on the table. "I've had enough of this, case dismissed." I was amazed. I never set out to achieve that, all I wanted was a scaled down charge.
Some years later I was discussing this case with the Captain and he stated that he thought that I overstepped the mark in the way I had treated the O.O.D. And the 1st Lt. "I must disagree Sir, that incident did this ship a power of good, and the fact that you dismissed the case because it had been badly handled raised your esteem in the eyes of the ships company. Remember the old lower deck saying "Put in a complaint and you finish up in the rattle.' Your decision helped to disperse that, and also the D.O's in this ship have much more prepared themselves for the more serious cases, after seeking the advice of Hartly Shawcross (which had become my nick name).

Finally, every officer in this ship will in future deal more thoroughly with ratings statements of complaint, either as his D.O. or as the officer dealing with his complaint.
I met the Captain some time after I retired and he immediately talked about this case. "My God Jack, you shook us all up that day, and taught me a lot".

Chapter 16

HONG KONG

Hong Kong, city of mystery
Or so the books all tell,
But Hong Kong to the average bloke,
Is just a town of smell.

Where one works all day,
With sticky perspiration,
But still us English were
A long drawn out suffering nation.

Where one develops lots of spots,
Blotches and prickly heat,
And plenty of boils and dhoby itch,
Not to mention Hong Kong feet.

These chaps who write these thing in books
And make then look so swell
Should try a summer in Hong Kong,
And then say "It is swell"

* * * * * *

Allenby Flisher recalls;-
I was born in September 1919 at Lydd in Kent, a small limb of the Cinque ports on the sixth continent - Romney Marsh.
I always wanted to join the Navy, but when I left school at 14, my father would not sign the necessary documents. I had to wait until I was eighteen and a man!
So it was on September 20th 1937 I reported to Chatham barracks for my basic training. After the completion of this I was delighted and excited to be drafted to **H.M.S. Westcott** operating with submarines in the Far East. A train load of us travelled to Southampton where we embarked in the troopship Dilwara.
Although I had a slight insight into sea training of one day on board **H.M.S. Wanderer**, the thing that gave me the biggest surprise was that we all had the need of a galvanised bucket this was a necessity to wash in, bathe in and do ones dhobeying (washing) in. We had to go out on to the upper deck and

pump the water into the bucket with a deck hand pump, this in all weathers. Hot water could be obtained from the galley, or by using a steam geyser in the canteen flat. The wash place had no fittings except a wooden bench on which to rest the bucket. However this did not detract from a clean ship and a smart ships company. Another thing that surprised me was the need for secondary lighting for at this time the old oil lamps were still in use. It was my job as a stoker to clean the glass, trim the wicks and fill them with sperm oil and light them when we went to sea. One of these lamps was situated beside each glass gauge on the boilers. We also had a polished brass lamp on the stokers mess deck.

Captain Lolly was the Commanding Officer until he was given an Admiralty appointment. The crew compliment was then between 70 an 80.

Captain Lolly was followed by Commander Firth who, after about three months on board was taken seriously ill and while we were at We-Hai-Wei he unfortunately died. The funeral took place on the island and representatives from the whole Eastern Fleet attended and of course most of our ships company.

A Commander Corrie-Hill then took over command. **Westcott** was often referred to in signals as Submarine **Westcott** followed by the name of the submarine. This was not surprising as we were attached to the 4th submarine flotilla. We were also part of the Hong Kong defence.

The ships role was to act as guard ship and communicator for the submarines, also as off shoot target and to accompany them when visiting foreign ports. For the offshoot target exercises our torpedo tubes were removed, along with the aft gun. In place of the Tubes we had wooden racks on which to store the torpedoes and a derrick with which to lift them on board. When we went out on exercise with a sub', they fired torpedoes and when the 'tin fish' stopped running its course a red dummy head would normally bring it floating to the surface in a vertical position where it would bob up and down. A ring bolt would enable the crew to hook a line on so that it could be lifted on board and stored, On return to harbour the tin fish were either returned by cutter to the depot ship H.M.S. Medway or transferred to the submarine directly if she happened to be tied up alongside the ship. Sometime when a group of six torpedoes had been fired only five could be found. In Deep Water Bay in Hong Kong divers had to be used to recover the sixth from the blue clay where it was stuck tail first. On one occasion, off the coast of Malaya the sub fired six 'tin fish', we recovered five. The RAF Were requested to assist in the search for the missing torpedo. On its last sweep that the plane carried out it took them overland. Surprise, surprise, the torpedo was about a mile inland being carried shoulder high by the local natives. It took a Naval party nearly a week to trundle it back through the jungle to the beach for recovery.

On another occasion we were sent to dispose of a derelict Junk which had become a hazard in the shipping lane. We fired shells but they went straight through it. A charge was put on board, but apart from splintering it, it still remained afloat, in the end it had to be towed inshore where it was beached.

One place we visited was Taingtao where I was surprised to see Japanese guards outside the principle buildings and banks. This did not affect us directly or our visit. though at nights we could see convoys of lorries laden with Japanese troops moving along the coast.

The next occasion we came across the Japanese was when we were sent up the Pel-Ho river to Taku to relieve HMS Diana. Before we could go up the river we had to have our Asdic dome removed and a blank plate fitted in its place. The river was very fast flowing and the whole length twisted and turned on its course. Our duty there was as protection vessel for British liners berthed at Taku. Apparently Japanese officers had been going on the liners and interfering with the state rooms. A naval rating was put on guard on the gangway, all he had was a trenching tool handle as a defence, it seemed to work. Less than a mile away was a large encampment of Japanese troops. On the other side of the river it was swamp and apparently home for bandits and pirates, so we too had armed guard on deck.

At the end of our stay, I was on deck, so I was able to watch our passage down river. It was amazing to see houses made of mud. One bend in the river was almost a right angle, to get round it meant letting the ship gently go into the sand bank ahead and then use the engines to go astern and swing the stern round at the same time, freeing the bow so that the ship was pointing down river again. It was a tense time, but apparently the manoeuvre is normal practice for ships coming down river.

The third time we were close to the Japanese was at Wei-Hai-Wei. We had been out on a day time exercise with a submarine and had been shadowed all day by the Japanese cruiser Itzumu. As we entered harbour followed by the submarine, the cruiser cut straight in front of us, forcing Westcott to go full astern to take avoiding action, the ship bounced up and down with the movement. It was amazing to think that whilst this was going on we were training Japanese Officers in Chatham Barracks.

In the crisis of 1938, when fear of war was imminent, we were sent to Singapore to have our gun and torpedo tubes replaced. We were then sent on patrol. We had to be darkened at night and closed down. The temperature was horrendous, ventilation almost non existent and it was terribly uncomfortable. As soon as the crisis was over we reverted to our original role

The **Westcott** was very busy visiting lots of places with one or two sub's for company. These are some of the places we visited. Miri, Labau, Surabaya, Malacca, Chefoo, Penang, Chinwanto, Peitaho, Port Swirtenham, Singapore and Batavia.
The **Westcott** paid off in April 1938. I had hoped that I would be able to stay on her, but it had been decided that as we had been on her for a full year we should come home.
One or two things that have stayed in my mind about **Westcott.** Around the rear of the superstructure door a frame had been built, on this was carved all the names of the submarines in the flotilla. The crew at that time also had a dog as a mascot. It used to fall in at the end of the row with the men going ashore, it was always first off the ship and it knew how to dodge the dockyard police when the men were marched from the ship to the dockyard gate and it was always the first out. It found its own way back and was never adrift.
I never expected to see Westcott again so soon, but when I was serving on the **Volunteer** in the first Norwegian campaign, she was present there too. We had a spell of screening H.M.S. Ark Royal, then with the Glorious, but because neither of us could keep up with her when she was at maximum speed to get her aircraft airborne. We were subsequently relieved by H.M.S Ardent and Acasta who sad to say were with the Glorious a few days later when they were all sunk.
After my foreign leave, I joined H.M.S. **Volunteer** to bring it up to sea worthy condition ready for King George V1's reserve fleet review at Weymouth in the August.
When we left there we all became H.M. Ships because war was now imminent and our destination was Milford Haven, from there to Liverpool where our first trip of the North Atlantic convoys began. We remained on the Atlantic convoys until the Norwegian campaign. On our last trip from there we called at Petsamo and escorted H.M.S, Devonshire bringing the Norwegian Royal Family and government out of Norway to the U.K.
Next we were engaged in the evacuation of Dunkirk, then a short spell of escorting convoys up and down the Channel, before returning to the North Atlantic. On one occasion our food rations were low, we were out of bread and meat, so our Commanding Officer decided to drop a depth charge to see if we could obtain some fresh fish. Not one measly fish came to the surface!! However a little later we made contact with a fishing vessel who supplied us with enough cod to feed all the crew. Every one was looking forward to dinner! It was soon after this that we were in collision with H.M.S Newark, her bows struck the port side of the stokers mess deck. I was asleep in my hammock when I was awakened by a 'flash and bang' and water on my face.

Four shipmates who were playing cards were immediately lost along with two men from the seamen's mess. I could see the sky through the ships side. The ladder to the upper deck was bent so I had to use hammock rails to pull myself across to get up to the deck I was left with what I had on when I went to sleep in my hammock - my vest and pants! Some of the seamen were already packing their gear I stood in the seamen's mess for a while, dazed, others too were standing in a dazed state. I swore and made my way to the upper deck, as I did so the Chief Stoker ordered me to help on the Dounton hand pump. The effort was in vain as the suction line had been damaged. At 0400 I was ordered to relieve the stoker on watch in the number one boiler room. As I climbed the ladder to the deck plates I was standing in two feet of water. When I saw the duty S.P.O. I had no qualms about being down below, for he stood by the pumps puffing away at his pipe as calm as could be, just as if nothing had happened, and giving great confidence to us youngsters. At 0800 when the boiler was shut down we went up on deck. I went into the engineers officers cabin and borrowed a pair of overalls. I also found a pair of rubber boots which I purloined. Being dressed made me feel much more comfortable. A tug was sent out to tow us to Belfast. Newark had limped home under her own steam and when we arrived we found Newark in the same dry dock!

On the **Volunteer** it meant that all compartments had to be pumped out, oil and ammunition removed, and a length of the keel cut off so that the rivet holes could be plugged. It was when the compartments were drained that we found the four stokers, unfortunately the two seamen were missing. Apart from one empty hammock, everything had gone, crockery, tables, lockers, bedding had all been washed away. The messdeck ladder was completely distorted which accounted for me not being able to get out of the mess. It took until September for the ship to be repaired and resume duty. It had cost me everything except the most precious thing - my life!

It was not long before we resumed duties in the North Atlantic, It was then that I was made up to Leading Stoker and Liverpool was made H.Q for Western Approaches. At this time escort ships were at a premium and there were times when **Volunteer** and **Witherington** were the only escorts for quite a large convoy.

It was early 1942 that I was drafted back to Chatham where I completed my P.O's course.

Chapter 17

1938

R.N. BARRACKS CHATHAM

The situation in Europe was becoming rather volatile. Germany who had already began rearming at an alarming rate and were producing U-boats as fast as possible also producing bomber and fighter aircraft, all contrary to previous international terms and conditions.

My introduction to the V&Ws.

At about -0200 on a Saturday in September 1938, I was sleeping in my hammock in 5GG mess R.N.B Chatham, when I was aroused by someone switching on the lights. It was an R.P.O, who was calling out from a list of names, and asking each one "Can you ride a Bike?" On receiving an affirmative, he was instructed to report to the main gate, where he would be sent round on a bicycle delivering call up messages to reservists in the Medway. One wit, hoping perhaps to avoid the task replied "No", only to be told to report to the main gate, where he would have to walk round delivering call up messages.

Before switching off the lights the R.P.O informed us, that due to the Munich crisis the Fleet was being mobilised, and that most of us would be drafted to ships that day. So much for the short week end leave that I was expecting.

That day in the barracks was one of watching and waiting. Watching the huge notice boards that had been placed in the drill shed and trying to find out which ship you had been sent to. I eventually found my name, I was posted to the **Whirlwind** a V&W destroyer. It was then a question of waiting, waiting until about 1600 hrs, when after much hanging around, we were marched to the dockyard to join **Whirlwind**. I was then an AB SG and was allocated to number two mess, top division, trainer of 'B' gun, and,, "Captain of the Heads", (toilets) a very privileged job, or so I thought until I saw it. They were in a terrible state, and to put it crudely Stunk! The ship had been in reserve for many years, and I do not think that any work had been done in the heads during that time.

The first night we stored ship, and the following day went to Shore Reach to ammunition ship. We then went to Portsmouth and spent the next few days at sea doing all the commissioning exercises.

Whenever possible I worked in the Heads, and got them up to a reasonable standard to satisfy myself and the chief of the mess decks. One bonus was that I had my own "Caboosh". There were two toilets marked, C.& P.O's and a third one with no marking. I decided that this was spare, and I rigged up a

nice little den for myself, with photographs, a line for my dhobeying and other personal items. I had the best caboosh in the ship. Alas it came to an end one day whilst at sea, when the Captain appeared in the galley flat and asked where his sea heads was. It was my caboosh. He naturally exploded when he opened the door and saw my dhobeying hanging there. That was it for me. I lost my Captaincy and was back working part of ship.
The commission only lasted for about a month, following Neville Chamberlain's return from Munich waving a piece of paper saying "Peace in our time". We paid off and it was back to R.N.B.

Chapter 18

WAR

Recollections of a thirty niner. Arthur Skelton.
October 1939 like so many others, I was sent to HMS Royal Arthur (Skegness). On completion of my training I was drafted to my depot Chatham on the fourth of December. By January 1940 I was out on the 'oggin as a "Dabtoe" aboard an old V&W destroyer on Atlantic convoys (ring job for the spew class). No sea clothing, just the issue overcoat and oilskin. Like a frozen turd on lookout, (before radar). Six inches of water on the mess deck, and water gushing out of the gun stanchions. No heating whilst at sea, in harbour we were allowed to light the combustion stove. Fresh water pump was at the port waist on the upper deck - not very handy in roughers, contents of bread locker mildewed after a couple of days. Steam Capstan on the forward mess - chip fryer and steam bath!! Coal fire galley. The cutlass stowed in the after wardroom flat with the muck sticks (rifles). Weather, always trying to miss the next one (wave) over. Eating pot mess with tin opener whilst wrapped round a stanchion. - Just my introduction to the **Vanquisher.**

* * * * * *

When the war broke out **Westcott** was in Singapore having 'Y' gun and the torpedo tubes refitted. From then on our time was spent patrolling the islands, we also took divers from H.M.S. Medway to Miri in North Borneo to lay charges under the oil pipes that ran out to sea.
We left Singapore in January 1940, stopping off at Penang, Aden, Alexandria, and spent some time in Malta from where we returned home with Glorious and others, arriving in Plymouth in April. We were given weekend leave while degaussing gear was fitted.
Then it was off to Norway where we patrolled off Narvik, we were bombed and shelled, some falling so close that the deck was washed down, we went as far North as Kirkenes and then down to Aalidalsness to take off the Marines during the night, at the time we were accompanied by **Walker,** Sheffield and Arethusa. The marines left a lot of Lewis guns and rifles behind, but we had to give them up when we arrived at Plymouth where we refitted.
On completion of the refit we took two French minesweepers over to Brest. On the way back we were sent to help one of our own boats, the 'Votaire' (there was no V&W by that name) who had had her bows blown off. After taking off all the survivors we sank her with torpedoes.

From there on it was North Atlantic convoy duty running from Liverpool and Londonderry. On one convoy a German aircraft was brought down by a 'Kite' being towed by one of the merchant ships. We were with a convoy when the Bismark broke out, she missed us by about 200 miles. The Westcott's skipper, Bockett Pugh had the torpedo tubes trained outboard just in case we met her. His intention was to go straight at her, 'Death or Glory' fashion, in this case it would have been death.

There was a time when we were told to clean up and get into our number one's and line up on the jetty. Winston Churchill arrived and walked along the rows and inspected us. We were at sea within the hour.

On another occasion we got an 'echo' at the same time as one of the Corvette's, our skipper signalled her saying "I'll take it", but she took no notice and ran into us, leaving a hole in our mess deck big enough to get a bus in. We crawled back to Londonderry where they patched us up with timber and cement to enable us to get to Liverpool and dry dock for repairs.

The 'Spiggot Mortar' (later to be called the 'hedgehog') was fitted and we spent some time carrying out trials off Large and Troon. Bob Blowers lost some fingers off his left hand when a 'spiggot' short circuited. I do not recall us ever sinking a sub with it, in fact one pattern that we fired blew up when it hit the water, the safety pins had been taken out so many times that the 'Keep' wires had parted.

Back to convoy duty again, we picked up a boat full of survivors from a merchant ship, they were in a bad way having been adrift for some time.

Whilst we were in Londonderry at some time in 1941, Earl Mountbatten brought three of the 'K' boats up the river Foyle for the week-end, Kelly, Kashmir, and Kandaha. On the Sunday morning we all had to march through Londonderry where he took the salute, immediately that was over they set sail for the Mediterranean. One of our Westcott lads, Bob Hurlet was on the Kelly when she was sunk, he went down with her.

Nearing Christmas 1941, we left Londonderry thinking we were going to Iceland with a fast convoy, instead we finished up in Gibraltar on Christmas Eve. Our duty there was mainly 'club' runs and Malta convoys. The 'club runs were escorting the carriers Eagle or the USS Wasp taking Spitfires to within flying distance of Malta. We would leave Gibraltar at night when there was no moon because the spies in La Linea always knew when we left, because we were always attacked as the Spitfires were taking off. Sometimes we would pick up the pilots who had to ditch on take off. We left 'Gib' for the Azores to pick up a troop ship, the Llangibby Castle which was laden with 1,000 British personnel. she had been struck by a torpedo which badly damaged her rudder and steering gear and had pulled into the Azores but under the three day rule she had to leave the harbour. We were accompanied

by the Exmoor and Croome. Exmoor took up station outside the Northern entrance and Croome the South We took up position outside the harbour for it was known that U-boats were in the area waiting for the troop ship to come out. Just as the forenoon watch was taking over, the alarm bells went, and there in front of us on the surface was a U-boat which appeared to be steering the same course as ourselves. We increased to full speed with the intentions of ramming her but only struck her a glancing bow. We soon overtook her and as we came alongside a depth charge pattern set shallow was dropped and as we turned The 'X' and 'Y' guns were able to get a few rounds off at her too. Skipper had intended to ram her, but thought better of it, however the collision damaged our stokers mess deck.
At this point the German U-boat crew were jumping over the side, we managed to haul forty one officers and men aboard including the Captain Pfeifer who when he arrived on board delivered a formal protest in writing. Meanwhile the remainder of the crew were put in one of the damaged stokers mess. We posted an armed rating to stand guard over the hatch to the mess.

The Protest

(1) When being followed up, boat got gradually water without influence of the enemy. The consequence was to rise to the surface as soon as possible. The boat was in distress at sea.
(2) According to our navigation (controlled by taking bearings on the coast) boat was four miles off the coast before the persecution, afterwards boat was steering East course for some time, later on when coming to the conclusion to emerge about ten minutes 70 degrees. After emerging boat was steaming on 70 degrees. The stream was setting NNE.
(3) The boat would have been ready with lay down 24 hours in a neutral port.
(4) In spite of the possibility to shoot, boat did not launch torpedoes. I made no use of the gun because it was the neutral zone.
(5) After having seen that the boat should be rammed by the destroyer or should be covered with depth charges I commanded. All men off the boat.
(6) The depth charges did not disturb the boat hardly because it was on the surface. I myself gave the order to sink the boat. It was flooded by the Chief Engineer who left the sinking boat with me.
(7) Of course of above we beg for delivery to a neutral country.

Pfeifer Kptlt.

While the survivors, more than forty in number were being picked up, the Commanding Officer of **Westcott,** Lt, Comdr. Bocket-Pugh had taken the opportunity of fixing the position.
Having ascertained that it was outside territorial waters, he rejected the protest.
With regard to the first item, unseaworthy U-boats, he considered should stay in harbour and, if at sea should show "Not under control lights". The second was very vague and proved nothing, and his comment on the third was "It would probably have been ready within one minute if the Llangibby Castle had been observed to sail".
As for the rest of the protest, it seemed to him that after the first attempt at ramming and the pattern of depth charges, that was justifiable enough, panic on board. The enemy realised that the outline of the U-boat had not been lost against the background of Pico Island as had been hoped, the torpedo tubes were not ready and the gun was out of action. Either through panic or because the U-boat was too damaged to be fought, they decided, before Westcott ran in for her second attack to abandon ship.
The three destroyer continued with their patrol until Llangibby Castle was observed to be heading into the Fayal Channel. Westcott steamed into the channel and signalled the liner to steer for the Southern end, which had been so satisfactorily cleared.
It was considered that there had been a U-boat at the Southern end of the Fayal Channel, so there would also be one at the Northern end. Therefore Westcott went ahead of the liner, telling her of the good news as she went by, and exhorting her to make for the open sea and to steam 'Like Hell'.
Llangibby Castle however was headstrong and was refusing to obey her Master and steer North, then went off to the West. Later she changed her mind and went East-South-East down the channel between Pico Island and San Jorge Island. She apparently knew better than her master, for there lurking off Ribeirinha Point was another U-boat, and it could do nothing but bring up the rear of the convoy as they passed between the two islands at 8 knots.
Out in the open sea the liner who had been steering by her engines felt the full force of a South-easterly wing and the Master decided to take a tow from the tug 'Thames' who had been standing by.
While the tow was being passed 'Croome' sighted a U-boat some five miles away as it was coming out of the channel. Exmoor and Croome carried out depth charge attacks, which may have discouraged it from continuing to pursue further.
On each of the following days U-boats were sighted, but Llangibby Castle was not attacked and arrived with all her passengers safely in Gibraltar.

Chapter 19

Soon after that fateful day in September 1939. The cinema's throughout the country were showing newsreels of troops marching through Sydney on their way to the docks to board great liners, the news reader was boasting of our gallant comrades of the British Empire, the Anzacs, who were boarding to come to "Blighty" to the defence of their Mother land. The First Sea Lord, Winston Churchill was furious. To think that we were broadcasting to the world at large and in particular our enemy that troop ships would soon be sailing, loaded with thousands of troops, on the only obvious route, with no escorts. Churchill immediately ordered H.M.S. Westcott who was fitted with Asdic and operating with the 4th submarine flotilla on the China station, to prepare and make all haste to escort these ships to their destination. Westcott, who had been stripped of her torpedo tubes to make way for gantry's to be fitted, thereby enabling her to recover the torpedoes fired by the submarines during their exercises.
Westcott proceeded to Singapore to have her torpedo tubes refitted and to ammunition ship before proceeding to take up station with the troopships. Another of the V&Ws, **Vendetta** also fitted with Asdic was in Haifa, she too was detailed to proceed to escort the troop ships. However, and thankfully their journey proved uneventful and they arrived in the Mediterranean unharmed.
After a brief stay at Alexandria 19th March 1940 **Westcott** sailed for Devonport, after a boiler clean she went off to Narvik where she bombarded the railway and tunnels and then evacuated many Norwegian civilians and Royal Marines to Scapa Flow. There Lower deck was cleared and we received a 'thank you' speech from a senior officer for what we had done. We thought we might get a few days leave, but no, although we were given an extra railway warrant for the year. Then it was off on Atlantic convoys during one of these a tanker was sunk and the sea became an inferno, many of those we rescued were covered in oil and many of their wounds were operated on in the wardroom.

* * * * * *

H.M.S. **Vanessa** (D29) A crew member writes:
It all began in 1938 when architects came off the reserved occupation list. Now I could fulfil my ambition to go to sea. There were three members of our staff who were like minded and wished to join the Royal Navy Volunteer Reserve, but the difficulty was getting to Newhaven to attend drills and instruction. But now we had a fourth who had a car, so the problem had been

overcome and we duly presented ourselves to the drill hall in Newhaven and signed on. And so with the prospect of war in the near future, we all (Geoffrey Price, architectural assistant, and clerical officers Cecil Scrivener, Stanley Frost and Archie Allen) joined the reserve.
We were all good keen sailors and did our best to learn all the things necessary to make us fit to go to sea with the Fleet.

* * * * * *

In July 1939, when the reserve fleet was taken out of moth balls for the review by the King, we all received our calling up papers for our annual fortnights sea training. What a fortnight that turned out to be.
The Sussex division was Portsmouth based, and to the famous H.M.S Victory. A large contingent from the division mustered, duly equipped with hammocks additional items of uniform, given a five pound note, and allocated to a mess for the night with instructions to muster in the morning for transport to various ports throughout the country to join the ships to which we had been appointed.
I was to go to Rosyth to join the old V&W class destroyer **Vanessa**. Scrivener Wren and Frost were to join **Verity** Allen went to a tug H.M.T St Fagan.
After out first night in hammocks we went our separate ways, I to board a train at Portsmouth docks, the next stop, Rosyth.
As this story is mine, it would be as well now to relate the ways of my office companions. It is a sad story. Stan Frost and Archie Allen were both killed in action in 1940. Allen died during the Dunkirk evacuation when his tug received a direct hit from a bomb, and shortly after this Frost, when the Wren was bombed and sunk in the channel. Cecil Scrivener became an Asdic operator in destroyers and frigates in the battle of the Atlantic and was awarded the D.S.M.
To continue. On arriving alongside the quay at Rosyth where three or four dirty old destroyers were berthed. One was H.M.S Vanessa, Her compliment had about fifteen seamen from the R.N.V.R Sussex division, most of us ordinary seamen or A.B's (Able Bodied) and not very knowledgeable about the routine of running a ship. This was soon learned, We also found that the mess decks were going to take some while to get used to. The seaman's mess was on a level with the upper deck and crowded. Each individual mess, which had one of the four corners of the area, was comprised of one leading seaman and 18 seamen, these were in turn divided into four parts of watches. Each day, in rotation one part of the watch became cook of the mess and were responsible for cleaning the mess deck and preparing the food, which

was cooked by the galley cooks. Each individual mess was responsible for its own catering for which some provisions were provided. The rest had to be bought from the N.A.A.F.I and accounted for by the leading hand, for this there was an allowance of one shilling and three pence a day per man. The food was good and eatable and, when we got used to it, conditions were good.

An O.D. Was paid thirty shillings a week, plus one and three pence kit allowance. (We were fully kitted up in the first place and from the on we had to maintain a full kit on this allowance. Also in those ships we received a shilling a day "Hard Lying" money. Incidentally when I was a full Lieutenant and in command of a minesweeper. I received the princely sum of thirty shillings per day with an additional two shillings hard lying and an additional two shilling command pay.

Having been allocated our watches and messes, we duly boarded the ship and were given tea and bread and jam, then we changed into overalls and were at once put to work painting ship. Here started the first of many incidents which were to enliven what could have been a rather dull routine. Another rating and I were put to work painting the ships side, The deck level to the water was about ten feet. I had noticed on the train that one very young Volunteer Reserve, by the name of Bishop, was very frightened indeed at the thought of the whole business of preparing for war. He had been given the job of painting the stantions and to do the outside meant standing outside the guard rail. He had an Epileptic fit and fell into the water alongside my companion and me as we were busy on a stage at water level, we realised what was up and went in after him. Anyone who has had to cope with a person having and epileptic fit will know how hard it is to restrain him, fortunately we had the stage to hold on to, and the boat attending the painter was close at hand. Bishop was duly revived and put on lighter duties until he could be fully examined and assessed. We dried off and changed into dry clothes and took our wet ones into the boiler room to dry. Then it was back to the stage and the paint pot after a short break when a much needed rum ration was served up. This was the first tot of my naval career. But all was not over. During the afternoon Bishop repeated the performance, exactly as before, except that he fell from the forecastle which was much higher than the after part of ship. We duly pulled him out and again were very soaked to the boots. This time when we had dried out we were summoned to the First Lieutenant's cabin and after a short talk during which he wanted to find out our occupation etc; he rewarded us with a large scotch. This I think, helped me to get ahead and gave me a more interesting job aboard than sweeping the deck and polishing the stern light and the handrails to "Y" gun. Later on I was put to doing some chart correcting, and assist the navigating officer.

There was plenty of work to do to get these ships into full working condition and much training of the raw crews. We were at it from dawn to duck, After the final trials of the ships, the small flotilla sailed from Rosyth through the North sea and the channel to Weymouth Bay. There were many seasick sailors when we first set out, but after a few days things settled down and a quite efficient crew seemed to emerge.

I give a fuller description of these ships and our crew further on in this account, but I did hear one Admiral say that he considered that the seamen in Nelson's ships had better living conditions.

July moved into August with the review by the King. Then came some really intense and concentrated training with gunnery practice, depth charge and anti submarine work, torpedo firing, boat work and flotilla manoeuvring etc; The ships company had settled down to a pretty fair body of men and one had to admire the chiefs and petty officers whose job it was to knock us into shape. Our duties rotated in order to give us the feel of the many tasks. I had turns as crew of the motor boat, an ancient relic powered by a petrol/paraffin engine, and all other parts of the ship. My daily task was a quarter deck man which entailed washing down the deck at the crack of dawn and keeping it clean during the day unless some other excitement intervened. I concentrated on the stern light and "Y" gun. They were always bright and gleaming. We did have plenty of time ashore and were able to see the lights of Weymouth and the Salvation Army hostel and to take walks to the hillside and through the town.

August moved into September and by the third of September we were at anchor in the Clyde when war was declared. On this day I learned one of the rules of survival. The Bosun came into the mess deck at about noon and asked if anyone could ride a bicycle, he got two offers, I and another V.R. found ourselves up the funnel painting out the flotilla markings. After this I was instructed to use the paint and paint the stern light grey and also the hand rails up to "Y" gun. War had really come to us.

The first alarm came that very day. The Athenea was torpedoed somewhere off the Irish coast and we joined in the search for possible U-boats. The ship was soon back in the Clyde and a day or two later we went out to join the escort of a large troop convoy.

From then on the work was all convoy escort. Based in Devonport or Milford Haven we took convoys out into the Atlantic and the met the homeward bound ships, escorting them to the Channel ports, sometimes as far as Dover. It was on one of the Channel runs that an amusing incident occurred which made me realise how well the officers knew the crew.

One of our Sussex seamen was a young carpenter called Drake. In a very patriotic moment his parents had christened him Francis. He was a quiet lad, not the brightest of the bright, and when things were not going too well he would comment "never mind eh". It became the "in" expression in the mess if things were not going well to say "never mind eh". I was on watch as a bridge lookout as we moved up the channel in thick for and were passing Beachy Head. I knew this as I had done some sailing in this part of the channel, having lived in Hastings. I knew that Beachy Head sounded a bell in foggy weather and we could also hear the Royal Sovereign light ship which had a distinctive, grunting fog horn. The Captain was on the bridge and turned and asked the navigator our position. He told the Captain that the fog horn was Beachy Head, whereupon I had the nerve to but in and correct the navigator, explaining my local knowledge. The navigator checked the chart and then confirmed that I was correct; the Captain commented "Well as Drake would say Never mind eh".

During this period of the cold war we had one trip with a troop ship to Quiberon Bay on the Atlantic coast of France. The ship was anchored off a small fishing harbour and as we had been at sea for quite a while we had run out of fresh meat. There was no refrigeration in those old ships. I was in the duty watch and a party was to go ashore and buy some meat. To ensure that I was in the shore party, I told the duty officer that I spoke French fluently. We went ashore with the liberty men in the whaler towed by the motor boat, and with the help of my fluent French bought four and a half carcasses of beef, which had to be carried on out backs to the landing stage, a distance of about two miles. After a wait of about two hours in the local tavern, the boats came for us and picked up the liberty men. A fairly strong off shore wind had risen and on the return journey to the ship the motor boat broke down. The whaler then took the motor boat in tow and we all manned the oars and eventually returned to the ship. After the boats were unloaded the whaler had to be taken to the port side of the ship, and to do this it was drifted round on its painter. But someone forgot to keep a firm hold of this painter, which saw myself and O.D Buxton drifting fast out to sea We tried hard to pull the boat back to the ship, but two oars do not make headway in a heavy boat and the ship had to "up anchor" and come and get us before we got to America. Two very cold and wet seamen were very happy to get "home".

Christmas saw us in Dover at anchor. I went ashore to a dead town, no pubs open and no where to go. However Buxton and I were outside an army drill hall where there was a party starting when the officer in charge turned up to join in the Christmas dinner. He was a good friend of mine from my hockey playing days in Folkestone and we were invited inside and well dined and wined. We returned to our ship with a large bag of left overs for our mess shipmates.

The winter of 1939/40 was to be one of the coldest and stormiest for many years and convoy work in the North Atlantic was pretty grim. Very rough, very wet and cold is all that I can say about it. At that time in the war the earnest ladies had not yet sharpened their knitting needles and the ship was desperately short of warm clothing. I happened to mention this to my brother Peter who was serving as an instructor (sergeant pilot) with the air force. He told his wife who in turn told a rich aunt and shortly after this I received 50 parcels in the post. Each one contained one Wolseley woollen vest and a pair of matching long johns. I had friends for life. These were sold on a ballot for five pounds a set and the money went into the ships fund, which bought such things as football boots and hockey sticks.
We did get some games in when in port, especially when in Milford Haven and I was in both the football and hockey teams.
Around about Christmas, we had a change of commanding officer and the first Lieutenant also transferred. Lt Comdr. Plumer who had commissioned the ship left. and Lt Comdr. (full ahead both) Stocker took over and Lt Michael Pollock replaced Lt Carey RNR. Both officers were popular with the crew and certainly knew their jobs.
Both of our commanding officers were on the reserve prior to the war. Lt Pollock was a regular officer and gunnery officer. I met him again in 1942 in Port Said when he was gunnery officer of the Arethusia. I have had intermittent correspondence with him during the past years. He named his daughter Venessa and finished his service as Admiral of the Fleet Sir Michael Pollock.
Just after Christmas, I'm not sure of the date, Vanessa had a desperate battle in a howling gale on a very dark night when on escort duty. This is the story of that attack on a U-boat in a winter gale in the North Atlantic January 1940.
We were escorting a West bound convoy. We were well out from the coast North of Ireland, the wind was at gale force with the sea running very high. Although still an OD, which is the very lowest of the low I had been put into the torpedo party and my watch station was on the bridge where the duties generally were to renew lamp bulbs, and when they blew replace the fuses. In action I handed over to the Chief Torpedo Officer and, in the event of depth charging, I worked with the party aft or at the throwers, In gun action I was part of the supply line to "X" gun at the aft end of the ship where, being tall I stood on a table in the ward room with my head and shoulders just above the deck and passed the ammunition up to the loaders for the gun.
The action started with an old merchant ship astern of the convoy being torpedoed and sunk and we were able to pick up an echo which turned out to be a U-boat. We went to depth charge stations, but before I was relieved on the bridge we had dropped a pattern which consisted of increasing to full

speed and dropping one charge astern, and then the two throwers and the a further charge astern, turning and sweeping again to pick up the echo. We dropped a lot of charges, after the first pattern I was relived from the bridge and went aft where a slight amount of pandemonium reigned.
Reloading the throwers and the stern charges is quite a performance even when the sea is calm, but with the ship rolling at 30 or 40 degrees and the sea coming aboard waist high it is anything but easy, A depth charge weighs about two hundredweight and has to be hoisted up from the magazine, fitted with a primer and then have the pistol placed and at the last moment the pistol pushed up to the primer and fixed and be ready for dropping or firing from the throwers in about five minutes, and the throwers have to be armed. Hard work. With the charges to be dropped aft and there was not time to fix them in the chutes and then careful position the pistols just before dropping. We armed them fully as they came out of the magazine, rolled them across the moving deck, held in position with two rope ends, kicking them over when we got the word. Very unsafe with the fulminate of mercury pistol already in contact with the primer.
However the charges all went off as required and we dropped about six patterns of four charges each, then much to everyone's surprise the U-boat came to the surface quite close to the ship and "A" and "X" gun opened fire. I do not think we hit the U-boat as the ship was dancing about like a jack rabbit. Anyway, she went down again and after a few more depth charges to help her on her way we continued on after the convoy. All very exciting, but we were very wet.
The ship was given a possible, but later in the war it was found that although badly damaged the U-boat got back to Germany and went into service again.

* * * * * *

My War

By Jack Stokes

When war was declared, I was serving on the Battleship Resolution in Portland, having arrived there the previous day after a two day exercise in the Atlantic. At that time I had been in the Navy just under four years and was an A.B. But waiting to be rated Leading Seaman, which happened just one month later.
The declaration of war was in many ways a relief as we had had the continual threat of war hovering over us for several years. I served a further four months on Resolution during which time we made two trips to Halifax in Canada escorting convoys, and the only excitement was chasing what we

thought was a German Pocket Battleship, but turned out to be a British armed cruiser. One other interesting fact was that our cargo consisted of the gold reserves of the country being taken to Canada. We did not at first know that these small and very heavy boxes contained the gold and out cargo must have been worth millions of pounds. I spent the first Christmas of the war on Resolution at Halifax. I left the ship in February 1940 and soon after that joined the destroyer HMS **Veteran**. Rightly named as she had been built in 1918.

I was a bit disgusted because I would have preferred to have joined one of the many destroyers recently built and which carried far more modern and efficient weapons. It took me some time to find her, as at each port we went to she had just left. We went first to Plymouth, then to Chatham, on to Rosyth and finally Scapa Flow in the Scottish Islands. There were six of us, all regular Navy (later three of those six lost their lives in **Veteran**) Our arrival on board was not very encouraging. We joined the ship at 0200 and with us came the ship's mail and so the ship's company were more interested in the mail than us. Our mess deck where we were to live was a nightmare. It was overpopulated and contained the steam capstan that operated the anchor, consequently the crammed space, hammocks slung and the steam capstan hissing away, we can hardly say that it was a welcoming arrival. There were no spare hammock billets and so I laid out my hammock on the mess table, fortunately the man I was relieving was leaving the next morning and then I took his space. Having been accustomed to the strict routine of a peace time battleship, I was horrified the next morning to see the hands fall in for the day's duties. They were dressed in nothing like the conventional uniform, and I and my colleagues were the only ones dressed in the correct naval uniform. It transpired that the ship had only been recently commissioned and that many of the crew were pensioners or reservists who had just recently been called up, and many had only one uniform and did not wear that for every day duties. I won't go into details but suffice it to say that the general standard of discipline was totally different to my peacetime experience. In fact I was horrified.

Our first trip was to Norway, where we were engaged against the Germans. We were escorting a troop convoy and as far as I can remember, nothing happened on the trip across. Our main duty once we arrived in Norway was to patrol the fjords and carry out bombardments on possible troop emplacements. Surprisingly this brought little response other than some high level bombings, which were not very accurate. We did have one near miss. It happened one afternoon when I was on watch on my gun. Throughout the watch a British Swordfish biplane kept zooming around us, rather showing off we thought but this one, we realised too late, had black crosses on its wings and was attacking us. I looked up to see what appeared to be a large number of small black balls hurtling towards me, and I well remember saying to myself “You’ve had it Jack”. I really thought that the bombs could not possibly miss, but they did and landed right along our port side, doing some damage, but luckily no casualties. We blazed away at it as it flew away from us and we last saw it emitting smoke, and we assumed that we had hit the plane, but we will never know, for we did not actually see it crash.

The next scare was as coxswain of the motor boat I was ordered to take an officer ashore and wait his return. I was horrified whilst waiting to see the ship up anchor and disappear round the bend. I began to visualise being taken as Prisoner of war and felt very isolated moored alongside the jetty. However after what seemed an interminable wait the ship reappeared. Then came the order to withdraw and evacuate the troops. This took four nights and three days, during which time we had very little sleep as we were closed up at action stations. All our meals were taken standing at our guns and consisted of corn beef sandwiches and soup. Our routine was to embark the troops during the day and go at full speed through the fjords and take the troops out to the waiting transports. On the last night we embarked a large number of French Foreign Legionnaire's who were in a bad way, having been fighting a rear guard action. They were dirty and unkempt, many with untreated wounds, very hungry. But they also had a large number of grenades, which they were busily throwing in the water and exploding them, and they also had a lot of brandy, which they were happily imbibing. With the ship bursting at the seams we set off on out last journey to the troop ships, and to my delight the Captain decided that we could fall out of action stations and break in to two watches. It was just midnight and I realised that I could turn in my hammock for four hours, but when I got to my hammock I found it occupied by a Legionnaire, what could I do? I hadn’t the heart to turn him out, so I found an odd space somewhere and tried to sleep, but after so long sleep just would not come. We eventually disembarked them to the transports and then formed up with the other destroyers to escort them back to Britain.

Our trip home was interrupted by a very sad event. We were ordered to leave the convoy and proceed at full speed to the Faeroe Islands, where we picked up 33 survivors from HMS Glorious, which had been sunk by German Battleship of the crew of 1500 these 33 were the only survivors. It seemed that 800 got away from the sinking ship, but four days in Arctic water meant that most died from the sheer ferocity of the cold sea. The 33 were in a bad way, and all had suffered from frostbite and were in agony as their bodies came to life again. They were crying with pain, but we had no doctor on

board, so there was little that we could do. I should have mentioned that with the carrier were two destroyers, who made heroic efforts to close the battleships and sink them with torpedoes, one did register a hit, but they were h blown out of the water, and only one man, (he was one of the 33) survived. The survivors told us some terrible stories of the way some men died. Beside the cold thirst was a big problem, some drank sea water and that was fatal one man remembered what the Bible said "You can drink your own piss and eat you own dung" and some of them did the former, again with fatal results. Sad for me though was a friend who joined the Navy when I did, was not a survivor. It was good to get back to Rosyth where a load of ambulances were waiting. I have often wondered how many of them survived.
From Rosyth we were ordered to Harwich to act as anti invasion force, as with the fall of France everybody expected that Britain would be invaded. On arrival at Harwich we were given 48 hours leave, and on that leave I married Edie, (a marriage that has lasted 58 years). We used to go out on patrol in the Channel practically every night looking for the expected invasion but it never came.
We had a few skirmishes with E-boats, they were very fast boats and it was all over very quickly, we were lucky if we got two rounds away. We did have one hectic excursion when we were ordered to Bologne with four other destroyers to destroy the invasion barges that were mustered there. We went right inside the harbour blazing away with all our guns, but the Germans did not realise it was ships bombarding thinking the attacks were coming from the air, and to start with nothing came our way, but once they realised it was ships, things got a bit hot. Having gone round the harbour once. I got somewhat scared when we were ordered to go round again. Only one of our ships was hit, and it was quite a relief when we headed for open water again. We were led to believe that we had caused a lot of damage to the invasion barges. We spent the whole summer doing that sort of patrol.
However we were sent to Chatham for our routing boiler clean, and this meant four day's leave. I left home after my four day's, and later in the day we steamed out of Chatham heading for Harwich again, but a short time after leaving there was a terrific bang, which did some considerable damage to our stern and we had to return to Chatham for repairs. We had detonated one of the new magnetic mines. This meant a few more day's leave.
In the October of 1940 the invasion scare was off and we were ordered to go to Liverpool to join the Atlantic convoy escort groups, but instead of going through the English Channel, we took the longer and safer route going northwards round the coast of Scotland. In all my experiences at sea it was one of the roughest trips that I have known. The **Veteran** had been in reserve for many years and we found that in very rough weather she leaked like a

sieve, consequently our mess deck was flooded up to about a foot of sea water. The worst storms were when we were passing through the Minches, the waves and winds were just unbelievable and we sometimes wondered if the old ship would master the elements, but she did and on many Atlantic convoys we were to experience equally rough storms.
After our very rough trip we arrived at Liverpool, topped up with stores and that same afternoon set sail for our first Atlantic convoy. In the next eighteen months we were to do many such trips. I never kept a diary during that period. I only wish that I had for so much happened, and it was by no means a success story. We just did not have enough escorts, we had no air support, no radar. The U-boats out numbered us and they would gather in packs and make concerted attacks on the convoy. At that time we had received on lease lend 50 old U.S destroyers, but at first they were of little use because they kept breaking down. Our only weapon against the U-boats was depth charges, which in those early days were not very effective. The Germans used Focke Wolf planes to shadow our convoys and radio to the U-boats our position, course and speed. The aircraft would fly over very low and out of gun range and there was little that we could do about it. Later we too had air cover and they were a match for the Focke Wolf's, our aircraft would also attack the U-boats on the surface as well as passing on information to the convoy escorts.
Those early months in the Atlantic were pretty disastrous, we lost a lot of merchant ships and had little success against the U-boats. The **Veteran** fired many depth charges, but scored no direct hits, we did pick up an awful lot of survivors. One I shall never forget, was when coming across a ships boat loaded with survivors. We had established a routine for picking them up, and my job was on a scrambling net hung over the side and then to assist the survivors to get aboard. On this particular day it was quite rough, and one moment when the boast was in the trough of the wave I would be looking down at then and then when it was on the crest I would be looking up at them. I therefor instructed them to jump for the scrambling net when I said so, One young lad (I was told afterwards that he was only 14) jumped too soon, missed the scrambling net and fell into the ocean, and as he did so a gigantic wave bashed the boat and his head against the ships side. We never saw him again. On another occasion we came across a boat load all dead. One humorous incident, we came across a single survivor sitting crossed leg on a raft which was just about big enough to seat him. It was windy and very rough and because of the heavy seas we could not get close enough to him to drag him aboard, We tried throwing lines to him but the wind made it almost impossible, and after many attempts this chap (he was a Canadian) called out "Say you guys, your not very good throwers, I wouldn't have you in my ball

team". It transpired that he had sat on that raft for forty eight hours. When we finally got him aboard he was in agony as he tried to straighten his legs, having sat cross legged for all that time. On another occasion as cox'n of the sea boat I was ordered away to pick up two survivors who were obviously in no condition to help themselves. They were Chinese and the only survivors of an oil tanker sunk by aircraft bombs. They had both been badly burnt and picking them up was not a very pleasant job. The tanker was one of our own convoy and had been sunk by an aircraft which flew in just as it was getting dark and despite all the weapons blazing away at him, he made straight for the centre of the convoy and scored a direct hit. There was a terrific explosion and when it all cleared all we could see was oil, some wreckage and these two survivors.

In those early days before we had radar, the U-boats would surface at night almost sink ships ad lib, with so few escorts we were helpless.

Towards the end of 1940 a new CinC was appointed. Admiral Sir Percy Noble and he decided before taking office, he would do one convoy trip in one of the escorts, and we were chosen. On one occasion he came in to our mess and sat and had a meal with us. I cannot remember, but it is possible that we had no plates or other utensils, because due to the extreme rough weather, all our crockery would get broken. We used to escort the convoy for about five days, then due to shortage of fuel we had to leave them and return to Liverpool, picking up another convoy on its home trip.

On Boxing day 1940 we were due in Liverpool, incidentally after a very rough trip Christmas day was wonderful flat calm, no wind and the sun shone. I remember it being so warm that while on my gun in the afternoon watch I was able to take my great coat off. We heard on the radio that Liverpool had been subject to air raids and as we neared the Mersey we could see heavy clouds of smoke from obvious bomb damage. It was worrying for me because Edie had come up to live there, and naturally I was concerned as to what might have happened to her. I was even more concerned when we were ordered not to enter but to go to Londonderry instead. We soon went out on another convoy, but this time on our return we were allowed to enter.

I went ashore to try and contact Edie, it was Wednesday when Edie usually did voluntary work at the Y.M.C.A. But no luck I was informed that they had not seen her since Christmas. That was a very worrying thought, and then I made my way to the place where we lodged, and I feared the worst when I found the road closed off and there was a lot of damage. The Warden could not tell me anything about casualties other than the fact that there had been some deaths and many injuries. I began to fear the worst, however he directed me to where I could get more information. Off I went, and then to my great relief I saw Edie walking along the road towards me! The house had been flattened by land mines, but as she was in an air raid shelter she had not suffered in any way. This was on Christmas day evening, and she had spent Christmas day in the local parish hall eating Lancashire hot pot for her Christmas dinner. Soon after this we obtained a three bed roomed house quite near the docks for thirty shilling a week. We shared with another chap from the ship, which meant that his wife and Edie had company when we were away. However the ship was transferred to Londonderry and Edie went back to her home in Wembley. Being based at Londonderry meant that we could escort the convoys a little longer and we did not have the problem of air raid when we were in harbour.

By this time we were getting escorts and air cover by a rather ugly looking aircraft called the Catalina. It was very economical on fuel and could remain with us for most of the daylight hours. They could also give us information about the U-boats on the surface. By now we also had radar and learnt with amazement that our radar had picked up a U-boat at 6,000 yards, we thought this incredible. This was in the latter part of 1941, and two incidents stick in my mind. One evening during the last dog watch (6-8pm) we were suddenly attacked by an aircraft, but I received no order to open fire, despite bombs being dropped. The next morning just as it was getting light, another aircraft zoomed in on us. I did not wait for any order this time and opened fire, at which an angry and stentorian voice from the bridge called "Captain of the gun report to the bridge". You see the aircraft was one of ours, a Sunderland flying boat. The Captain gave me a roasting, including saying "It is grinning apes like you that are loosing us this war". However when I mentioned what had happened the night before he withdrew his reprimand and congratulated me on my initiative. The story goes that the aircraft signalled to us "Good shooting Navy, but you definitely spoilt my breakfast" The time when a certain kill of a U-boat was not a kill, we got a definite echo and dropped depth charges only to see a whale surface and make off at high speed. Our first kill did come in the latter part of '41 by which time we had a new skipper, Commander Eames. We received a report that a submarine had been sighted on the surface just off Iceland, and **Veteran** and an ex American destroyer Leamington were dispatched to investigate, we soon found her and attacked with depth charges and were pretty certain that we had hit her, this was confirmed when oil and other debris appeared on the surface, later we were told that it was U207. In sixteen months of convoy escorting and attacking numerous U-boats that was our only kill. How different it all was when I next went to sea. I left my beloved **Veteran** in February 1942, by that time I was Petty Officer and went back to gunnery school at Chatham to qualify as gunnery instructor.

In September of 1943 I was drafted to another destroyer HMS Duncan based in Londonderry and once again on Atlantic convoys, but how different it was, plenty of escorts, better weapons, far more efficient Radar and improved Asdic's, in addition we had air cover almost continuously.

Chapter 20

Built after the first world war, a "Half Leader" of the V&W class **Wolverine** was the first British warship in action, within thirty minutes of Neville Chamberlain making his speech declaring war on Nazi Germany.
We were at our "War Station" at Milford Haven carrying out the normal sweep when we were given the last known position of a U-boat by a Sunderland Flying boat, who had attacked it whilst on the surface, the Sunderland herself had been hit by the fire from the enemy U-boat and when it attempted to descend at its base it crashed killing all of the crew, they must have been the first casualties of the war. **Wolverine** carried out an attack on the U-boat, but was unable to claim a kill. However **Wolverine** was later to ram and sink a U-boat commanded by the third Reich hero Von Prein, who had carried out the successful attack on the Battleship "Royal Oak" whilst she lay at anchor in Scapa Flow.
Whilst on invasion patrol duty, **Wolverine** was ordered to rendezvous with the latest and crack flotilla of Tribal class boats for an urgent U-boat sweep in the North sea. Whether she was included because the tribals were one short, or because she had the two best Asdic operators in the Navy we don't know. When assembled the racing flotilla was soon away, **Wolverine** being astutely stationed second last of the line ahead formation; with three boilers alight and "full speed ahead" on the telegraph she set the speed of the line.
John Richardson, CPO Mechanition remembered:- Conditions below included a "hooligan" in the boiler room, and a deafening ring, plus a "fry up" in the engine room, all at a sustained speed of 29.9 knots, I remember having to watch the shuttle gear of the port air pump as it frequently stuck at high speed. From this lonely station down between the condensers, I could only see the caps of the Chief "Tiffy" and of Mr Brown, the ex Boy Artificer, now a commissioned Engineer. Mr Brown was very tense, but exceptionally able as the Officer responsible for the whole of the "works" of the ship from the oil consumption to distilled water, and for the records of the engine room personnel to repair lists, all kept up to date for the ships next brief "alongside" or docking. In action or on entering or leaving harbour Mr Brown usually took station at one of the throttles, these were now fully open as both shafts spun with an endless ring and we surged through the Channel Northwards.
Off the Tyne the flotilla changed formation to line abreast and carried out a U-boat sweep widely to the North. No enemy showed up, not one single "ping" so we topped the British Isles then through the plush green Hebrides, once more rushing in line ahead. At that furrowing speed the depot was soon

reached, Wolverine had thunderously kept station with her eight younger sisters, living up to her famous efficiency reputation.
The names of the other boats were hardly dry in comparison to the little old V&W or when it comes to wounds received during service for **Wolverine** still showed scars inflicted when on river patrol in China, by an ancient gun barrel set up on a river bank hump and filled with rusty nails, bricks and scrap iron. When a landing party went ashore to investigate they found the gun deserted, and the ships log records "We duly spiked the gun".
Still whilst on invasion patrol **Wolverine** attacked a U-boat until it made a record dive or sank to the bottom of the deepest Cornish bay, not confirmed except a minesweeper brought from Falmouth dragged a special contact mine over the position where our marker flag lay and there was an explosion, but nothing came to the surface.
Still on invasion patrol from Lands End to the White Cliffs of Dover **Wolverine** manoeuvred close to the Cornish rocks to look for possible survivors from a Hurricane and a German reconnaissance plane which appeared to have shot each other down, for we found the planes floating side by side. The German plane was upside down the underside of the wings were painted sky blue with the red German crosses on them. The British fighter in light and dark green camouflage. Both seemed to be mainly intact but there was no sign of life. We left them wallowing in the now quiet waters of the rocky inlet.
Wolverine was engaged in Western Approaches defence and convoying in extreme and prolonged bad weather conditions answering many calls to action stations day and night, as a result we became a little bomb happy.
Under the command of Captain Craske who had organised and led out 150 ships from L'Orient from right under the noses of the advancing German Panzer columns, who were only four miles from the port. In doing so they had to go through a field of magnetic mines in the Barry Roads when the "James Magee" blew up, she had not been fitted with degaussing gear. **Wolverine** promptly rescued the survivors. This event showed us that early in the war out friends overseas were supporting us as the James Magee was under American charter, flying the Panamanian flag with a Canadian crew and a Welsh skipper, who was the only casualty having broken his nose. When first organising the vast merchant fleet at L'Orient Captain Craske brought his ship up to one of the larger vessels, the "Athol Star" and yelled through the loud hailer "Are you the Commodore?" No sir came the reply. The Captain then ordered with the reply "You now are sir, take over". The ships were surprisingly ready to be led out in a short space of time. With the little destroyer ahead zig zagging to locate any possible enemy craft, six long lines of Allied merchant ships made their slow way from the French port into

the Bay of Biscay and after a week of strict radio silence arrived off the West coast of Britain.
The next incident occurred, still while on invasion patrol, **Wolverine** dashed from Lands End to a position just off Weymouth to rescue the "Meknes" survivors. She had been close to this brilliantly lit ship some hours before, her name and purpose was in a large clear signs. By the time we reached the scene, which was during the forenoon watch of the next day there was no sign of the liner Ex French Naval Officers and men were widely scattered over the ocean, and we spent some time searching for them and getting them aboard. A few were already dead, others were completely exhausted and ravenously hungry. We collected their Kapok life jackets, because they looked a lot safer and piled them on one of the beef screens, later we found them to be lousy, so later they were burnt on the dockside. We were packed to the gunnel with French seamen and glad to have the drifters take them off our hands. We speculated who sank this brightly illuminated ship.
Arriving in Norway at a critical point in the Norwegian campaign, **Wolverine** was given charge of the Norwegian ship "Chroby" a 20,000 ton liner packed with troops for an assault on Bodo from seaward. Powerful British ships including anti aircraft cruisers were there at the time of our arrival, but only the little Frigate "Stork" was with us. The attack on Bodo should have opened up at 2400 hrs, but at 2345 an intrepid German squadron leader detached from his flight and machine gunned the packed decks of the "Chroby", then as the aircraft flew on, the rear gunner took up the slaughter, after making a half loop the German aircraft crossed above the bridge of the liner and hit the bridge with incendiary and high explosive bomb. All the Army officers were having their final briefing as the bomb burst among them, all were killed with the exception of one Major who was severely wounded. **Wolverine** raced alongside the blazing liner, taking off 695. Stork went along the other side and rescued the rest. One of those who came aboard was the wounded Major I helped carry him forward cradling his floppy leg in my arms whilst three soldiers carried the rest of him (I learned later that he recovered). Between the decks of the blazing liner men were dashing into smoke filled passages and collapsing, their mates on the freer side were running in and pulling them out. Sadly as we steamed away from the carnage, about 70 figures appeared on the forecastle out of the smoke and flames. We were unable to save them. Years after I learnt that the "Chroby" had run aground.
During the evacuation of Namsos in Norway, a German Heinkel seaplane, flying at wave height and at a safe distance spotted us and must have reported our approach. Whilst under air attack **Wolverine** took in artillery and brought men out. The accuracy of the enemy bombing was thwarted by

Captain Craske, he had one of the bridge lookouts to lay on his back, and as the planes passed overhead he would shout "Bombs Away!!" The Captain would then order the rudder to be heeled over. The combination of bombs dropping and the ship heeling over was nerve shaking, especially to those in the boiler rooms. When we grated alongside the damaged jetty among the smouldering ruins of Namsos the first of the British troops came staggering aboard, one, leaning heavily on my shoulder gasped out "I used to be a Harrier, but one of the officers passed me going like a train coming down that mountain. He also said that the German aircraft had been hunting and machine gunning them for days.

Wolverine drew astern rapidly from the jetty and manoeuvred to leave the ill fated town of which only a few houses that were nearer the back drop of the mountains seemed to have survived. In the town centre were the burning ruins of the church, where 200 Namsos folk lay dead.

The Penal Battalion of the French Foreign Legion were rumoured to have shot 400 German parachutist before they reached the ground. One of our crew said that he had seen a Legion NCO shoot two legionaries in the act of looting. Our own lads were luckier as one had to be dissuaded from bringing a motorcycle aboard, while a "dustman" (stoker) planted a large wicker chair at the break of the foc'sle and with a bottle of wine in each hand was doing a fair imitation of Vera Lynn. As we sped along the Fjord towards the open sea the hollow booming sound of the bombs began again. The last event I recall in the fjord was that of a lone defiant seaman high on the bridge of a French merchant ship armed with what looked like a Maxim gun blasting away at the enemy aircraft. In a very dramatic fashion, **Wolverine** sank a U-boat as it crept out of the sound at Plymouth to escape a small fleet of ships which had been alerted of its presence.

The boat of the daring commander had been lying in wait in the river mouth for the return to sea of the battleship Valiant after her 30 month D2 refit (complete strip down and rebuild).

After the U-boat had been spotted laying in wait off Drakes Island by a patrolling seaplane, all kinds of ships were rushed into the area, some smaller craft rigged a marker buoy over the enemies position. It was hoped to capture her 'alive', but in the dusk she made for the open sea. When she was about to gain open water, Wolverine located her and attacked with depth charges whilst on the turn and at low speed of fifteen knots. The full pattern of depth charges put out our own lights, just as the secondary lights came on Wolverine made a crashing leap out of the sea. Our leading sparker looked green in the pale light and missed his footing at the top of the engine room ladder and descend to the diamond plate with a crash and a loud comment before fleeing to put the generator 'back on the board'. It was said that when divers found the sub her hull was squashed together. I was then drafted to Devonport for the leading stokers course. I also heard later that **Wolverine** had been engaged in a two hour battle with Von Priens U-boat during which many charges had been fired. (off watch we used to help haul them up to the quarter deck through a large round hatch over which the wardroom carpet was normally spread).

Twice Von Prein brought his boat up and fought the tenacious destroyer on the surface, during all the manoeuvres, ex heavy weight boxer 'Bill Bailly' and sinuous Stoker P.O. 'Cock' Orme in charge of the destroyer's boiler room never allowed the steam pressure to move of the 'red mark'. They were both mentioned in despatches.

Finally **Wolverine** avenged the Royal Oak by ramming the U-boat. I last saw my ship in Guz (Gosport) about fifteen feet of her bows had been torn back. The lads would be going on a well deserved leave. As old stoker 'Pike' used to say "Uz dern't want terbaccy leaf Nicky, uz want Xmas leaf".

As it should be Captain Craske was the main mover in **Wolverine's** success. He was a four ringer with great skill, courage and long experience. On his way to and from the bridge he often paused for a few words with us 'dustmen' as we took a few gasps of fresh air at the 'stokers bridge' (the low wash plate before the engine room hatch). I remember him on the night of the 'Chroby', when I had been relieved from the first watch and told by my relief, "take my place on the foc'sle Rick. The Captain was leaning out from the port side of the bridge, directing the rescue, his face blistering in the heat. His cool but intent command was steadying to me, because I had reached the airlock at the top of the boiler room ladder, after the heavy crashes that we had heard below. I assumed that we had reached Bodo pier and that the firing, screams and din beyond the outer airlock door were from the Germans having boarded us, and I had to make myself in the second pause, get out on deck where troops were already making death leaps down on to our deck from the blazing liner. The ones who jumped too far and went in to the drink were the worst off for just after a brief immersion they were groaning with shock and cold as they were hauled aboard.

How far sighted someone at the top must have been to have the old V&Ws mothballed. Interesting records were broken when the British yards built the amazing sea boats, even if we did say "Give me the boats and a bucket". They were built on the 'jig' system and at the rate of one off the slips a day. I believe this rate of building was not equalled until the second world war. (These are John Richardson's figures)

Wolverine was often accompanied by **Whitehall** or **Valentine**. I remember the names of most of the V&Ws. Before the second world war began, I worked with other stokers and the rest of our crew at Rosyth preserving

them. We did every kind of check, cleaning and painting compartments, turning propeller shafts by hand gear, (six of us hauling on a rope knotted at intervals and attached to a lever and worm gearing until we had moved the shafts on a quarter of a turn. All the work we did proved worthwhile, and I will never forget the sight of the flotilla of freshly enamelled destroyers steaming out from the Fourth, funnel markings clear on the 'Woodbine' and 'Cigar stump' stacks.
The last proof of our work was when each of these smart ships broke their own speed records.
I never saw these nine flotillas again, as demands of war meant that they worked alone, or with other 'chummy' ships. BUT HOW WELL THEY ALL DID!!

Ode to the Wolverine

If, my lords you would employ a
Most efficient old destroyer
And should want one, that is clean
Send at once for Wolverine
**

If it's crew must know their stuff,
And can take it, calm and rough,
One who's motto is "Ich Dien"
It must be Wolverine
**

If the job's unloading ships,
Whilst the diving bomber dips
Over the flames that light the scene
Send at once for Wolverine
**

If a ship requires a tow,
Through U-boats waiting in a row,
And there's no destroyer screen
Call upon the Wolverine.
**

If without the slightest ripple,
Lurking deep there is a hippel,
And the Asdic's chance is lean,
What you want is Wolverine
**

If the Huns are out in packs,
Pressing home their night attacks,
Or produce a second Prien,
Whistle up the Wolverine.

**

If a convoy can't be found,
And there's fog for miles around
There's no need to scratch your bean,
All you need is Wolverine.

**

If it's picking up survivors,
Or providing corpse revivers,
Of all the escorts, choose the Queen,
Obviously - Wolverine.

From "Stand by to Ram" 1943

* * * * *

At the outset of September of 1939 H.M.S. **Walpole** was at sea and was involved in the very early detection of U-boats. Leading Seaman William Hutchins relates:- Saturday night on the 2nd of September 1939 we were in asdic contact with two submarines and assumed that they were German U-boats. Contact was lost with one and on hearing of the sinking of the ss Athenia on the 3rd September, we believed that this was the U-boat that had sunk her, as it was not too far away when the Athenia was attacked. War had not been declared therefore **Walpole** did not drop depth charges. We remained in contact with the second one until the announcement of the declaration of war at 1100 hrs 3rd September. At 1103 we attacked with depth charges and assumed that these attacks had been successful. (never verified). The other destroyers which were in company were - **Vanquisher** and **Wolfhound** and one other Leading Seaman Henry Martin recalls:- on one trip to 13 degrees West (actually 10.52 West) a torpedo passed under the **Walpole.** I saw it as clear as if it were daylight although it was night time. The torpedo ran on and struck a ship called ss Bronte and she settled down on the bows. Before the dust had settled the crew of Bronte were alongside us. Our Commanding Officer was none too happy, so he sent over a crew from Walpole and they, in true matelot fashion, porloined a lot of their navigational equipment. The boarding party then returned and reported that the Bronte was fir to sail. So, back went the crew of the Bronte and the C.O. Decided to take her in tow. We secured the Bronte's hawser from her stern and took the strain,- guess what? These hawsers had “Liverpool splices” in them and pulled straight out. Our skipper went berserk, so we employed our wires and once again took up the strain and proceeded to tow her. After towing her for some time the weather deteriorated and the ss Bronte broke up and sank, taking the remains of a prize bull with her. We rescued all of Bronte’s crew and returned them to Liverpool, Whilst going to and fro from Liverpool we had an asdic contact and dropped twenty five depth charges, we had to fit pistols with detonators flying about and load them into carriers, on the bridge the skipper was going mad, but we managed it all.

P.O. Stoker Arthur Suffolk writes:- The Bronte was carrying a prize bull destined for the Argentina. **Walpole’s** First Lieutenant went over to the Bronte to shoot the bull as it was felt that it would be more humane than to leave the poor beast to drown. Unfortunately the officer failed to take any ammunition for the revolver with him and had to return for some! Eventually with mission accomplished the Bronte afterwards soon sank.
A few days after the sinking of the Bronte the C.O Lt, Comdr A.F Burnell-Nugent RN DSC wrote to a fellow officer as follows:-
“My Dear Hoar, Thank you very much for your letter which I was pleased to get and hear all your news. I sympathise with you not being at sea but no doubt it would be fatal if everybody in important jobs like yours all left at once.
I suppose I am damned lucky to be in command of a destroyer in war time, which is the job that I have always wanted. But I had no idea what a hell of a sweat it would be. We are employed entirely on convoy work in the Atlantic and do seven days out and two days in harbour, and so on. It would be grand if the weather at this time of year was not always so bloody awful. I am writing this in my sea cabin. Last night we had the worst gale that I have ever met, hove to all night quite helpless and everything getting bust, thank God in the morning we met another destroyer who took charge of me, otherwise I should have no idea which way to go to find the convoy again.
My Officers are a Lieutenant RNR, two acting subs (sub lieutenants), an acting Gunner and a Midshipman. Very decent fellows, but not very experienced at keeping station at night without lights, but they do it damn well on the whole.Crew are almost all reservists, mostly men who left after twelve years, but there are a few who are pensioners, the oldest is 54. We also have a few very young RNVR seamen ages about 18, very willing but it is absolute cruelty to send the very young, or the very old on a job like this.
What rather gets me down is the paper work - when one gets back to harbour and expect a ‘stand easy’ about twenty bags of different official mail arrive mostly ticking us off!

One has incredible adventures. Last trip we brought back 42 survivors from a British ship (the Bronte) that had been torpedoed. I tried to tow it back to harbour stern first, but a gale came up and the bloody thing sank only 60 miles from harbour after two days towing. Maddening, for I had hoped for a spot of salvage money.
I have shared a U-boat (the C.O. has mistaken her as the U-boat that attacked Bronte was U34 but it must have survived because in July 1940 U34 sank H.M.S. **Whirlwind** off Lands End). (By coincidence, **Whirlwind** was one of the destroyers engaged in escorting the convoy) but it is not a very pleasing business as I felt sorry for the fellows trapped inside.
There is a good deal of semi -confidential stuff in this, but as you are in the reserve I reckon it will be all right. Anyhow I will censor it myself. But don't show it to everyone you meet.
It is still blowing like stink but clear weather.
My job certainly teaches one to rely on oneself and I have learnt more since this war began than in years of peace.
Always delighted to hear from you. I hear that your sister had married some nice Naval Officer but I'm ashamed to say that I don't know who it is".

Chapter 21

1940

At the end of 1939 I decided to join the Andrew as a short service rating, and after passing my medical and educational exams at Whitehall recruiting office in October I was finally sent my papers to join the Navy on the 23rd January 1940.
From Whitehall I was put on a coach and whisked off to Skegness to join the crew of HMS Royal Arthur, which like many others, I found to be a very cold, damp and miserable Butlins holiday camp, with no heating in the chalets, there were notices everywhere forbidding any heaters under the penalty of the glasshouse. The instructor was the infamous Dusty Miller, P.O. Gunners Mate, a most awful person to all new arrivals.
We had no uniforms for three weeks, except boots, the R.N. Had run out of stock, due to the amount of bodies called up at short notice, so we FROZE!. (I have never been to a Butlins or any other holiday camp since, or wanted to).
27th February 1940 At last we finished our introduction to Navy life and we were all split up to various Naval Depots of our choice. So I found myself on another coach on my way to Chatham. On arrival at HMS Collingwood, I was delighted to find that we were billeted in a proper barrack room, and I actually had a bed to myself, for at Skegness it was a double and a single bed to a chalet, and I had to share a double bed with a lad from Wales, fortunately he was normal next day we were introduced to our instructor, a pensioner who had been recalled for the duration of hostilities who had a big chip on his shoulder. Another P.O.G.M. named Rose, who in no time had us all doubling around the main parade ground for talking in the 'Tunnel'. We doubled for three hours complete with gas mask and rifles at the slope, it did keep us warm though on a very cold February afternoon.
By the 17th May our training finished we were all, hopefully, fit to call ourselves seamen, and I was immediately given a draft to HMS Boadicea which had just come in to the dock yard for some repairs.
At the start of the Dunkirk evacuation we were almost ready for sea, and expecting to join the throng but at the last moment our orders were cancelled in order to have our mess deck portholes taken out and larger escape ones fitted. This was due to so many lives being lost by crews of destroyers being unable to get free when sinking. This took a few days extra, and by the time we were ammunitioned at Sheerness, Dunkirk was just about over. We were sent to Le Havre with Bulldog and ambuscade to carry out rescue operations

there, on arriving at the French coast we split up, Boadicea going to St Roses en Traux, where we found the beach full of soldiers of the 51st Highland Division and numerous French civilians. Whilst collecting them we were attacked by 13 Junker 87's and hit with three bombs which stopped us where we were. God was on our side, for from then on thick fog came down and enveloped us thus stopping the Hun from doing any further damage, and allowing our motor boat with whaler in tow to finish the evacuation. Ambuscade received our S.O.S and managed to find us and although we were sunk to our midship gunnels, managed to tow us back to Portsmouth, still in thick fog. I would add that as soon as we within a couple of miles of Pompey, the fog lifted and once more it was a sunny day.

Autumn 1941 I was recommended for a gunnery course and returned to the RNB where I qualified as an AA. 3 on the 9th October 1941 and drafted to Liverpool to serve as a gun layer on HMS **Westcott** on the 2 pounder Pom pom mounting, with 'Lofty' Jarvis as trainer, he being a leading Seaman AA 2.

After a couple of escort duties bringing back convoys across the Atlantic we were sent to Greenock and had fitted a Bofors on the stern in lieu of a 4.7 gun mounting, and a Hedgehog we spent numerous days with the inventor, a Sub Lieut onboard doing trials. The first time we fired the thing I was at defence stations on B gun, and as I saw the first bombs go skyways and turn over to come down again, I saw a glove come off one of the bombs, or so I thought, on looking over B gun flare I saw A.B. Blowers holding his wrist where his hand used to be, and realised that our new toy had claimed it's first victim due to a premature firing. After that all bombs had to be lowered into position with the aid of a stick.

On completion of trials we were sent to Gibraltar to join the Toc H force as it was then known, and took part in numerous runs to Malta, and the invasion of the North African landings at Oran.

The first big job we were sent on was to rescue the S.S. Llangibby Castle who had been torpedoed which blew her steering gear and rudder away. This is reported earlier.

We then continued with the Malta convoys helping to top up the airforce compliment of fighter planes for Malta and attempting to get through badly needed supplies to the Island, and finalising our 'holiday' in the Med' assisting in the North African landings.

We got our orders to sail home for Christmas 1942 with a final bag of 3 Axis subs, one Italian torpedo bomber, which was shot down by A.B. Alf Beckett who was awarded the D.S.M. The other crew members said if he had not shot the dive bomber down, they would have shot him!

Westcott also helped in the saving of HMS Liverpool from being sunk.

Our collection of medals from all these operations was;- One DSO two DSC's, Five DSM's and eleven Mention in despatches, plus a lot of experience.
On the 14th November 1941 whilst on the **Westcott** I passed and was rated leading seaman after just one year and ten months service and passed as Petty Officer after two years and six months, on the 22nd July, but due to an A.F.O (Admiralty Fleet Order) restricting advancement to P.O. To ratings with less than three years service, I could not be made up until December 1942 just before leaving for the U.K. Consequently I was more than happy with my time on the **Westcott.**

Chapter 22

The situation in France and Belgium was becoming very serious, the Allied armies were in retreat before what seemed at the time an invincible German army and were all making for the coastal ports of Belgium and the most famous of all escape routes, Dunkirk. Here the old V&Ws were to prove invaluable, but not without tragic loss. The first casualty of WW11 was H.M.S **Valentine** who was attacked by aircraft and severely damaged, so much so that she had to be beached and abandoned in the Scheldt Estuary on the 15th May 1940. In fact 1940 was to prove a disastrous year for the old boats a total of seven were to meet their doom. After **Valentine, Whitley** too was to suffer a similar fate on the 19th May quickly followed five days later by the **Wessex,** all from heavy German air attacks.
Wakeful, who was loaded with troops was the next to succumb to the German air attacks, she was sunk with a total loss of life.

THE PIONEER OF DUNKIRK
As recalled by Bert Kidd of HMS Wolfhound

Admiral Sir William Tennant, a famous son of Worcestershire and a great Naval Hero, played a key role in the Dunkirk evacuation.
He was beach master, spearheading the operation which resulted in the 'miracle' rescue of 378,829 servicemen from the French shores.
It was May 1940 that 'Bill' Tennant received the order to take charge of the evacuation from the beaches of Dunkirk.
He was the head of a Naval beach and pier party of 12 officers and 160 men aboard the destroyer **Wolfhound** which sailed from Dover on the 27th May, suffering minor damage en route from aircraft attack. On arrival, the area was too dangerous to set up the operation planned and she re-routed east of the harbour. After landing the beach party she took aboard 130 troops She was again attacked but survived and later took an early part in the evacuation of the Dunkirk beaches, bringing back hundreds of troops.
The following day, Captain Tennant signalled for 'every available craft' setting in motion the famous armada of little ships to accomplish a miracle, the rescue of more than a third of a million troops, 120,000 of them French.
Years later a colleague wrote, 'Bill Tennant's tall athletic figure in blue strode fearlessly over the beaches giving orders to largely demoralised 'brown jobs' and being obeyed.
At 11.30 pm on the 2nd June 1940 Captain Tennant was able to report "Operation completed, returning to Dover". But first, he patrolled the water

front calling out through the darkness, “Are there any British soldiers still ashore?”
Another senior colleague was to declare, “Without Tennant and his men the troops would have been like lost sheep.”
For his action at Dunkirk, Capt, Tennant was awarded the C.B. (Companion of the Bath), the French Legion of Honour, and the Croix de Guerre with Palms.
He later commanded the equally mammoth operation and large armada of tugs and ships which towed the two vast ‘Mulberry’ floating harbours across the Channel for the 1944 D-day landings. He was in charge too of laying the cross channel ‘Pluto’ fuel pipe line for the same Normandy landings.
From June 1940 onwards **Wolfhound** was mostly on East Coast convoys. On the 3rd September she was attacked by JU-88 aircraft whilst escorting FS84. A near miss forward caused severe damage and the forward part of the ship broke away and sank near the southern end of the Dudgeon Shoal, fifteen miles off the Norfolk coast. The remaining part was taken in tow and was berthed at Immingham on the 4th September. She was eventually repaired and re-commissioned on 31st March 1943, but her condition was such that she could no longer take part in any major action. At the end of the war, she was used as courier ship to Norway.
Placed in reserve 18th February; 1948 she was sold and broken up at Granton.

******

I would like to follow this up with my story says Len Wadsworth of H.M.S. **Wolfhound**-
After being landed ashore at Immingham, we were marched, some with trousers, many bereft of clothing, to the Naval Establishment. There we were kitted out with brand new uniforms, all creased in the wrong direction. One inch of pussers hard (soap), one shaving brush, one razor (cut throat), one towel.
The washroom was along a building with rows of metal sinks, with running water (cold). Some of us, including myself had quite a lot of oil fuel on us, so, trying to wash and shave presented problems, namely oil, and cut throat razor, I don’t know about anyone else, but I’m sure my razor is where I left it
Then we were given 10/- and pointed to the nearest watering hole where we spent the evening singing a few well known songs, ditty’s, poems and monologues.
Wolfhound was a Chatham ship and all the crew were sent there. Myself and a bunting tosser were in Captain ‘D’s’ pool at Rosyth.

We were both given travel warrants to Rosyth and told, in no uncertain terms, not to mention what happened, or even to mention the ship's name.
Can you now picture both of us at Grimsby station, dressed as we were, faces still showing streaks of oil. Most of all, looking lost. If ever there were two who had just landed off a sub, we were it.
The M.P.s (Military Police) at the station went spare when they saw us. This routine also took place at Crewe, Carlisle and Edinburgh. We even had a compartment to ourselves most of the way, nobody wanted to know us.
The climax came as we entered the dockyard at Rosyth. We had to let everyone else go in front. When we arrived at the gate, no identity, only our rail ticket. It does not take a lot to imagine what happened then. I think someone said "Shoot the B*****'s.
We were eventually sent to Cochrane, where we were taken to the Captains cabin, After being asked what happened we were given 14 days survivors leave, had our 'tot' and then went home. My home then was in Stirling.
I cannot remember the bunting tossers name. I wonder did they ever salvage the fore part of **Wolfhound.** My ditty box is in it!
Vanquisher, **Venomous, Venetia, Vimera Verity, Vimy**, **Vivacious, Wessex, Whitshed, Wild Swan, Windsor, Wolfhound, Wolsey, and Worcester** were all to take part in the evacuation of troops from Dunkirk in May 1940. The following are accounts of the experiences of those who were there. Army as well as Navy.

May 13th 1940.

Admiral Ramsey ordered HMS **Windsor** and HMS Codrington to go to a small jetty west of La Panne to evacuate some civilian personnel. Both destroyers approached the area with caution, as it was not known if the group would still be there or not, it was also getting dark. As the two destroyers approached the jetty they could see some civilians, so they came alongside the jetty and took the passengers aboard. We wasted no time in getting away. Later, when approaching Dover we found out that our passengers were the Dutch government and members of the Dutch Royal Family. They had with them a nanny who was carrying a small baby. That baby is now Queen Beatrix of Holland.
May 23rd At 2130 hours Admiral Ramsey ordered **Windsor** who, at the time was off Calais to proceed to Boulogne. She arrived almost an hour after the others had departed. Despite the confusion she managed to get alongside and take aboard some 600 troops as well as all the wounded and the rest of the demolition party without damage to herself there were still more troops

there so Ramsey ordered two more destroyers, the **Vimera** and **Wessex** to assist.
May 25th. Windsor and **Verity** left Dover to cover the withdrawal of small vessels waiting off Calais to carry out the evacuation when ordered.
May 26th; 0140 off Calais. **Windsor** picked up three soldiers from a raft. At 0300 It was decided not to evacuate Calais, so assisted **Verity** to escort small craft back to Dover.
0645 An attack by dive bombers, no hits due to the expert handling of the ship by the skipper.
0745. Anchored in the Downs disembarked the three soldiers into a boat from the Fervent.
1700 Hrs Returned to Dover.
May 27th 0635 Left Dover to patrol: 0904, closed Mona's Isle who was loaded full of soldiers, she had been machine gunned so we escorted her back to Dover then resumed patrol at 1515.
May 28th: 1145. We were close to number one buoy (near south Goodwin light house vessel) with several hundred soldiers aboard when we were attacked by fifteen dive bombers supported by ten fighters. No direct hits but we received extensive damage from bomb splinters and bullets, the wireless telegraph was out of action, the violent evasive action made things rather precarious, again we were attacked but managed to avoid all the bombs aimed at us, but a near miss caused some damage to the boiler room and there were between twenty and thirty casualties on her crowded decks. We made Dover harbour and repairs were put in hand immediately.
May 30th 0930 we sailed from Dover for Dunkirk arriving at La Panne at 1330 and proceeded to embark troops from small boats for the journey to Dover.
1530: Rear Admiral Dover transferred his staff from M/S Hebe to the **Windsor,** and he was landed at La Panne to visit Lord Gort to discuss the situation. At 1700 the Rear Admiral and his staff were transferred to the **Worcester** so Windsor proceeded back to Dover, landing 606 more troops.
May 31st 0200 **Windsor** sailed from Dover once again bound for Dunkirk arriving at 0600 and began embarking more troops, returning to Dover at 1000 and disembarked another 658 soldiers.
Within two hours she was once again on her way back to Dunkirk and on arrival secured alongside the Icarus which was alongside the East Pier taking aboard yet more troops, returning to Dover with 588 of the tired out soldiers.
June 1st ; 0545 departed from Dover on now the familiar run to Dunkirk this time tied up alongside the **Vanquisher** and Icarus and the P/V Maid or Orleans. During the night of the 1st-2nd June, due to the fact that the German

heavy guns had now the control of all three routes into Dunkirk, which meant that the final stages of the evacuation had to be carried out under the cover of darkness.

Admiral Ramsey reported that there were many more troops ashore, and more ships were required, but there would never be enough.

During the night, the destroyers **Codrington, Sabre, Whitshed, Windsor** and **Winchelsea** managed to bring out a large number of those stranded troops of which there was a large assortment, French and Belgian besides our own, it was impossible to tell which regiments they belonged.

June 2nd The German U-boats were still at work and one of their victims was the anti-submarine trawler Blackrover. She was torpedoed and sunk near "T" buoy at 1618. Her sister ship Westella went to her rescue, and whilst picking up survivors she too received the same treatment by the same U-boat. Because of the urgency of the operation accidents were bound to happen and sure enough two of the destroyers were damaged when they were in collision damaging the bows and propeller of the **Malcolm, Whitshed** collided with the Java but both carried on with their desperate task despite the damage they had received. Eleven destroyers, which included **Venomous, Winchelsea** and **Windsor** with the help of thirteen personnel ships which included the King George V, the Rouen, Royal Sovereign and St Helier between them they brought back to Dover 26,257 men. Sadly some ships had to return empty as the troops failed to show up. BY 2330 Capt Tennent who was ashore was able to send the signal "B.E.F Evacuated".

H.M.S. **Windsor** herself brought back 8,991 troops in seven trips across the channel. She was one of the first to go to Dunkirk and one of the last to leave. An achievement to be proud of.

H.M.S. **Vanquisher** I (T. Robinson) was at action stations aboard the **Vanquisher** in the crows nest as a look out. The crows nest was a splendid place to be, because one had such a wonderful view of all that was going on. We were alongside the Mole which had been breached by a bomb. A narrow walk way had been put across the gap and the troops were filing across in single file to reach the ladders that led down to our decks.

Two French Poilu appeared pushing a bicycle which was supporting a safe carefully balanced on the cross bar. They had obviously been doing a bit of looting and hoped that the safe contained a fortune. Their problem was how to get the bicycle across and more importantly the safe across the abyss? They were holding up the whole proceedings at a time when time was the essence and everyone was being urged to get a move on. The problem was soon solved for them when someone had the sense to push the bicycle and its load into the sea! The evacuation then continued and the poor Poilu's were left in tears. I thought the whole incident rather amusing.

Another **Vanquisher** shipmate Ted Loughlin, remembers:-

In May 1940 I was serving on a V&W destroyer, H.M.S. **Vanquisher**, this ship had been in service in the 1914-1918 war. It was quite small and with a ships company of approximately 100, there was little space to spare. The armament comprised of four 4 inch guns a 3 pounder (A/A.gun) six torpedo tubes and two Lewis machine guns, when required she could produce a maximum speed of 30 knots.

In late May we were despatched from North Atlantic convoy duties and directed to Dover. On our arrival there it was a hive of activity. We were refuelled taking aboard provisions and ammunition then topped up with fuel. We immediately made our way across the channel to Dunkirk. During our North Atlantic convoy duties were aware of the problems in the Low Countries, but never envisaged the true picture. We were quickly brought up to date on the situation.

I was bridge lookout and shortly after leaving Dover I could clearly see the smoke and fire ahead to which we were sailing. It was anything but friendly.

The Captain addressed the ships company over the Tannoy system. By the time he had finished speaking we had no doubt of the magnitude of the task that lay ahead.

We were then closed up for action stations in preparation of attacks by the enemy aircraft, E-boats and by the constant threat of mines, magnetic and otherwise which had been laid continually by the German forces. We were to remain in this state of readiness every time we left Dover.

The scene that greeted us as we arrived off Dunkirk was truly horrific. The beaches were full of soldiers, lines of abandoned vehicles, and in the background, huge pillars of fire and smoke from the burning of storage tanks. On one side of Dunkirk harbour was a very long wooden mole (jetty) which stretched from the shore. It was at least three quarters of a mile long. Moving slowly along this were hundreds of soldiers, who at the end clambered on to the destroyers tied up alongside. In addition to the personnel using the mole, small boats of every description were picking up the soldiers from the beech and conveying them to other craft in deeper waters. During all this activity, large numbers of enemy aircraft were continually strafing the harbour and dropping bombs on the beeches and harbour areas.

Whilst waiting our turn just outside the harbour to go alongside, we were subjected to incessant bombardment from the enemy aircraft. It was commonplace for forty or more to be attacking us at one time. The screening from the high pitched engines of the Stuka dive-bombers, and the accompanying explosions of the bombs, and the gunfire, was something that those present, will I am sure, never forget. As well as the bombing of the

beaches, ships both large and small were receiving direct hits. Many of which were embarking the troops at the time.
It was during a temporary lull in the attacks that the Mones Queen, an Isle of Man ferry was hit by a magnetic mine, she broke her back, causing her to turn over and sink in a very short space of time. We were close by and our whaler managed to pick up survivors off the hull before she went under. Fortunately, like us, she had been waiting to go into harbour, thus no soldiers were on board.
When our turn came, we went alongside the Mole and took on as many soldiers as we could carry. As I have earlier mentioned, we were a small destroyer and cramped for space. At the time these ships were being built, the armament was put in first, before the question of where shall we put the crew was addressed!
Amazingly on each of our visits to the beaches of Dunkirk we always returned with just short of a thousand soldiers. When loading was completed we quickly pulled out, and another V&W destroyer would take our place. Once clear of the harbour and wrecks, it was full steam ahead for Dover.
On arrival it was a case of rapid disembarkation of the repatriated soldiers and replenishing oil and ammunition before taking off again across the channel. After the initial taking on of provisions, repeat stocking up of this commodity was a rarity. We had no time to eat, and cigarettes were the prime requisite. Due to the large numbers on board, our mess decks, heads and washrooms became untenable. It meant a quick visit to the facilities on the jetty, before making our way back to Dunkirk. This meant cat naps around the guns as opposed to proper sleep. This was to be the formula for the next six trips. Each journey was full of incidents. On one occasion we passed the bow of H.M.S. **Wakeful** (a chummy ship), sticking out of the water. It was a most sobering and solemn moment to see this tragic sight. We learnt later that she had been attacked by a large number of enemy aircraft that had scored direst hits Her sinking was a tragic and huge loss of life.
On another occasion, having endured severe air attacks we tied up alongside the Mole, we had expended all our ammunition, but fortunately over the preceding days we had collected quite a few Bren guns, and was thus able to make a bit of noise if nothing else. We had a tea chest on board into which the soldiers put their ammunition. This was quickly utilised in repelling low level attacks from the enemy aircraft. Our ability to maintain some sort of fire power enhanced moral.
As the evacuation of the British Expeditionary Force from the beaches of Dunkirk continued, we were discovering greater numbers of mines on our short route across the Channel. As a result we had to make a lengthy detour past the North Fore land, across the Belgian coast and thence to Dunkirk. On

one of these detours we ran aground on the infamous Goodwin Sands. That too was to be a never to be forgotten experience. The ships engines were put to full astern, and apart from the terrible vibrations, we remained stuck. All hands were then summoned aft and instructed to jump up and down simultaneously. After what seemed an eternity of jumping up and down, and the engines at full astern, we eventually slid off the sands into deep water. We later discovered that in affecting our rescue from the Goodwin Sands we had left our Asdic Dome as a momento of our visit. On several occasions we had passed the Goodwins at low water and saw the masts of the ships that had floundered there in the past.

Going into Dunkirk at night, is best described as a 'hairy experience' The fires and smoke from the oil storage tanks, intermingled with the flash of gunfire on the outskirts of the town, provided an awesome backdrop, liken I imagine to Dante's inferno. In the foreground were the masts and hulks of sunken ships with the general flotsam floating by. During all this time we were ever conscious of the continual long lines of soldiers still waiting to be taken off.

On our last visit to Dunkirk, to allow for more space for personnel to be taken on board, the soldiers were ordered to throw their rifles into the sea. The Mole as a result of continuous bombing was now in a dangerous state. It was potted with holes and there were large parts missing, making passage along it very precarious, and the embarkation of the troops thereby slowed down.

The continued efforts over this stressful and dangerous period, gradually took its toll. Various members of the crew became hospitalised through injuries and exhaustion., these were quickly replaced by ratings sent from the barracks. Quite a number of senior officers were also replaced, but there was to be no let up in what was called 'Operation Dynamo'.

There were of course lighter moments. On one occasion, barges full of soldiers were being towed by a tug came past us. One of the barges bore the sign 'Pickfords - we can carry anything anywhere'. If only I had a camera with me at the time, I think I could have earned myself a very good pay day!

Towards the last of our visits to Dunkirk we embarked French soldiers, when we arrived back at Dover, one of the Frenchmen as he was leaving the ship embraced me and placed in my hand a Rosary with a St Christopher on it. I gave the Rosary to my Mother, and the St Christopher has travelled everywhere with me since, I still have it to this day.

Another sight that will forever remain in my memory, was seeing an extremely tired and dispirited company of Guardsmen hobbling down our ships gangway at Dover. A Sergeant Major, immaculately turned out, complete with pace stick, marshalled them together, and in parade ground

HMS Vanquisher dashing across the Channel to Dunkirk

Approaching Dunkirk

Making their way aft

HMS Vanquisher inside the Mole.
Note the scrambling net ready for anyone in the water

Troops queuing along the Mole ready to board

Loading from the Mole at low tide, hence the ladders

Glad to be aboard

We even provided light entertainment with A. Skelton on the drum, who provided the photographs

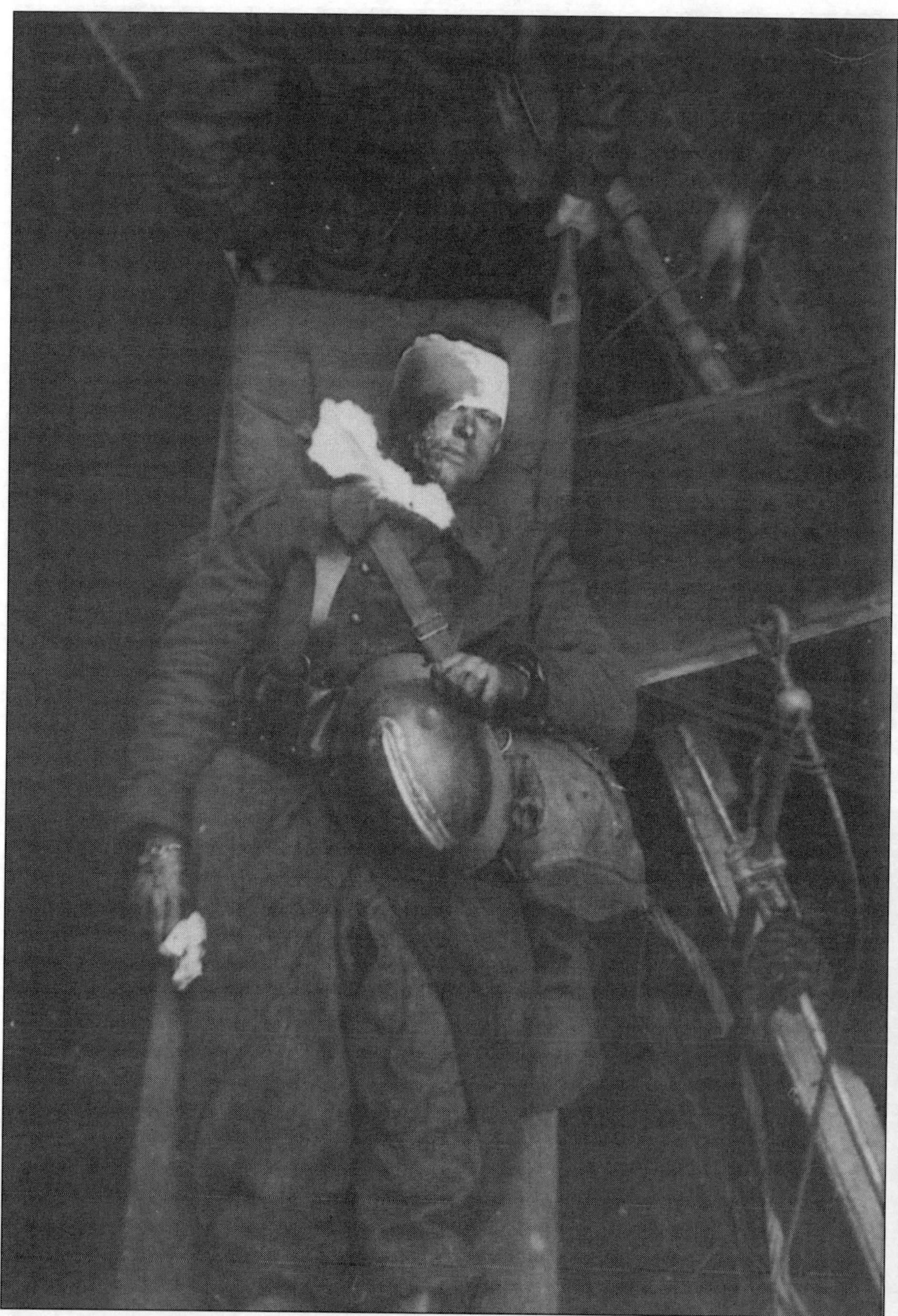

One of the French wounded being carried aboard

Unloading at Dover, three of the Vanquisher's crew in the foreground

A tight squeeze

voice shouted 'Guards!'. As if by magic, they straightened to attention as one and marched off in ceremonial parade ground style. They were desperately tired, hungry, and unwashed, but most importantly they had retained their pride, and the spirit to march when the Sergeant Major gave the command, as the disciplined body that they were, they rose to the occasion.
At 0240 on the 4th June 1940, HMS **Vanquisher**, pulled away from the mole (a wooden jetty) at Dunkirk, laden with members of the British Expeditionary Force, the town and harbour were silhouetted by the many fires that were burning out of control, plus the continuous Explosions taking place ashore. The plight of the soldiers ashore was now desperate, the German Army were now on the outskirts of the town and closing in.
This was to be our seventh and final voyage to Dunkirk, a few hours later we were informed that Dunkirk had fallen and that the German Army were in control.
Having disembarked the soldiers at Dover, we were ordered to Chatham, and were informed that the whole ships company would be granted three day's leave on arrival, whilst the ship was cleaned and fumigated. Having carried thousands of soldiers in the past week, conditions, particularly below decks, were in a dreadful state; the Heads, wash area and mess decks were untenable. The ship being small, it was always cramped for space, even with our normal crew numbering about one hundred. We the crew looked as dirty as the ship, for there had been little time for personal hygiene over the past seven days.
On arriving at Chatham and having secured the ship, we braved the filth and stench of the mess decks and retrieved our best uniforms and small cases etc; and went to the dockyard toilets and showers, after making ourselves presentable we put all our dirty clothing in our cases, we were given railway warrants and off we went on three day's leave which, was mainly spent in sleeping and eating. We had been at action stations continuously for the past week and apart for the occasional 'cat naps' a good sleep had been non existent, therefore sleep was a wonderful pick me up.
On returning to the ship, it was much cleaner and wholesome, with a distinct smell of disinfectant. It was then a case of back to work, bringing on board ammunition and provisions etc: At this time a number of Sappers, Explosive Experts and civilians came on board, we were then engaged in man handling a large amount of explosives on board that we secured on the upper deck.
We then cast off and once more returned to the war, and action stations, as darkness fell we arrived at our destination, our mission this time was the dockyard installations on the French coast, which were to be destroyed. Having landed the soldiers and the civilian passengers together with their

previsions and explosives at various points, our last port of call was La Rochelle, we then returned to Dover, once again counting our lucky stars that we had not encountered any serious problems during these clandestine operations.
On arriving at Dover, it was now daylight, we refuelled and managed to get some sleep. We had been at action stations since leaving England. We were then informed that we would be leaving harbour later that evening.
We were once again off out to sea and headed yet again for the coast of France, we were then joined by two other V&W destroyers. It was then that we were told by the Captain over the Tannoy, that there were several allied ships in Bordeaux Harbour, and that we were going to try and enter the harbour and get them out, but in order to achieve this we would have to travel up the river Gironde, which was nine miles long, and before the river we would have to negotiate the estuary, which was fortified on both sides of the entrance to the river by Forts with six and four inch guns. The Captain carried on to say that if we came under attack from the smaller guns we would reply, but if the larger guns attacked us we would have to get out the best way that we could. He continued to give encouraging words, then clinched his message with a mention of making 'Supreme Sacrifices' and concluded by wishing us luck. The tannoy was then switched off.
On hearing this we all became very quiet and extremely vigilant, the adrenaline was now flowing. He was of course preparing us for an impending bloody action, so having heard the bad news, I being the eternal optimist thought surely nothing could get worse, but to cheer myself up, hoped that things could only turn for the better.
When we approached the mouth of the estuary, the two other destroyers remained outside, ready to cover our retreat.
It was now dark, we commenced making smoke, our cover being supplemented by smoke canisters on the forecastle, for although it was a pitch black night, a wandering searchlight might pick out the ship, the smoke made that eventuality more difficult. We proceeded through the estuary, unchallenged into the River Gironde, now that we were in the river our speed had to be reduced. Then began the longest nine miles I have ever known, being in the middle of the river with limited space to manoeuvre was not the best place to be if action was to be fought. I was bridge lookout, and believe me it was strange going past built up areas on the river bank, I could see some lights, but the thought upper most in my mind that by the same token they could also see us. Which was not a comforting thought.
We eventually arrived in the harbour, and I could see that there were several ships at anchor, it was soon apparent that they were expecting someone for they all had steam up, we went alongside them in turn, the Captain through

his megaphone identified us, and told them that they were to slip their anchor cables at an appointed time and follow us out. During this time there was a considerable amount of activity on the dockside and in the ships moored alongside. It seemed impossible that we had not been seen.

Eventually, at the appointed time, the ships all slipped their cables, to hear the anchor cables splashing in to the water, to us seemed a terrible din. Being all tensed up, it sounded loud enough to 'awaken the dead' let alone the enemy.

We then led the ships out of the harbour into the river and began the slow journey back down to the sea, it seemed impossible that we would not be challenged and attacked, the throb of the engines to us seemed magnified, but of course we who were all in a state of readiness were awaiting the first burst of gun fire, which would pronounce our discovery and the battle would commence.

Amazingly we completed our journey to the estuary, and into the sea without incident and met our two friends, the destroyers, who took over the ships for the final part of the journey to England. We were then despatched enroute to Dover, at long last we could all now light up the cigarettes which we had craved for, as we used to say 'to steady the nerves'.

On reaching Dover we once again refuelled and caught up with some sleep, as by now it was again daylight, and we had experienced what might be called a heavy night. Later that day we were despatched to Devonport, we were most cheered by this news, the prospect of a couple of nights in harbour, and probably some shore leave certainly lifted our spirits.

These thoughts however proved to be a flight of fancy, for on our arrival in the Hoe, we saw units of the French Fleet anchored inside. We were instructed to anchor near a French destroyer and then we went to action stations, training our guns on the said French destroyer.

We were informed that some of the French crews, wanted to return to their homeland, however, the powers that be decided to take this action to ensure that the French ships did not leave their anchorage, we then went watch and watch readiness and remained so until the politics of this situation had been settled. It was truly an amazing sight to see all the British units, aiming their guns at the French Fleet.

After some time we were stood down, and the ship ordered back to our base at Liverpool, this was great news. On arrival we were informed that there would be night leave (4pm-8am) to forty per cent of the ship's company if their watch was due for leave, this meant eggs and chips at a service run establishment, a visit to the pictures and then back on board ship. 'They' being in their teens were not allowed ashore later than 10pm. On reflection this did us a power of good, we all needed a good night's sleep.

In conclusion I would add that in a few short months, the RNVR and HO ratings, had changed from being willing, but untrained seamen, and had together, with the regulars and reservists, been moulded into an efficient and battle hardened crew, ready to face the trials and tribulations of the war years that followed. I am sure that their experiences helped many of us to survive the remainder of the war.

Ted Loughlin
HMS **Vanquisher.**

* * * * *

Sitting at home one evening the telephone rang and a voice said I've been waiting over 55 years to say this "Thank you for saving my life" Blimey I thought, I'm a hero, but whose life had I saved? He went on "You won't know me, but I was a 'Pongo'. You took me off the beaches at Dunkirk". Now, I was too young to have been at Dunkirk, it was the crew of H.M.S **Worcester** he wished to thank. He was replying to an advert that I had for any V&W shipmates.
This is his story:-

GNR: S.T.Kester. R.H.Q 53rd Medium Reg't Royal Artillery.

The first time I saw H.M.S. **Worcester** was on the evening of the 30th May 1940 off the beach at La Panne.
We had been holding the line at Nieuport for two days as makeshift infantry until relieved by the Royal Fusiliers.
We were told to make our way to La Panne where the Navy would pick us up. We got there in the early hours of the morning.
During the day an assortment of ships were picking up troops, but we did not get lucky until H.M.S **Worcester** appeared. They sent us out in small boats and we had to board via a rope ladder, it was a job for me as I had been wounded in my right arm and shoulder. Progress up that ladder was very slow, when I got near the top a sailor looked over and said "Come on mate, your holding the cinema queue up." Then he saw the reason and leant over the side and grabbed my webbing braces and lifted me bodily on to the deck. He then said to me "Walking wounded in the stern, you can sit down there." I then asked him if that was the back end of the boat. I cannot put in to print his comment.
We sailed at 2200 hrs but not before a German bomber came over, it was pitch dark, but it was that low we could see the outline of the plane. By this time there must have been over 600 troops on board, but there was complete

silence, until one of the Oerlikons opened up. I believe it was the Captain who made the comments which followed. In plain English it was "Why don't you send him a postcard and tell him we are here." In actual fact I have never heard so many swear words put in to one short sentence. I think it must have even frightened the German because he did not come back.

I got talking to one of the gun crew, an old sweat, and I got a quick history of the ship, including the fact that she had won the destroyer trials in the 1930s. He was very proud of her.

I dropped off to sleep, when I awoke there was a sailor swinging the lead and calling the depth up to the bridge. The ship was first going forward and then astern, after repeating this operation several times we then shot forward and picked up speed.

I asked the gunner what had happened. He told me that we had run aground on a sand bank, I made a remark about bad driving, he then said "You missed the fun." A German torpedo boat fired two torpedoes at us and in taking evasive action we had run aground.

As dawn broke we were going at full speed, my friend the gunner came along with a steaming mug which he gave to me, it looked like cocoa, but it was thick and the spoon was 'standing to attention', and it smelt like rum, I think he called it "Pussers Kye." Whatever it was it was a great drink.

We entered Dover at about 0730 on the 31st May, as we went into the harbour every destroyer there sounded their sirens, when they finished the **Worcester** replied. I was nineteen years old at the time, but even now if I hear those sirens it sends a shiver down my spine.

As I went down the gangway I looked for my sailor pal, but none of the ships company were to be seen, so I could not thank anybody for bringing me home - I did thank the ship.

I do know that the next day **Worcester** was dive bombed and suffered a lot of casualties. Later when I read of the German capital ships and the 'Channel Dash' I felt a great sense of pride when I learnt that **Worcester** had played a brave part in the action.

Just before the Normandy invasion we had some nineteen year olds posted to the Regiment. One day one of them said to me "You were at Dunkirk, how did you get home?" I simply said to him, "La Panne to Dover via **Worcester"** I think that he is till trying to work that one out.

In closing this story I would like to quote a drill sergeant I had when I first joined the army in 1938. When the squad did not perform to his liking he would say, "When I look at you lot, I say to myself, thank God we have got a Navy". I said those words to myself in 1940.

In defeat most of us have reached an all time low, we felt let down by our own Generals, the French, the Belgians and most of all the R.A.F. (at that

time). What we did not question was the statement that the Navy will pick you up. I think that the **Worcester** was one of the finest ships ever to fly the White Ensign. (All of us who served in the V&Ws feel the same about our own ship).
I know I have gone on a bit, but it has been in me for the past 57 years waiting to come out.

VENOMOUS ENCOUNTER

My encounter with H.M.S. **Venomous** was brief, dramatic and left a memory which will stay with me for the rest of my life. To relate how she came into it I must go back to June 1940 when, as a Sergeant in the 3rd mortar platoon of the Fifth Battalion the Green Howards, I arrived at Bray Dunes. This was about half way between Dunkirk and La Panne. On the night of the 1st June at about 10pm we started to move towards Dunkirk. The distance was about six miles, and it took all night. We moved in pitch dark, in single file, carrying our rifles and holding on to the man in front. Sometimes in deep soft sand, sometimes up to our knees in the sea. Captain Whittaker, (later Sir J.M. Whittaker) who was wounded at Bray Dunes, wrote in the 'Scarborough Evening News' some ten years later. "Those who were there that night will never forget it, though many of them were sleeping as they marched. Incidents that will long stay in their memories."
And so we came to the Mole, where chaos and confusion reigned. Shells were falling, dive bombers screaming, and then the words came down, "No more boats tonight, everybody back on the beach." More chaos. All I remember is getting back onto the beach, finding a hole in the sand and falling asleep.
With daylight on the 2nd the bombing and shelling started again. I left my hole and tried to find other Green Howards. The Mole had been hit several times and there seemed to be bodies everywhere. I found some Howards, and we eventually came to the place where the C.O., Col. Bush, had set up his head quarters. It was there that the officers and staff officer organised a bayonet cordon to police the embarkation that evening, and to prevent the chaos of the previous night. And so it was that I found myself one of a hundred other ranks and four officers controlling the embarkation.
It is impossible to describe what happened. There was a Major from the R.E's who seemed to appear from nowhere and who organised a rota. Somehow he found out the various groups and units and gave them all a time to embark. It seemed impossible, but it worked like a dream, and even the French troops co-operated. So well did our cordon work that, just after midnight, we were told that all British troops had passed through the cordon

onto the Mole, and had been picked up by the Naval boats waiting in the dark. We were told that there was also a chance that we could also get away, and we should proceed to the Mole at once as there was a destroyer ready to pick us up. The Mole itself had been badly damaged which made getting a hundred men along it quickly and in the dark a very daunting task. I remember seeing the shadowy shape of the destroyer at the side of the Mole, and thinking 'Thank God I've made it.'

However there was not time to think as two crew members took charge of me and one said "Now Jump!" I jumped. It was dark and seemed so very unreal as the deck seemed to come up to meet me. Then another crew member told me to put my rifle on a pile of others, and led me down to a mess deck. I did not know it at the time, but I was on board H.M.S. **Venomous.** Members of the crew came round with pails of water, which was very welcome as we had not shaved, washed or even eaten for several days. I could hear the engines, and gunfire, and feel the motion of the ship, but I had no idea if we were at sea or still at Dunkirk.

Eventually we left the mess deck and were amazed to see the White Cliffs of Dover. We were back home.

I do not know if **Venomous** went back, but many naval ships did, and 26,000 were evacuated that night. When on the 4th June records show that the 18th German army at last captured Dunkirk, some 40,000 French were taken prisoner. These were the men who had held out much longer than expected and helped to make the Operation Dynamo such a success. In all some 338.226 Allied troops, including 143,000 French, were evacuated from Dunkirk, on more than 800 ships of every size and kind. Losses were heavy, including nine destroyers. I am told that H.M.S. **Venomous** survived to be sold and broken up in July 1947.

Ex. 4390283 Sgt L. F. Warn
5th Bn the Green Howards

Chapter 23

OPERATION LUCID
OCTOBER 1940.

I was on leave after Dunkirk when I was appointed First Lieutenant of a fire ship laying at Sheerness It was an old Norwegian tanker named Mytilus.
The ship's company had guessed our role, some having joined at Portsmouth dockyard where the ship had been fitted out, as it transpired to indifferently and too hastily. They totalled twelve. One Chief Engine Room Artificer, one stoker P.O. And four stokers, one seaman P.O. And four seamen and a signal man who acted as cook and cabin hand for the three officers. The ship was loaded, having taken on its deadly cargo at Hambledon. Captain Agar V.C. was in overall command.
He came aboard the next day and addressed us. He told us that our task was to steam across the channel to attack certain harbours, which, he did not reveal, get as close as possible and then set off the time fuse to ignite the mixture and then abandon ship. This would be into motor launches, which would come alongside while the ship was still steaming on by itself with the steering wheel lashed amidships. He explained that the meteorological conditions of tide, moon and wind had to be favourable, while the Royal Air Force would make diversionary raids. He assured us that three other tankers would be joining us shortly, we would not have to operate alone. Once we sailed there would be a covering force of destroyers, minesweepers, motor torpedo and motor launches from Harwich and the Thames estuary to escort us and give protection from enemy surface interference. Smoke laying may also be used. We were left unimpressed except for the Sub Lieutenant who regarded it as a tremendous adventure and with enthusiasm.
In fact only two ships were available for the first attempt against Boulogne on the night of the 25/26th September. War Nawab and War Nizam. War Nawab had only left Portsmouth that morning and was only capable of six knots and was leaking in many places. Captain Agar had embarked in Campbell, the leader of the 21st flotilla, and as we passed War Nizam in the Edinburgh Channel, she was seen to be making thick black smoke an allowing in the sea that was running. Her patched up boilers were giving trouble and she was down to four ½ knots. It was obvious to Agar that neither ship would reach the rendezvous position and, indeed, the wind was coming from an unsuitable quarter and the motor torpedo boats were unable to operate in such conditions. Accordingly the Admiralty called the operation off, being reluctant to waste such a promising weapon so early on.
For the next attempt on the 4/5 October, Agar was hopeful of having three tankers available, namely, War Nizam, Oakfield and Mytilus. War Nizam

had had some of her glaring faults remedied at Sheerness Dockyard and the Oakfield had been completed at Chatham Dockyard. They loaded their cargo on the 2nd October. Mytilus had remained at anchor fully fuelled awaiting her chance. This time the allocation of duties was War Nizam and Mytilus to Calais and Oakfield to Boulogne. Agar was with this force in the hunt class destroyer Hambledon. Again the operation had to be postponed because of an unfavourable south west wind and the promised bomber support to cause a diversion had been cancelled. By now the crews were becoming highly tensed up. The prospect of living on these floating furnaces and making their escape before the wall of flame cut them off was increasingly daunting. They needed a break. The next attempt was planned for the night of 7/8 October. Ill luck continued to dog Lucid. The War Nawab unloaded her mixture and this was the reloaded to top up Oakfield and War Nizam. Her crew was reduced while she remained at Sheerness with Mytilus, who had been ruled out because of unseaworthiness. Oakfield was again allocated to Boulogne and Agar again embarked in Hambledon. The Calais force was some way astern when Hambledon struck a mine and was badly damaged. This meant that the Calais force might have to enter newly mined waters and Agar was forced to lose another of his escorts, by ordering **Vesper** to tow Hambledon back to port. Again the wind failed to veer. Lucid was again postponed until 1st November.

In fact, Lucid never did sail again. The idea was killed off due to a combination of badly prepared ships, lack of destroyers and the advent of unpredictable stormy weather. Remember, too, the new magnetic mine had arrived and destroyers and merchant vessels on the East Coast were being lost. The stormy weather also made a German invasion an unlikely operation. They had missed their chance.

Destroyers that were also involved in the operation:-

Campbell (Captain 'D' 21) Mackay, Walpole, Venetia, Witch, Veteran, Venomous, Wild Swan, Wolverine,, Beagle, Vesper, and the Hunt Class Cottesmore, Garth and Hambledon.

Minesweepers;- Salamander, Selkirk, Sutton, Elgin, Hussar and Speedwell.

J.R. Gower
HMS **Winchester.**

* * * *

Memories of H.M.S. Worcester
By Harold Barnett E.R.A.

I Joined **Worcester** in Sheerness dockyard on the 24th April 1940. She was at the end of a fairly extensive refit. The Engineer Officer was Mr Smillie, commissioned Warrant Officer, the C.E.R.A was Sid Silkins, and the watch keeping E.R.A's (Engine Room Artificer) were in order of seniority Ron Brenton, Bill Peters, and George Angus I came bottom of the pile, supernumerary 5th. Our skipper was commander Allinson.

I had a lot to learn, and was given a large book and a 'Pussers' notebook and sent off to trace the source of oil and water, main and auxiliary steam, pumping and flooding systems, identify valves, the bits of the machinery and their valves in the engine room and boiler room. Then after spending all day crawling through bilges and under deck heads of the machinery spaces, find a quiet corner in the mess to make fair sketches and write details of my days work. This was presented to the Chief and the Engineer the next morning, who both questioned me closely to make certain that I had learnt something, before sending me off to clamber over or under something else. Hard men to please, but looking back they were fair, and making sure that I had learnt my trade thoroughly, and become a good member of, what was, in the end, a good team.

The refit complete, we were soon at sea, what we were doing, or who we belonged to I had no idea. I do remember going into Portsmouth and then steaming over to Le Havre for some reason, then back to Portland.

May 27/28th we were steaming down the western end of the English Channel when we increased speed, steaming East through the night, we were off Dover early in the morning. And were ordered straight to Dunkirk.

We were berthed alongside another V&W who's name I cannot recall at the extreme end of the Western Mole, we immediately started to embark troops and, at the same time transfer oil from our neighbour, it seems that we were running pretty low after our fast run up the Channel. I seem to remember it was very noisy, but troops continued to come aboard in an orderly fashion. How long it took I know not, but we were back in Dover harbour with over 500 troops at 2000hrs.

Time meant very little during the next five days, we were back and forth, Dover - Dunkirk, picking up troops and survivors from ships that had been hit along the beech or whilst they were at the mole. By the morning of June 1st we had landed some 3,200 men at Dover. On our way back over that day we came upon a motor cruiser which was being attacked by three German fighter aircraft, they sheered off when we joined in, leaving the cruiser to continue her way to Dunkirk. When we arrived there things were rather hectic, and I believe that all the destroyers had been ordered to return to harbour during that afternoon. We continued entering Dunkirk harbour. The skipper decided that it didn't make sense to return without taking on as many as we could. So eventually packed with our precious human load we pulled away at about 1700hrs. We immediately came under attack from Stuka dive bombers, they were a very determined lot, wave after wave they came at us dropping over 100 bombs. Due to Commander Allison's brilliant way that he handled the ship we received no direct hits. There were plenty of near misses which sent huge columns of water over the ship and our sides and upper works were riddled with splinters. By the time the attack eased off, sadly there were 46 dead and 180 wounded. Most were of course the lads that we had picked up from the Mole. Unfortunately Mr Smillie was one of the fatalities. He had been at the top of the engine room hatch the whole time during the attack.

We were far from being out of trouble, for whilst we were taking evasive action in the shallow waters of Dunkirk we must have hit the bottom or some submerged object damaging our propellers. Quite how badly was not discovered until we were dry docked later. However whilst we were making our way to our berth at Dover Western dock, the ship was not responding as she should and we collided with the Channel steamer 'Maid of Orleans', our bows striking her just forward of her bridge, her way ahead heeled us over at an alarming angle, shooting some of the poor soldiers over the side into the water. We remained at this perilous angle until our engines, going astern took the desired effect and we became upright again. We finally berthed at 2115hrs and landed 947 troops, bringing our total up to 3350. Thus ended my first six weeks in a sea going ship.

We then took the ship to Gravesend to undergo repairs, after which we were soon back at sea with the 16th destroyer flotilla based at Harwich. We had a new skipper. Lt Cmdr E.C.Coates, and our new Engineer was Commissioned Warrant Officer Griffiths.

A little aside on our collision with the 'Maid of Orleans'. Some years ago, my son and his family moved close to Dover where our two Grand daughters attended the village school, there they became 'best friends' with two sisters of their own age. One day my son was entertaining the parents and grandparents of these two young girls in the garden, we two Grand Dads were back in the shade of the pear tree 'swinging the lamp' to discover that Ernie was an apprentice seaman aboard the 'Maid' when we ploughed into her.

Chapter 24

We settled down to the drudgery of the East Coast convoys and I continued to learn my trade resulting in being promoted to fourth in January 1941. Chief and Mr Griffiths seemed to think that I was beginning to 'catch on' which was confirmed in March of that year. Having got my 'sums' right they must have persuaded the base Engineer Commander that I was worth the risk, I was given my engine room ticket in April 1941, so now, at last I was on the watch bill. Ron Brenton left soon after that, so now we were back to three watches, but at least I was no longer 'supernumerary'

I have no clear memory of the next nineteen months after we left Gravesend, except that we were alongside a repair ship in Scapa Flow after a trip up to near Iceland.

Christmas 1940 we were hiding away in the Faroes with a tanker for a few days, why I cannot remember, (if I ever knew) part of some large strategy I have no doubt.

Christmas 1941 found us sampling the delights of Greenock, when all the locals were only interested in was the approaching New Year.

All this of course was interspersed with the periodic five days boiler cleaning alongside at Harwich or in dock at Chatham, and of course chasing the odd E-boat away from our convoy, and picking up the pieces of the ones we missed.

The story of **Worcester** continues: by another shipmate:-

After making my own way from H.M.S. Victory I joined **Worcester** in the late afternoon one day in June 1941 and was taken to see the temporary Officer Of the Day. I was then given my mess and being joined up as part of ship, I was left to my own devices until the bulk of the crew returned about five days later.

When the full time 'Bosun' returned I was given various jobs and was delegated number three on 'A' gun a low loading 4.7 separate ammunition gun. I stayed with this job for over a year until I was transferred to the torpedo party awaiting a draft chit to a torpedo party school.

The Leading Seaman in charge of 'A' gun had been a Petty Officer but had been reduced to L/S for having machined gunned Japanese seamen.

The crew was made up of about three R.N. Regulars and 23 Hostility Only (HO's) who, like me had been called up. We had at least four amateur boxers among them, so, we had to be careful who we quarrelled with or you would soon get a 'right ear full'.

One thing of interest that I learned was that the First Lieutenant had been a survivor of the Thetis which had been lost in the Mersey. For some reason the Captain refused to speak to him, they used a signalman to pass notes from one to the other on the bridge!

During my stay on the **Worcester** we took part in all sorts of operations, going round the British Isles more than once. On the afternoon of the 27th July 1941 we were sent out in a mad rush to the assistance of H.M.S **Malcolm** who had been damaged during a bombing raid by Junkers 88's, another of the V&Ws, the **Wren** had been sunk in the same raid. We made fast alongside the **Malcolm** and towed her into Harwich.

Chapter 25

Wren was named just after the demobilisation of the 1917-1919 W.R.N.S, and although there was no indication that the name was intended as a compliment to the Wrens, the Association of Wrens claimed her as their own and provided boat badges and silk ensign and other tokens of affection.
After her loss, the Second Sea Lord, Admiral Little, suggested officially that the naming of a new ship **Wren** would be an encouragement to the Wrens, who were already doing excellent service, and furthermore, proposed that the Director of WRENS should launch the ship.
Permission was obtained to allow Wrens to give towards the building of the ship and a sum of over £4,000 was voluntarily subscribed, made up very small sums. Representative parties of WRNS were allowed to go to the launching, and with a large number from the nearby ports of Glasgow and Greenock it was a real Wrens day.
Messrs Denny, the builders (who had built many of the original V&Ws) gave a grand luncheon in pre-war style.
To launch a ship is an unforgettable experience, to feel her come alive, to move, to be released from captivity.
To her right element. And this was a very special ship; something took to sea with her of the love of the British women for the service which has made their country's history.
The Wren was a sloop and although that sounds smaller than a modern destroyer, she was actually considerably bigger than her predecessor. She became one of the famous Second Escort Group under the late Captain F. J. Walker. On one of my happy visits on board, where I was always received like a queen and everyone felt that she was the Wrens own ship. I was told by then the Captain (Lieut, Comdr., S.J. Woods RNR) of the great reception given them when the group had come into Liverpool from one of their famous 'kills'. But the thing that had touched them most was when a squad of Wrens had had marched along the quayside, eyes righting proudly as the passed their name-ship.

Dame Vera Laughton Mathews D.B.E.

Chapter 26

We had a number of scrapes during the time I was aboard the **Worcester** yet we only had one casualty A.M Farlane who was hit by pieces of an Oerlikon shell fried from our own gun.
I left **Worcester** in September 1941 to go to H.M.S. Vernon at Portsmouth, in the following February she was involved in the 'Channel Dash' operation and was severely damaged. I still wonder sixty years on, what happened to 'A' gun's crew.

* * * * * *

On the 5th July 1940 **H.M.S, Whirlwind** together with **H.M.S. Westcott** were ordered to carry out a U-boat hunt off Lands End, whilst doing this the **Whirlwind** was torpedoed and badly damaged by U-34 some 120 miles off Lands End and after taking off the crew she had to be sunk by gunfire from H.M.S **Westcott** who returned to Falmouth with the survivors.
During August 1940 **Westcott** formed part of the escort for convoys OG 40, HG 40, OB 201, and SC2. Then after undergoing repairs she joined the 5th Escort Group, Western Approaches Command operating out of Liverpool.
In December 1940 she escorted convoys OB 253, Hg 48, and OG 48, In January 1941 she escorted convoys SC18. On 28th January, whilst escorting OE1, she was in collision with the corvette Bluebell and returned to Liverpool for repairs. She was then allocated to the 7th Escort Group.

* * * * * *

Lucky Wrestler

Operation Catapult
Oran Mers-el Kebir
North Africa

Wrestler Joined force'H' under Admiral Somerville aboard HMS Hood, also along were HMS Valiant Resolution, Arethusa, Enterprise the Aircraft carrier Ark Royal and two flotilla's of destroyers.
We set sail from Gibraltar at 1400hrs on July 2nd.
The first action occurred at about 2345hrs when a torpedo exploded ahead of the destroyer **Vortigern,** she along with **Vidette** carried out a search, there was then much coming and goings between Admiral Somerville and Admiral Gensoul's emissaries to try and determine the outcome of the French Fleet which was now berthed at Mers-el-Kebir and Oran.

becoming obvious that the demands of the Admiralty for the French Fleet to surrender to the British were not going to be met. At 1730 hrs It was 'Action Stations' and we were detailed to close the entrance to the harbour to intercept any submarine activity.
Soon the 15 inch shells from the Hood were whistling overhead causing explosions among the French Fleet with smoke and flames rising several hundred feet in the air. The shore batteries were beginning to find our range and shells were falling all around us, they seemed to be of different colours, each shore battery must have had its own colour scheme.
Admiral Somerville ordered the **Wrestler** "To get out and retire out of range". Not before time too for we were being straddled, but 'Lucky' **Wrestler** came out unharmed.
The Battle cruiser Strasbourg and some destroyers escaped, we gave chase for a while but due to the shortage of fuel compelled us to retire and were recalled to the Fleet, we picked up the crews of two Swordfish which had been shot down.
With Force 'H' back in Gibraltar it was found that we had lost three Swordfish and two Skua's were lost but only one Skua's crew was lost. Of the Vichy French - enough said.
Wrestler had become the home of a legion of cockroaches, but I reckon we had the cheapest and most successful way of helping them on their way to Davy Jones Locker, but I don't claim copyright.
A jam jar strategically placed in several messes, burnt coffee placed in the bottom of the jar smeared with grease (preferably butter), they gave themselves up in droves, tip over the side, and R.I.P.
Later the skipper made it up to us when a signal said that we must carry out a boiler clean in Bermuda instead of Liverpool. Each mess was given a weeks ration of our own island. What a break!, talk about Captain Hook and Long John Silver. They could have had nothing on us, we lived like pirates for a week. What fun!. Old Joe was the oldest among us but what a good mate to have around when it came to tent pegging, camp fires and cooking. Best to end on a happy note!!

Laurie Conlon

* * * * *

December 1941. The tragedy of the sinking of the Prince of Wales and the Repulse in Far Eastern waters has been well documented, but what was little publicised is, that in that Naval force there were also four destroyers escorting the Capital ships, one of which was **Vampire.** When the battleships had been sunk the destroyers rescued 2.000 officers and men and returned them to Singapore.

The graves of HMS Worcester's casualties from the epic "Channel Dash" operation, lying in the churchyard of St Mary the Virgin, Shotley

The graves of HMS Vortigern lying in Lowestoft Cemetary. Vortigern was torpedoed in E-boat alley 15th March 1942

Chapter 27

Channel Dash

Worcester had just completed a boiler clean alongside at Harwich, and on the 12th February 1942 we happened to be exercising together with our flotilla leader H.M.S. Mackay, Captain P.J. Wright and two other V&Ws **Whitshed** and **Walpole** Captain 'D' of the 21st flotilla was Captain Pizey and as senior Officer he was in command in H.M.S **Campbell,** also of the 21st was **Vivacious**. We were just off Harwich. I was keeping the forenoon watch. Some time towards the end of the watch the bridge ordered an increase of rev's and by the time I had handed over the watch, we were very close to full power. It was about then that the skipper told us what we were about to do.
It seemed that we were on our way to intercept three German capital ships off the Scheld estuary. The only way possible according to all accounts meant crossing an unidentified minefield, a risk Captain Pizey was prepared to take with his six ships. It was a dull murky day with poor visibility. About mid afternoon we were closed up at action stations. Word went round that we had two big ships on the Radar at about nine miles range.
Twenty minutes later the enemy was in sight at about four miles. **Walpole** had turned back earlier with engine trouble (condenseritis) I believe, an endemic disease in V&Ws, that left just the five of us to carry out the attack. The two large ships turned out to be Scharnhorst and Gneisenau. The poor visibility had so far helped to cover our approach, but now we came under heavy fire**, Campbell** and **Vivacious** who were ahead of us had fired their torpedoes at about 3,000 yards, when out of the murk came the Prinz Eugen. We came under fire from her, but we set course to intercept and fire our torpedoes at 2.00 yards and as we made our approach and turn we were hit several times. As a result, 'A' & 'B' guns were put out of action. The bridge, radio room and sick bay were badly damaged, and we were on fire from right forward to abaft the bridge.
My action station at that time was with the forward fire and repair party. As we started to fight the fires, we were hit and straddled by another salvo, it seemed to me at the time that this had the effect of reducing the fire, whether it was the deluge of water from the straddle, or concussion from the explosion, who knows? But the fire was reduced and the fire party was bringing it under control. Only trouble was, the hit as we made our turn, and after firing our torpedoes, had added to our problems, and this took me away from the fire. A shell had entered the forward boiler room at the base of the forward funnel Port side, it had gone across the boiler room and exploded in the Starboard boiler water feed tank, blowing a hole in our ships side. We of

course lost all of our feed water and the boiler room started to flood. The Stoker PO And his stoker were able to shut down main and auxiliary steam and the isolating valves between the forward and the after boiler rooms before evacuating. We sealed the hatches and reported the damage and our actions to the Engineer. He sent me to the bridge to report the damage and the situation to the Skipper. It was then that I saw the damage that we had suffered forward and on the bridge and the casualties that we had sustained, they were quite considerable.

The immediate task was to secure the bulkhead between the forward and after boiler rooms. In the after boiler room this was in hand and I joined in when I got back from the bridge.

Shrapnel had pierced the bulkhead and water was leaking through. We managed to plug these holes and reduce the level of water by using hand pumps. All the damage we had suffered meant that we had lost steam and had stopped. But now we were able to commence raising steam again, trouble was we had no distilled water for the boiler feed, so were forced to use salt water. "To be done only in extreme emergency" as the engineering manual puts it. We figured we had one.

By now it was completely dark. **Campbell** who had been standing by us for a long time, and fought off one attack from the R.A.F. However she had been ordered back to base. When we had raised enough steam, we set course slowly back to Harwich, over the minefield again.

The next twelve to fifteen hours is a vague jumble of things we had to do. Spells at the evaporator trying to make distilled water to dilute the salt to reduce the salt damaging our machinery. A hopeless task really, that evaporator was a temperamental beast at the best of times, but we had to try. Spells at the throttle whilst the other E.R.A's were off doing some other essential tasks. Blowing down boilers to get rid of the deposits left by the salt water, and so to keep them priming, inspecting the damaged bulkhead and re-plugging the holes as required. There was so much to do and not many of us on our feet to do it.

We brought the ship into Harwich at about 1800hrs on the 13th and put her alongside at Parkeston Quay where the base staff immediately put salvage pumps aboard as we proceeded to shut down.

They worked on tidying away the damage and getting her reasonably seaworthy for us to take to dock, meanwhile we were able to rest and reflect on what had overtaken us.

Our casualties were high, we had lost 27 killed or died of their wounds on our way in, 46 seriously injures and 24 slightly wounded.

We buried our dead in the little churchyard at Shotley close to H.M.S. Ganges. One poor lad had married whilst we were on the five day boiler

clean leave. I quite distinctly heard his young wife say as his coffin was lowered into the grave, "He'll get cold down there". There she was, sweetheart, bride, and now widow all in about ten days, and possibly mother too before the war was over. The white poppy wearers say we old fellows glorify war on Remembrance Sunday. They have no idea, have they?
When the ship was ready, we took her into dry dock in London docks. The damage to her was so great that it meant that she would be there for some considerable time, so she was paid off and those not 'standing by' were returned to depot. We came into R.N.B. Pompey on the 18th February 1952.
I think of **Worcester** with a great deal of affection. She was my first ship, and I definitely 'grew up' in her.
When her story was published in the newspapers they called her "The ship that refused to die". A great deal of effort and dedication went into keeping her alive. In some ways I am sorry that I did not go back to her when she sailed again. But I may not have been quite so lucky next time round.
During our set to off Dunkirk, I was in the engine room with the Chief who told me to keep my eye on the water level of the drain tank. It had no practical use, because the watch keeper was doing it anyway.
It was simply giving me something to do and to keep my mind off what was going on up top. When we were back in Dover, I was following him around as we were shutting down (part of learning process) he took me aside and said "You are not to worry about what has gone on today, when this is all over and you are back home, you'll tend to think only of the good times" for me that is largely true, but I often think of Mr Smillie and that young widow at Shotley in her distress.
"Thanks Sid". I would not have dared to call him that way back in 1940 - 42.

Chapter 28

APRIL 1941

The German army had invaded Greece and were having great success and the Allied troops were being pushed towards the southern coast. It was obvious that another evacuation operation had to be planned, although there was no question of a 'Dunkirk' with the help of the 'little ships' and so it was that on the 24th April 1941 ships of the Royal Navy with transports ships and others, including nineteen destroyers set about the task of getting the troops off. One of the transport ships was attacked by a large number of German dive bombers and sunk. The destroyers Diamond and **Wryneck** set about the task of rescuing the troops. However the survivors elation at being rescued was short lived, for only a few hours later they too were sunk by the dive bombers. There were to be only fifty survivors from these ships.

******

March 1941

On the 7-8th March H.M.S **Worcester** was escorting a convoy in the North Sea (E-boat Alley) going North and passing a convoy going South. There had been heavy air activity for two days and the crews had been at action stations for long periods. Just after nightfall at 2030hrs they were attacked by two flotilla's of E-boats. Seven merchant ships were lost. Commander Coats the new skipper of the Worcester complained bitterly that the escorts were using radio telephone communications which meant that the enemy could pick up the signals and detect the position of the ships.

The Loss of H.M.S. Vortigern

I joined the **Vortigern** at Rosyth in early '41 after passing out as S/T at Vernon and Roedean college Brighton.
We did a lot of convoy duties and at one time we were escorting a cruiser from Dundee, going South. We picked up a young drafter there, the weather was terrible, no one was allowed fore or aft unless absolutely necessary, but this young lad, on his very first trip was washed overboard and was lost. I never even got to know him.
Whilst proceeding South we received a signal to proceed to the Channel. Three German battleships were trying to break out. Our sister ship **Worcester** was hit and one of my shipmates, Jim Adams was injured.

At the time of our sinking, we had left Portsmouth on Sunday 13th March to meet up with the convoy. The weather was again bad, corned beef sandwiches was all we could have.

On the night we were torpedoed, we were at action stations, I was on duty middle watch, luckily. I had just switched on the degaussing motor forward for we knew there was trouble in store because merchant ships were being blown up.

My duty was right aft with the depth charge party, keeping in touch with the bridge by manning the telephone.

The night was pitch black, all we could see was the silouhettes of the merchant ships.

At about 0200 we were hit forward. I always thought that it was two torpedoes, because the ship went down so very quickly. I managed to free a carley raft which was lashed around upright by a thick sling. I had to punch the wood toggle out with my fist. I damaged my hand but did not notice it.

These rafts had a lamp aboard which was activated on contact with the sea, so we had a light.

I remember the officers steward who had his quarters aft came up to me on the deck and I told him to jump overboard, we had no order to abandon ship because all those forward had been killed. He said to me "I've got to go back to retrieve something". I never saw him again. I took my duffle coat off, all I had on was a boiler suit and my rubber safety ring. I jumped in and managed to swim to the raft. I helped some of the others to get on. The oil fuel and the sea were so very cold. Quite a few died and slipped away. Our First Lieutenant was hanging on, but he too died and drifted away. Two others died on the raft, one named 'Sharky' Ward our L/S LTO also a three badge A.B. Sharky had only got married on his last leave. He came from Liverpool.

We must have been adrift for about eight hours, after a lot of singing and talking about different things just to keep ourselves awake.

We were of course overjoyed to see a corvette, H.M.S. Guillemotte on the horizon, they had been searching for survivors.

I tried climbing the scrambling nets, but I was too cold, however I was hauled aboard, put in the shower room and scrubbed down with hard brushes to bring back the circulation. The M.O. refused us rum because we had swallowed oil fuel.

We were then taken to Lowestoft hospital. I was there for three days, my feet and legs were very bad. Luckily I got over it and was allowed home on leave.

I received a telegram to go to Lowestoft to help identify the shipmates that are now buried there. I was met at the station by two Nuns, and taken to a 'mock up mortuary' a tin hut. It really upset me to see the lads laid out there.

Then I was called to the Admiralty, and before Admirals and other high ranking officers had to answer questions about the sinking.
I finished my Naval career as a L/S LTO on two carriers, the Argus on the North African landings and the HMS Indefatigable out in the Pacific.

Bill Bradshaw.

* * * * *

The sinking of the **Vortigern** and the loss of life, was the biggest loss on the East Coast Convoys.
Those who are buried in the Lowestoft cemetery are;-

Lt Comdr., R.S. Howlett D.S.C.
Lt, P.A.B. Powell
Sub Lt, J. Gilmour
A/B J Muir
A/B D. McLeod
Wierman R.C. Nutt
A/B L.W. Grace.
92
A/B J Flynn
A/B J.H. Jones
A/B H. Smith
A/B J.R. Leigh
A/B J.L. Stewart
A/B D. Mcleod
H. Farrow.

Petty Officer George Blundell's body was washed up at Cromer one month later. He is buried in Cromer cemetery.

R.I.P.

Chapter 29

Traditionally, the destroyer is the first of all fighting ships to leave port, the first to fight and the last to return to the relative inactivity of an anchorage. There is the vivid instance of H.M.S. **Vimy** which lost a screw when ramming a U-boat, and escorted a convoy 6,000 miles to North Africa before putting in for repairs. Again there is the amazing mileage of the old **Windsor,** one of the first destroyers to reach Dunkirk for the evacuation of our troops from France. In eight months she steamed 30,000 miles and in one month completed 4,060 miles. In 1941 a six month commission involved 16,000 miles and in 1942 she logged another 24,000. One of her sister ships H.M.S. **Woolston** celebrated her 25th birthday by escorting a convoy towards the landing beaches in Sicily. "The army is dependant on us. We will not let them down". Lieut. F. W. Hawkins had told his ships company. For nine days the **Woolston** patrolled for lurking U-boats off Sicily, brought enemy planes crashing in flames, and of 62 days, spent 60 of them at sea!

A TRIBUTE TO THOSE LOST IN DESTROYERS

Dear Friends when your thoughts they would wander away
To think of the deeds that's been done
Let them stay for a while,
With the lads that have gone,
With their duty so nobly done.
The lads that have gone beyond recall
Were sailors so bold and brave,
Who managed our destroyers with courage and skill,
Who fought with the hun and the waves.
Our Empire they guarded since war was begun,
Their vigilance kept to the end,
With never a murmur of hardships endured,
But a cheerful reply for their friends.
With mine or torpedo's destruction came,
And called them away from our side,
Both old and young their duty was done,
And their spirits float with the tide.
To the Harwich flotilla, we take off our caps.
They are surely one of the best
We pay our respects to the braves that have gone,
To their well earned and glorious rest.

This poem was found in a Matelot's 'Ditty' box after he had 'Slipped the cable' from wounds received in battle.

Chapter 30

NARVIK

Narvik was the scene of some very remarkable events at the onset of the war. It was here that Hitler's Germany suffered its first defeat it was May 1940. It was their first and only defeat during the first three years of the war.
Narvik because of the Gulf Stream was ice free all the year round and was invaded on the 9th April 1940. Under the cover of a thick blizzard ten German destroyers entered the harbour and immediately sank the two armoured battleships, 'Norge' and 'Eidsvoll'. Narvik was taken and the invaders then controlled the most vital resource to the war industry, iron ore.
A few days later the Royal Navy reached Narvik and set about annihilating the German fleet that were there, in the course of two violent battles.
These two battles severely reduced German Naval potential and may well have contributed to the aborting of the German invasion plans from across the Channel.
One notable incident remembered by Ernie Humphries of HMS **Westcott.** When her 4 inch gun crew scored a direct hit on a German howitzer which was mounted on rails, it came to the mouth of the tunnel, fired at houses the other side of the Fjord and then retreated into the tunnel, **Westcott's** gun crew put a stop to that.
They were also the prelude to a campaign fought largely in the Arctic Circle, which became known as the North West Expeditionary Force, lasting from April to June 1940 in which three V.C's were won and 2,300, mainly British sailors lost their lives.
Many hard lessons were learned in that hostile environment, not least that British Naval supremacy was compromised by the land based Luftwaffe.

COPY OF A SPEECH GIVEN BY MR JENS CHR; HAUGE, BARRISTER - AT - LAW ON THE OCCASION OF THE UNVEILING OF THE NATIONAL LIBERTY MONUMENT NARVIK 7TH MAY 1995

"There are excellent reasons why Norway should erect this national liberty monument here in Narvik, and declare it a permanent symbol of Norway's gratitude to our Allies.
Here, for the first time in the second world war, Hitler's Germany came up against joint Allied resistance. However improvised it was joint. Norwegian, British, French, and Polish forces set themselves the objective of retaking Narvik and northern Norway, it would, for all of them be part of the struggle for liberation.

At sea looking forward from 'Y' gun

With life-lines rigged

Oiling at sea in calm weather

Looking aft from the flag deck

Depth charge attack

Narvik was retaken, There are veterans from the four countries present today who took part in that fighting. The Poles, Frenchmen, Britons and Norwegians who gave their lives for liberty, and for us, are also with us in spirit. Their graves, too, are liberty monuments. Four leader come particularly to mind: Norway's Fleischer, Poland's Scyszk-Bokuez, France's Bethouart, and Britain's Cork and Orrery.
The drama played out up here, in those late May and early June days of 1940, was to prove fatal.
The Allied forces retook Narvik. And slowly but surely they drove the German Dietl and his mountain troops towards the Swedish border. They were perhaps within twenty-four hours of being forced to enter Sweden and being interned.
Hitler was nervous!
But the advancing Allies had an even shorter, even more remorseless deadline, set by the Allies Supreme War Council. It had decided that the Allied forces must be withdrawn from Northern Norway, just a few hours before Dietl's impending destruction. The reason? The Allies were in danger of losing the whole war in Europe.
So the struggle up here in the north in the spring of 1940 must have been in vain?
The struggle up here in the north in 1940 was **NOT** in vain. In the darkest hours, it showed that the Germans were not invincible. That gave new hope and new courage. And the losses the Allies inflicted on Germans in this area were to have unimagined consequences later in the war.
Hitler's bold leap to the North appeared to have been a huge triumph. Ten destroyers from the German battle fleet, each carrying an extra contingent of 120 mountain troops, took Narvik on the morning of the 9th April. Dietl became known in Germany as the 'Hero of Narvik'. But in the sharp light of later study, experts have seen the Norwegian campaign as a strategic mistake, entailing the dissipation of German forces and contributing to the defeat of Hitler's Germany, in Russia, in Africa, in France, on the seas, and in the air.
On this ocassion, we may wish especially to recall the following points:-

From the 9th to the 13th April, the British Fleet destroyed or sank all the ten destroyers with which Dietl had reached Narvik. One name in particular must be mentioned in that connection: That of Captain Warburton-Lee. The German navy was so weakened that it was unable to play a part in subsequent events, which determined the course of the war. Between the 26th May and the 4th June 1940 Britain had to evacuate 340,000 British, French and Polish soldiers from Dunkirk. The German navy was incapable of intervening, because, here in Vestfjorden, it had lost so many ships of the type needed. German military history relates that, when asked to help to prevent the evacuation from Dunkirk, the German Chief of Naval Staff replied:

"The losses incurred in the occupation of Norway necessitate restraint. Further losses would restrict the freedom of operation of all units from battleships to submarines. Where destroyers and torpedo boats are concerned, the current position is that we can scarcely muster the numbers absolutely necessary for major transport operations to Norway and for the operations on the larger units".

When the German Army Command wanted to cross the Channel to crush England, Grand Admiral Raeder, who more than anyone else had pressed for the operation against Norway, said that he did not have suitable vessels with which to protect the Channel crossing,. No, the Allied campaign up here in the North in the spring of 1940 was certainly **NOT** fought in vain. Both for us who are here, and for those who lost loved ones here, that is a truth to remember.

Chapter 31

1941

My association with my first V&W commenced in January 1941 when I returned to Chatham Barracks soon after Christmas 1940 from a spell of survivors leave following the sinking in the North Atlantic of H.M.S Forfar, an armed merchant cruiser. The night before my leave ended, I had witnessed the awesome sight of one of the heaviest raids on the city of London from high ground near my parents home in Charlton SE7. I was somewhat relieved when told that my next draft was to a destroyer of the Rosyth Escort Force although some of the old 'barrack stantions' did their best to cheer me up with pointed remarks about the perils of 'E-boat Alley', as part of the convoy route was known. At least a destroyer has speed and 'teeth' H.M.S. **Verdun** was to be my home for almost the next three years. She had been named after the French town of that name, the scene of much desperate fighting in 1916. The ship's motto 'Ils ne Passeront Pas' which means 'They shall not pass' was the battle cry of the French defenders which they upheld until the bitter end. It was most appropriate therefore that she should be chosen to carry the body of 'The Unknown Soldier' across the channel on the afternoon of 10th November 1920. A brass plaque was fixed aft to commemorate the occasion.

Thus begun one of the most momentous and best remembered periods of my life. This comradeship was something the like of which I have not experienced before or since. My immediate boss was a regular Navy Petty Officer Telegraphist, an expert in all aspects of his job with a never failing sense of humour and the ability to get the best out of people by example and encouragement.

The Captain was a regular Navy Lieutenant Commander, slightly built and quietly spoken, he instinctively inspired confidence and loyalty and was greatly respected and admired by all of us, so much so that when he was drafted, the chips company presented his wife (gifts to officers were forbidden under KR's and AI's (Kings Regulations and Admiralty Instructions), with an inscribed silver salver, something which our hard bitten and long serving Coxswain had never known happen before.

Life on North Sea - East Coast convoys was a mixture of roughly 10 per cent action and 90 per cent suspense and boredom. The suspense came from the ever present threat of mines, contact, magnetic and finally acoustic which were liberally distributed by German aircraft and E-boats in the narrow, shallow shipping lanes particularly from the Humber southwards. Despite all the efforts of our minesweeping colleagues, they still claimed their victims. Skirmishes with enemy aircraft and E-boats were infrequent but could be quite hair raising while they lasted. In between, we passed the time in the less dangerous stretches of water listening to record requests on the ships sound reproduction equipment, (including, naturally, Vera Lynn and also more surprisingly movements from Tchaikovsky's Piano Concerto and Beethoven, 5th symphony), the occasional quiz programme and brains trust, and I can even recall organising a scrum practice on the quarter deck for the ship's rugby team - without a ball of course! A few of us used to endeavour to keep fit by pacing up and down the length of the iron deck when the sea was not too rough.

Living conditions on board were somewhat cramped and uncomfortable, but generally speaking good humour somehow managed to prevail.

In the course of my duties I handled hundreds of signals, including a number not addressed to the ship, such as those telling us of the sinking of H.M.S. Hood and the subsequent chase and sinking of the Bismark. But those I find easiest to recall are the humorous ones.

Except in emergency we were under strict orders not to break W/T silence, but we did have to make one signal every trip towards the Northern end of the convoy run from Sheerness; this was our expected time of arrival (ETA) off Methill. To confuse the enemy code breakers we were instructed to vary the wording of our routine signals as much as possible. Ships vied with one another in the search for originality with quotations from the Bible, Shakespeare etc; in consequence signals grew longer and longer. Eventually Captain 'D', Rosyth Escort Force felt compelled to intervene. A plain language signal was sent to all the ships in his force when they were next in harbour which went like this;-

"Fun is fun and I don't mind a bit
Your rhymes and ETA's to fit
But don't o'er do the signal chit
For brevity is the soul of wit."

On another occasion we were delayed in arriving back to Rosyth. Half the ship's company were due for an eagerly awaited four days boiler cleaning leave and it was obvious that if we proceeded into the destroyer pens there was no chance of the liberty men catching the day train from Edinburgh to the South where most of us lived. So without as much as by your leave the Captain hove to under the Forth Bridge and the lucky lads were landed at South Queens Ferry, using the ships motor boat and whaler, in time to catch the train. This provoked the following from Captain 'D' -"Your manoeuvre under the Forth Bridge this morning very well executed. Do NOT repeat Not repeat".

Finally as a variation to our normal convoy duty, we were detailed briefly from the escort force and detailed to act as part of the anti-submarine screen for a brand new battleship undergoing speed trials.

It was soon evident that we lacked the legs of the new ship and we began to fall behind which caused the battleship to tersely signal, "You are losing station" to which our Captain literally flashed back "I am 25 years old". Nevertheless there was life in the old ship yet as she proved right up to the end of the war.

Chapter 32

Westcott v **Bismarck**

We were in charge of a very large convoy in the region of Iceland when the news came through of the sinking of the Hood by the Bismarck. We were about 100 nautical miles from the incident, and the convoy had orders to scatter, and ships steamed off in all directions.

Over the tannoy, our Captain addressed the ships company. "I have news" he said "That Bismarck might possibly be heading this way, we are going at full speed to the last known position of Bismarck. Torpedo tubes will be trained over the ships side, and should we be lucky enough to meet up with her, we might be able to get in a strike."

It was akin to a death sentence! Pitting tiny **Westcott** against the mighty Bismarck was like putting a peanut under a sledge hammer.

A hush descended on the ship, anxious eyes scanned the horizon. A lookout was dispatched to the crows nest, as **Westcott** carried no radar. Strange thoughts entered my mind. Was this the end of the line? Would I ever again see my beloved family? Would I ever again see football at Roker Park? Would I ever ride my bike over Weramouth Bridge on my way to work? And so on.

After what seemed an age the tannoy crackled out again. "There is no need for further vigilance. I have news that Bismarck is now heading away from us."

A cheer went up. We and **Westcott** were to live to fight another day. I swear the only disappointed man was the Captain. What glory would have been his if those torpedoes had wended their way to Bismarck!

Slinger Woods.

Chapter 33

Early in 1941 merchant ship losses were becoming increasingly and disastrously high. The U-boat aces were having a very successful time, until the V&Ws took a hand. in March of that year. First on the 8th March H.M.S. **Wolverine** commanded by Commander J.M. Rowland whilst escorting convoy OB 293 attacked and sunk U- 70. Off the South of Iceland.
Next, convoy HX 112 was attacked when off the Hebrides when H.M.S. **Walker** who's Captain was Captain Donald Macintyre, sighted the wake of what could only be a U-boat and immediately attacked with depth charges, shortly after the explosion of the depth charges there was another with an orange flash spread across the surface, we were quite confident that we had made a 'kill'. About half an hour later she again had an Asdic contact and again attacked with depth charges. **Vanoc** joined in the attack. Whilst this was going on lights had been spotted in the distance, these could only be lifeboats or similar, so making sure of the position **Walker** and **Vanoc** set forth to investigate. They were indeed the lifeboats of one of the merchant ships that had been sunk. While **Vanoc** kept vigil the **Walker** proceeded to pick up the survivors from the lifeboats. When they had the survivors on board they proceeded to return to the scene of the attack. **Walker** noticed that **Vanoc**, contrary to previous orders was going at full speed, a few moments later **Vanoc** signalled to **Walker** "Have rammed and sunk U-boat". It was almost unbelievable that so many U-boats should be nearby, but it was not to be long before, once again Asdic contact was made. So once again depth charge attacks began, soon after **Vanoc** signalled to **Walker** "U-boat surfaced astern of me". Both ships after illuminating the U-boat opened fire with their 4 inch guns. A flashing light from the U-boat read "We are sunken". The U-boat crew were taking to the water, and were picked up by the British destroyers.
In picking up the German survivors it was discovered that their Captain was the much decorated U-boat Ace Otto Kretschner. It was also discovered that the U- 100 was commanded by yet another of the Germans Ace's, Joachim Schepke.
So in just three actions over a short period the old V&Ws had disposed of three of Germany's U-boat aces and had made a huge contribution to the outcome of the 'Battle of the Atlantic'.
18th July 1941, Whilst forming part of the escort to the Atlantic convoy OB 346 **Westcott** sustained slight hull damage whilst putting out a fire aboard the SS Pilar de Larrinaga which had been bombed that morning in position 54 degrees North, 16 degrees West. After putting the fire out she escorted the

merchant vessel to Swansea, and then proceeded to Liverpool for repairs and refit which were completed on the 25th August.
The role of the 16th and 21st destroyer flotilla's based at Harwich and Sheerness was to provide additional protection against E-boats and aircraft to the East Coast convoys as they rounded the East Anglian bulge.
Leaving Harwich, one evening in the summer of 1941 H.M.S. **Worcester** joined up with a North bound convoy. She then dropped back to sink a floating mine that had been spotted.
While the crew were mildly enjoying themselves taking pot shots at it with rifles, 'Action Stations' sounded. We closed up to the pom-poms as it appeared that three Hurricanes were pursuing a Junkers 88 above us, and we enthusiastically joined in only to hear Check, Check Check Down came the word from the bridge that in fact it was our convoy's escorting Blenheim being attacked by three ME 109F's, (which had never been seen in the area before). The Blenheim flew in a tight circle around **Worcester** who put up all it could at the ME's and they flew off trailing smoke. The R.A.F. Pilot lived to tell the tale and we received a message of thanks from his air station. Following this bizarre episode Blenheims were no longer employed as convoy protection.

******

Joe Curbishly writes**:**
I joined **Versatile** at Dover in June 1940 just after Dunkirk as an A.B. lS.D. (asdic rating) after spending a year in another destroyer H.M.S. Firedrake. That summer we convoyed up and down the English Channel. It was then that Goering decided to try out his mass bombing of the convoys.
Ninety planes in three waves of thirty attacked us. Our skipper decided to race up and down the convoy firing everything we had got including the 4.7's. We were the only destroyer as was usual in those early days. Six Hurricanes appeared and flew straight into the bomber formations and scattered them all over the sky. In less than five minutes there was not a plane to be seen. Our only casualty was an A.B. Who looked up with his mouth wide open and a shitehawk promptly filled it!
We then operated from Liverpool on the Atlantic convoys until one bright soul ordered us to join in the escort of a troopship convoy bound for the East via Capetown.at top speed all went well until a gale blew up and we sailed into the teeth of it, hitting milestones every minute, shipping water through strained deck head plates into the mess decks. We struggled on until the skipper had to ask permission to turn back or risk going under. We Limped into Londonderry which was not then a Naval port, for emergency repairs. After these had been carried out we sailed around Scotland to Wallsend

slipway on the Tyne for extensive repairs.
On the first nights leave a group of us from the North West caught a train from Newcastle to Manchester. I remember playing cards most of the time and winning a few quid, or did I lose? Going over the Pennines that night the train stopped, blacked out of course, and we watched Manchester being bombed. Not until early morning did we reach London Road station. I picked my way over to Central Station which was dark and deserted, but a railway 'bobby' opened up a waiting room so that I could get my 'head down'.
In the morning light I emerged to find that there was an unexploded bomb in the railway arches outside the station and no trains were running. It was not until the late afternoon that the 'all clear' was given. I arrived home at 2000hrs thankful and relieved and very glad to see my wife again. In the summer of '41 I left Versatile to do the H.S.D course at 'Osprey' and spent the rest of the war in Flower Class Corvettes and instructing at Osprey.

Chapter 34

1942

H.M.S. Wishart

After the two most famous convoys, Harpoon and Pedestal and the eighth army had beaten Rommel's Africa Corps, we then took a convoy through to Alexandria, the first for a few years.

On arrival we were given a few days leave, so down to the race course we went. We stayed at a hotel in Mohammed Ali Square and really lived it up. We mixed in with some army lads who were buying up bales of silk and souvenirs, as there were about thirty troop ships in the harbour, the 'buzz' was going round that they were going home, and of course we thought that we would be escorting them and going home as well.

I was mess caterer and managed to get hold of a few bags of Egyptian potatoes and gammon hocks. A couple of days before we set sail I managed to get tonsillitis, so I had to sling my hammock on the upper deck alongside the Pom-poms.

We set sail about 0400 as dawn was breaking. All the troop ships and cruisers were on the move. The Captain came on the tannoy. "Gentlemen" he said "You know bloody well we will not be going home."

So we were off for the invasion of Sicily. As I went down to my mess the surgeon saw me and wanted to know what I was doing out of my hammock, I told him that I was not going to get shot at! One of my mess mates brought me my dinner of the lovely ham and potatoes that I had acquired. I just could not eat it. That broke my heart, tho' I did manage to get my tot down.

I felt sorry for those troops who had bought those bales of silk thinking that they were on their way home. They must have had them packed in their haversacks.

We went to Salerno for the landings, there were rocket firing ships beyond us I said "I hope they know what they are doing" because the rockets were flying over our heads. Suddenly we peeled off and made our way to Malta, refuelled etc; and then off we went to Taranto. Italy had just surrendered. On our arrival at Taranto we went alongside the 42,000 ton Battleship Le Vittoria, pride of the Italian navy. One officer, one P.O. And five ratings, including me, were armed with 303 Lee Enfield rifles. We were to board her. "What do we do if they don't want to surrender?" Asked someone. "Oh you'll be all right, just sort it out" we were told. Thank God we did not have to use our rifles!

That night laying at anchor, ahead of us lay the mine laying cruiser HMS Abdial, at about 0200 there was an explosion. She got rid of her mines and had Royal Marine Commandoes and their equipment, including trucks on board that had been picked up at Algiers. Whether it was a mine, human torpedo or a saboteur that could have been picked up at Algiers we did not know. We put out scrambling nets and picked up a few survivors, up anchor and crashed out of the harbour.
However we eventually arrived back in Gibraltar via Catalina, Salerno and Taranto.
Whilst ashore I met up with an old shipmate who was on the Hurricane, they were going home, so I asked him to take the bale of silk and other goodies to give to my Mother, but they were sunk in the Bay of Biscay on Christmas day.
Soon after we went back home to have radar towers fitted, we were in Newport South Wales for about four days, we then again returned to Gib' where **Wishart, Westcott, Witherington, Wivern Verity, Velox**, Antelope and Antony were detailed to do a Radar shoot, by then all the destroyers had been fitted with Radar. **Wishart** was detailed to provide a target marking party consisting of a Warrant Gunner and four ratings aboard the trawler. As I was not the flavour of the month, I was to be one of the four aboard the target towing trawler.
The first salvo came right through the trawlers rigging. The Radar operators in those days were all seamen who had had no real training on how to operate the Radar.
One of the trawlers officers came and had a word with the Warrant Gunner, it seemed that one of the stokers had been taken ill. "Don't worry, I'll get one of my men to take his place" - Well you can guess who that was going to be. I thought that I could twiddle a few knobs and valves and I'll be out of the Gunner's way. The trouble was that when I got down to the boiler room, there was a shovel and about three tons of coal!. I wonder, have we got any shipmates or seamen who have had to shovel coal.
I eventually arrived home just before "D" day.

Doug Lochead.

* * * *

Able seaman Jock Falconer was a typical example of a pre-war three badged 'stripey'. Utterly reliable whilst on board, except perhaps where rum was concerned, a first class seaman, and with the ability, but not the interest to rise to higher ranks.

However, ashore, Jock was a different character, as his service papers so clearly showed, ie; deprived, restored, deprived etc.
He went ashore one day in Londonderry, on ordinary night leave, due to expire 0700 the following morning, but he failed to return, and it was two days later when he reappeared at the gangway. He looked awful, his uniform was all creases and in a filthy state, his collar was torn, he was unshaven and all in all looked most unkempt.
As the duty Petty Officer I lined him up before the duty Officer Of the Day, a young R.N. Sub Lieutenant and read out the charge. "Able seaman Falconer Sir, did remain absent over leave 48 hours, namely from etc."
"Well" said the O.O.D. "What happened Jock?" in all seriousness he replied "The alarm failed to go off Sir". It was such a ludicrous reply that both the O.O.D. And the P.O. Burst out laughing. What happened at the Captains table? Perhaps Jock thought of a more suitable reply.
Sad to say Jock lost his life when **Veteran** was sunk in the Atlantic in 1942.

Chapter 35

Early in the war the Admiralty expected the Germans to carry out a magnetic mine campaign, we did not have any effective sweeping gear. It was hoped that the counter mining with depth charges would set the mine off, but this did not work. The destroyer **Wivern** tried steaming at full speed around the wreck of a merchant vessel that had been sunk by a magnetic mine, to see if she could set another mine off and to use her speed to get clear of the explosion. She was unable to obtain a result, which was just as well, although her crew had been reduced to the minimum for this experiment. I joined the **Wivern** on the 2nd October 1941 at Sierra Leone as a replacement for and E.R.A that had gone sick with the inevitable malaria. At the time **Wivern** was under the command of Lt Cmdr M.D. Meyrick, who later as Commander Meyrick was Captain of the destroyer Savage, involved in the sinking of the Scharnhorst.

After a few weeks escorting convoys and carrying out anti submarine patrols in the South Atlantic, **Wivern** returned to her home base at Portsmouth for a refit and the fitting of the latest Radar.

We called at Bathurst, (now Banjul) Gambia and Gibraltar on the way home. During the time in Portsmouth I recall a meeting of dockyard matey's being addressed by the current Minister of Labour, Ernest Bevin. One of the matey's called. "We want more air raid shelters." Without but a slight hesitation, Bevin replied "You cannot work in air raid shelters, we want more effort to repair our warships." The meeting then went very quiet and broke up shortly afterwards.

After the refit, **Wivern** sailed to Londonderry and was then involved in escorting the battleship H.M.S. Duke of York, with Winston Churchill on board on his way to meet President Roosevelt for another Atlantic Conference. The weather during this voyage was the worst that I can recall, hurricane force winds and of course heavy seas. The destroyers of the escort, requested permission to reduce speed but was refused obviously due to the importance of the Duke of York's passengers.

Most of the destroyers were damaged, the **Wivern** had cracks in the upper deck and had to go to Greenock on her return to have them welded. In a book on the history of Winston Churchill it states that he had a very uncomfortable journey aboard the Duke of York and decided to fly back to this country via Bermuda.

The **Wivern** then escorted a convoy to Freetown. This convoy was obviously an important one as part of the convoy consisted of the two liners that always seemed to be part of the fast troop convoys. The Polish Liner Batury and the French Liner Louis Pasteur.

From Freetown. **Wivern** joined in the escorting of convoys and carried out Anti Submarine (A/S) patrols in the South Atlantic, refuelling at Bathurst, Takoradi Accra or Lagos.
In June 1942 **Wivern** was dispatched at high speed to an abandoned merchant vessel, the Empire Arun, formerly the Italian ship Savoia, which had been captured earlier in the war and now used by the Allies. The vessel was located and a boarding party put aboard then a tow line was passed over and the vessel was towed to Freetown. All the **Wivern** crew shared the salvage money in varying proportions.
Another exciting episode was a thirty one knot dash to Liberia and back to Freetown with survivors from torpedoed merchant ships.
In August 1942, Wivern was involved in the escorting of a troop convoy carrying reinforcements for the British at Alamein, the Batory and Pasteur appeared again. As the **Wivern** had not been converted to a long range escort, and still had the third boiler instead of extra fuel tanks, refuelling the ship had to be made at Bathurst, Lagos, Point Noire, Walvis Bay, Simonstown and Durban. **Wivern** then left the convoy and went out to Durban where we were greeted by usual South African hospitality, including being taken home by families for three or four days where we were made most welcome, no rationing or blackout, so it was 'Bright Lights and Big Eats' all round.
Then it was Simonstown for boiler cleaning, with more hospitality in Capetown and suburbs with families that took us on tours of the local sights and best restaurants. All this of course had to come to an end and so she returned to Freetown calling at St Helena on the way back.
Soon after returning to Freetown, **Wivern** visited the Portuguese Azores for the permitted twenty four hours, we were besieged by the local population offering a British one pound note and a Half crown for every West African pound note. **Wivern** then steamed to Gibraltar. From there she was involved in patrolling the Straits and convoy escorting, and was responsible for the capture of the Vichy French blockade runner the Courdebec. A prize crew were put on board and escorted it to Gibraltar.
Following the escorting of the Armada for the 'Torch' landings in Algeria. **Wivern** was at the Oran/Mers el Kebir section of the invasion. After the landings she carried out A/S patrols and assisted in the sinking of a U-boat, Our whaler picked up some of the survivors, including the Captain, who strutted along the deck like a little Hitler, a real dyed in the wool Nazi.
Then came the escorting of a convoy of captured French liners and Merchant ships en route to the U.K. Just after passing through the Straits of Gibraltar, at 1056 on the 2nd February 1943, The Canadian Corvette Weyburn struck a mine four miles off Cape Spartel (35.46N 06.02W) and started to sink.

H.M.S. **Wivern** now under the command of Lieutenant Hay, formerly the First Lieutenant went alongside Weyburn to take off survivors. Lt, Hay called across to the Captain of the Weyburn "Are your depth charges set to safe?" the reply was not heard, but assume it was the affirmative, as the rescue work continued, including lowering the whaler to recover survivors from the water. As the Weyburn sank her depth charges exploded lifting the **Wivern's** forecastle a foot out of the water, causing many casualties to the **Wivern** crew and Weyburn's survivors that were gathered forward. Petty Officer Stoker 'Nobby' Clark was killed after trying to save the Captain of the Weyburn. Both were killed by the depth charges whilst in the water as Weyburn sank Nobby was with me when we stayed with South African families. He was a sad loss. He was buried at sea in Gibraltar Bay. I was one of the lucky ones, as just before the Weyburn sank, I went down to the engine room to see if the watch-keeper needed a hand on the throttles whilst manoeuvring. As I reached the foot plates, the Chief Engine Room Artificer (C.E.R.A) called out, 'would I contact the Chief Stoker and ask him to ensure that we were using a full fuel tank while we were manoeuvring. Just as I climbed the ladder and reached the upper deck the depth charges detonated, if this had occurred a few seconds earlier I would have finished up in the bilges where the foot plates came up.

Wivern lost all power with only emergency lighting available as both dynamos were laying on their sides, a list to Starboard was noticeable and the ship started to drift towards the coast of Morocco. A Frigate came out to our rescue, I believe it was the Black Swan, and was able to prevent us from drifting nearer to the coast until a paddle tug came out from Gibraltar and lashed herself to **Wivern's** Starboard side and took us the fifty or so miles to Gibraltar harbour.

After the casualties had been taken to hospital, those of us that were left were billeted overnight in just what we stood up in, the **Wivern** was put into dockyard hands. We returned next morning to find that our belongings had been rifled and money and items of value had been stolen.

Whilst we were in dock we were able to visit our shipmates in hospital, and join the burial party for our friend Nobby who, as mentioned earlier, was buried in Gibraltar Bay.

All of the **Wivern's** crew received a copy of a letter from the Canadian Naval Authorities thanking us for our efforts in saving as many of the Wyburn's crew as possible, and expressing regret for the damage and casualties caused to H.M.S. **Wivern.**

After patching up, and with only a skeleton crew, **Wivern** was taken in tow by a deep sea tug, the 'Destiny'. As we left Gibraltar a signal was received which read "Good Luck **Wivern,** Your Destiny is ahead." How very apt. We

arrived at Devonport on the 17th March 1943 after some twelve days under tow, unescorted. My role during the voyage was to keep the large diesel driven pump operating to control the ingress of water from various leaks, a full time job which took ones mind off the slow speed of the journey.
A few weeks in Devonport and the Wivern paid off. We all went our various ways. Later I was pleasantly surprised to find that Wivern had rejoined the fleet, as I thought she would have been considered a constructional total loss in 1943.

DEPARTMENT OF NATIONAL DEFENCE NAVAL SERVICE
H.M.C.S. VILLE DE QUEBEC
2ND MARCH 1943

Sir,

I feel confident that I conform to the wishes of my Admiral in writing to you to express the deep gratitude of the Royal Canadian Navy to the Commanding Officer, Officers and ships company of H.M.S. **Wivern** who performed such a fine rescue and saved practically all hands of H.M.C.S Weyburn.
My regret is that H.M.S. **Wivern** should sustain casualties and damage.
I have the honour to be Sir,
Yours faithfully
A.R.E. Coleman
Lt Cdr R.C.N.R
Commanding Officer.

* * * *

At sometime in 1942 **Wolfhound** was detailed to deal with a ship which had hit a mine whilst in convoy off the Great Yarmouth coast and was on fire. We took off the crew and sent a boarding party to deal with the fire, and prepare to take her in tow.
As an A.B. Q.O. I did not get to know quite what was going on. However I do know that we took the ship in tow and took her to either Cromer or Sherringham where the lifeboat and the National Fire Service took over. It was then that the fire took hold which presented a beacon for the enemy planes, we, that is the Captain was ordered to sink her, whereupon our 'A' gun put a couple of rounds into her just below the water line. The ship went down and rested on the bottom with just her superstructure visible. I have often wondered about the full story and the outcome of this event.

Chapter 36

February 1942

The Channel Dash

J.F.N. Wedge, on board the **Worcester**
Following a boiler clean alongside at Parkeston Quay, we had been coming to 15 minutes notice for steam each evening, though at my lowly level I did not know why. It was therefore something of a welcome change that the 16th destroyer flotilla sailed on the morning of the 12th February sailed in the morning for gunnery practice at sea with a tug-towed target.
As Officer of quarters Pom-Poms mine was a passive role, but my mental peace was severely shattered when Sub' Lieut; Bill Bowmer R.N.V.R. Came down from the bridge to say "Roll on my ***** V.C."Proceed in execution of previous orders." We are to intercept the pocket battle ships!!!
I went down the hatch in the iron deck to my cabin to get my bible, which fell open at an agreeable reassuring passage.
We crashed our way at full speed through a choppy sea under low cloud, with little said,aircraft appeared through the clouds every now and again, mainly British and some apparently of the opinion that we were German.
"Enemy In sight" battle ensign hoisted, and a tense silence as the pom-poms which had earlier been in action against threatening aircraft. Dark shapes in the misty distance and our 4.7's began firing and the flotilla attacked. As I recollect **Worcester** was centre ship of the five and thus became the main target for the enemy. The others released their torpedoes, but Lt, Comdr., E.C. 'Dreamy' Coats R.N. pressed on for what seemed an eternity before firing our torpedoes. The last R.D.F (Radio Direction Finder) reading was just over 2,000 yards.
We were already being hit, but it was a relief at least to be turning away. However we continued to be straddled and hit and quite shortly we were lying stopped. The shelling ceased. In the silence which followed no one appeared to move. From the Pom-Pom it seemed inconceivable that anyone on the bridge could still be alive, given the battering that the structure had taken. I walked aft to the twelve pounder, which had been hit. Gunner 'T' L.G.C. Wellman R.N. Was lying on the deck, conscious and not too badly wounded. For a moment I thought he and I were the only Officers left alive, but miraculously our Number one Lieut; Anthony Taudevi R.N.V.R appeared, and then began to take some sort of shape, unhappily not before some people had gone over the side.

As we wallowed, a Junkers 88 flew above, firing recognition flares, then later an R.A.F. plane dropped torpedoes, aimed at us!
Quiet bodies lay in flats, and Surgeon Lieut D.C. Jackson R.N.V.R. And the S.B.A. (Sick Bay Attendant) Shelley worked heroically on the wounded in various parts of the ship.
The Chief Commissioned Engineer, Hugh Griffiths R.N. And his team were achieving miracles, and an engine started turning, two destroyers approached, **Vivacious** and **Campbell** (not German ones sent to finish us off as I had feared) and rescued some of the survivors from the sea. On satisfying himself (Captain Mark Pizey in the **Campbell,** the flotilla leader) that we were under way they returned to Harwich to replenish their torpedoes etc: Later we lost power again and languished very anxiously in the dark before the engine room again triumphed. The slowly but surely we made our way home to Harwich.
It had been a long, cold and a very uncomfortable night on the Pom-Poms, and throughout the ship. As we approached land a 16th Destroyer Flotilla, Hunt Class destroyer, 'Hambledon' appeared and offered assistance, this was proudly turned down by the Captain who indicated that we had managed so far on our own and would like to finish the job.
Alongside at Parkeston and after the sad disembarkation of the dead and wounded, we were all checked over by a medical team. I was completely deaf for a time, someone even tried semaphore to talk to me! Most of my hearing returned sufficiently, along with Bill Bowser and Sub Lt; Guy Agard-Butler R.N. Incongruously to play word games that evening in the Railway Hotel with Beatrice Lilly, her agent and her sister, after they had performed at an E.N.S.A concert.
Among those killed was telegraphist Denis Gibson in the W/T office which was in part of the Bridge structure that had been so badly damaged. Denis and I had trained together at the beginning of the war after mobilisation of the R.N.V.R.
Of the officers of **'Worcester'** Lieut W.F.L. Winterbottom R.N. was later to lose his life in a submarine. Guy Agard-Butler died whilst serving in the Fleet Air Arm at Gibraltar., and Bill Bowmer was lost in H.M.S. Martin off the North African Coast. 'Dreamy Coats became a Commander and went to a shore job. Anthony Taudevin eventually commanded a 'Captain' Class frigate as a Lieut Cmdr R.N.V.R. 'Doc' David Jackson went on to HMS Dolphin and after the war returned to Australia to practice in Brisbane,. It was there that he wrote the book "One Ship, One Company" which is a history of all the seven R.N. Ships named **'Worcester'** and his own fascinating account of the 'Channel Dash'.

Here follows an extract from Doctor David Jackson's book:

"In Bello In Pace Fidelis"

I saw the enemy at very much the same time as the first sighting, although the ships had been picked up by Radar a short time before. The visibility was bad, and the range then was about four miles. Almost at once the destroyers came under heavy fire from everything that the enemy had, but by a miracle there were no hits; in fact in the whole attack the **Worcester** was the only British ship to be hit. What happened to the German destroyers I never knew. But at any rate, for some extraordinary reason they kept out of the way and we had a clear approach. The range must have closed very rapidly, and at about 3,000 yards the **Campbell** and **Vivacious** turned away to port and fired their torpedoes. I do not know how the **Mackay** and **Whitshed a**ttacked, but, after the two leaders had turned, the Worcester held on towards the enemy. At just over 2,000 yards she too, turned away to port and fired her torpedoes, and as she turned she was hit.

This was the hit that I saw. One shell went through the deck abreast of the 12 pounder gun and exploded in the Sub Lieut's cabin, some fragments going through the engine room bulkhead. I think all the 12 pounder's crew were either killed or wounded, but Guns (Gunnery Officer) and the ratings manning the torpedo tubes which were just forward of the 12 pounder, escaped and all three torpedoes were fired.

During the turn to port there were other bad hits on the Starboard side. Apparently a shell exploded on hitting the water just short of the ship and about level with the wardroom; for the ships side there was full of holes varying in size from six inches to two feet across, both above and below the waterline. The wardroom was completely wrecked, and the after 'supply and repair' party suffered a lot of severe casualties. Just forward of the torpedo-tubes on the Starboard side there was a hole which looked big enough to drive a car through, extending from half way across the deck to below the waterline, so that the after boiler room was completely wrecked and flooded. Forward of this, again there was another large hole from the deck half way to the waterline, and the shell had penetrated the other boiler-room.

On the starboard side of the forecastle deck and about fifteen feet from the sick bay there had been a large locker containing Oerlikon ammunition. This locker completely disappeared, the surrounding deck was buckled, the bridge supports twisted, and everything in the vicinity, including the sick bay filled as full of holes as a colander. It we subsequently decided that the locker had received a direct hit.

There were also hits on the port side, so I assume that the ship must have carried her way after the first hits disabled her, and made almost a complete circle, presenting her port side to the enemy. A shell went through the side right in the bow, exploding in the paint locker and starting a fire that flamed out like a blow lamp, and there had been another hit at the base of the fore side of the fore funnel. This made a hole in the funnel casing about four feet across and also broke the mast about six feet above the deck. The mast fell backwards squarely against the top of the funnel where it remained supported, but all the rigging was hanging loose, and the butt ends of the mast were swaying to and fro near the port forecastle ladder. The ship had received seven hits in all.

Just how all this happened I never learnt, and I doubt if anyone ever knew, for the people on the bridge could see nothing. The ship was completely ringed by a solid curtain of shell splashes. Perhaps that concealment help to save us, but all sight of the enemy was lost, and nobody could see what happened to our torpedoes.

Nor do I know how long I remained on the deck of the sick-bay. It seemed to me to be only a few seconds, but judging from all that had happened before I got out on deck again. I think I may have been knocked out for a while, which would account for the rumour reaching some parts of the ship that everybody in the sick-bay had been killed. Anyhow I picked myself up and went to help the rather dazed S.B.A. And we both attended the rating who had come through the door and was laying unconscious.

The screen door was laying wide open and there was a fire on the deck outside, so I judged our side of the ship to be unhealthy. We carried our casualty through the lobby to the cabin on the port side that corresponded to the sick bay. We put him on the bunk, and I dashed back to the sick-bay, grabbed as many dressing as I could carry, put two bottles of morphia in my pocket, and by some inspiration also took a torch. Then I attended to my patient and some wounded men from 'A' and 'B' gun's crews who appeared grinning apologetically at the door.

I did not realise then that the noise had ceased and that the ship was stopped. The reason of course was that I was almost completely deaf (indeed we all went round shouting at each other for some time) and that the noise or the lack of noise had ceased to register. However my patients gave me to understand that there was a badly wounded man at 'B' gun, so I went out onto the forecastle.

It was then that I saw that we were lying stopped, and that there were a couple of Carley rafts with men hanging onto them about fifty yards from the ship. My first thought was that one of the other ships must have been lost, but then, Carley's. with a rather nasty shock, I recognised our own ratings on the

Then I saw the hole in the funnel and the broken mast swaying as the ship rolled, and saw too that the ship was down by the stern and listing heavily to starboard.

I must have looked quite bewildered, but fortunately at that moment Number One appeared at my elbow, and after thanking heaven for my safety, told me that we were not abandoning ship, and then went aft, as calmly as if he just ordered 'Hands Fall In.' So I told my small group of patients in a loud, and I hope, firm voice that we were not abandoning ship, and they were to stay under cover and sit down. Then I set about my business.

It is hard to give any connected account of that business. It went on for so long and took me to all parts of the ship, and I have no clear recollection of where I went or in what sequence. Wherever I might be there seemed to be an urgent call to go somewhere else. Nobody seemed to know where there might not be wounded men; below deck everything was in complete darkness and on deck everything was in a terrible mess. A destroyer is a pretty crowded machine at the best of times, but now there was wreckage, splinter holes and jagged steel everywhere. In no time my hands were torn and bleeding, and always wherever I was, there came a call to be elsewhere.

After attending to the man on 'B' gun and another bad casualty in the wheel house, I must have gone down to the waist of the ship and worked my way along the upper deck on the port side where a lot of wounded had collected, sitting or lying under the palm- palms and beside the torpedo tubes. The life seemed to have gone out of the ship and she was wallowing in the heavy swell. Although she was listing heavily to starboard, every now and then a sea would curl and break along the deck on the port side, and from time to time the pom-poms would open fire above us, which was a bit disconcerting.

Presently, however, I was greatly heartened to see the **Campbell** and the **Vivacious** approaching. I did not know until afterwards that shortly before this a German destroyer had come back to finish us off. She would have had an easy job, for all our guns except the Oerlikons and pom-poms were out of action. Luckily for us the **Campbell** and the **Vivacious** appeared out of the mist and the German turned tail and fled.

The two ships lay off for a while and began picking up our men from the Carley rafts and out of the water. I should explain how these men came to be there. At some time the order 'Prepare to abandon ship' had been passed. Every one was deaf, and by the time the order reached the after part of the ship it had become 'Abandon ship.' The quarter deck was then awash, so it was no wonder that when the Carley rafts were over the side a good many men, including some wounded, were put onto them. They drifted away from the ship, and as we could not steam, they could not be recovered until the two destroyers arrived. Unhappily, while these were stopped and rescuing our men, three of our own Beauforts appeared out of the clouds and fired torpedoes. The Campbell with a number of exhausted men still in the water near her stern, had to go full speed astern to avoid being hit.

Beside the twelve pounder there were men lying on the deck so still and alone that I knew that I need not stop, so I went to the after superstructure, where there were some dreadful casualties among the men of the supply and repair party. When I got round to the port side again the Campbell was talking to us through a loud hailer. I could not make out much of what was being said, and in any case I was more interested in the signs of life returning to our own ship. For smoke was pouring from the after funnel, there was a noise from the engines, steam was issuing from the great rent in the starboard side, and soon we began to move slowly ahead.

I cannot tell what the Chief and his men had done below, but it must have been something terrific. Long afterwards I heard him telling the story in technical language to a fellow 'plumber.' It was a language I could not entirely understand, but even without the expression on the other's face I could tell that it was an epic. All that remains in my mind is that for much of the time they were up to their waists in water.

When we began to steam, the Campbell and Vivacious left us, and we were alone once more, but I was still too busy to take much notice, or to wonder much about why and wherefore, so I carried on until it seemed that I had been to all parts of the ship. Finally I made my painful way up the shattered ladder to the bridge to give the Captain my report. But when I tried to tell of things, I found that I could not. However the fresh air, aided by some spirits revived me, and after giving what account I could I returned to work.

By now all of the bad casualties had had some sort of first aid, and the next task was to place them in reasonable comfort, and to do what more was possible in the way of treatment. I found to my relief that the cabin flat had been opened up, the holes in the bulkhead between it and the wardroom plugged with wooden leak stoppers, and best of all, that the light were in order. So there was somewhere with light and bedding that I could work. The cabin flat was at the bottom of a vertical ladder down which it was very difficult to get a wounded man. Moreover, many of those aft had compound fractures of the legs, which made it difficult to move them at all. Still, we bedded down such as we could, and established a dressing station in the Captain's day cabin, where the S.B.A dealt with those who were now leaving their duties, many of them only after repeated orders, and coming aft for treatment of what they regarded as minor injuries. While he carried on, I returned to the more serious cases on deck, and slowly and with wonderful gentleness their shipmates carried them to such places of shelter as could be found. There I examined them and did what more I could, which was little enough, but while I was thus engaged I realised that the sound of the engines had ceased and we were lying stopped once more.

How long we remained stopped I do not know, but it seemed a long time, and beyond all doubt it was, for me at any rate, the worst time of all. The heat of action had passed and with it the unthinking, almost automatic, state of doing desperately and as quickly as possible the work that lay to hand. Now I was able to take in our position in full.

We were alone, disabled and perhaps sinking, about ten miles off the Dutch coast and inside the enemy's mine barrier.

The wind was rising and darkness was falling upon the sea. The black smoke from the funnel, driving away into the murk to leeward, somehow made the waste of water look even more lonely and desolate. Once again the ship had that feeling of being weary unto death. She rolled, and with a horrible lifeless roll, heavily over to starboard and slowly, slowly righted.

Then and for long afterwards, my chief private horror was wondering what I could do with the wounded men when the ship sank, even though in that cold sea survival for anyone would have been brief indeed.

But the ship did not sink. Again the chief and the men below triumphed, and after a long time the noise of the engines began once more, the pumps got some of the water out of the ship, and the list became less alarming.

It was now quite dark, so there was very little more that I could do except see to the comfort and shelter of the various groups of wounded. The night was bitterly cold and the best we had been able to do for some of those aft was to place them in the lee of the officers galley, but they were well covered with blankets and seemed to keep fairly comfortable. There were others in the galley itself, in the lobby above the cabin flat, and in the galley flat forward. The sick-bay was in too much of a shambles to use, and the lobby outside it was full of an awful smell of burning and cordite fumes, but the little cabin forward gave shelter to a few. Others we could not move very far, so that they lay in ones and two's in all parts of the ship from the wheel house to the engine room.

The first half of my night was filled by the slow and repeated visits to all these places, but by midnight a great silence had fallen on the ship. The engines kept up their labouring, it is true, and there were groans from the battered ship as she rolled, but human activity seemed to cease save for those silent on watch. Most of the wounded were sleeping and comfortable, and some never woke.

As the night wore on hope returned. We were making about eight or nine knots, which was a good speed under the circumstances, and the sea seemed to have moderated. Perhaps the weather, though it seemed unkind at first, had helped to save us, for the low cloud had screened us from aircraft, and the rising sea at dusk may have kept the E-boats at home. And now the darkness covered us, and as each hour took us nearer home, the sea became smoother. About three or four o'clock I must have fallen asleep, my head on the Captain's table. Just before dawn I awoke to find a very weary looking Number One standing in the doorway.

"How are we doing" I asked, and his reply was about the most cheering I have ever heard. "Fine! We're just coming up to the sunk." The sunk Light vessel, so we were almost home!

When we went on deck together it was still dark, but by the time I had done my round, the sea and sky were beginning to colour, and as the light of the new day brightened, there on the port bow lay the low coast of England.

The wireless had been wrecked, but during the night, goodness know how or where, one of the surviving telegraphist had produced something that would work, and now we could signal the number of our casualties and ask for ambulances to meet the ship. As I gave the information to the Captain the familiar spectacle of a south bound convoy was showing up. It looked secure and reassuring, and though itself part of the grim picture of war it was to us a familiar, almost homely thing, as welcome as if we were waking to reality after a nightmare.

One of the escorting destroyers was signalling to us; did we need assistance? But the offer was declined with thanks, and with the first dawning pride that was beginning to emerge from dumb wonder at survival, and the explanation that we had come from Holland and could manage the rest of the trip alone.

I cannot remember much about our approach to Harwich, nor just what time it was when at last we were steaming up the harbour. We could see groups of patients and nurses on the hill at Shotley sick quarters, and the ship must have been a sight to see - still listing heavily, full of holes, steam issuing from odd places, and the broken mast leaning back against the funnel, with the battle ensign still at the masthead from whence it was impossible to move it.

Slowly she steamed right up the anchorage, alone and without help; for although two tugs were waiting they lay off till the time came for berthing. And as we came up among the ships we saw that they had 'cleared lower deck,' their ship's companies were fallen in aft, and as we drew abreast of each they cheered and cheered.

I was near to weeping then, with a great lump in my throat. It was partly the reaction of relief, of course, but also it was due to a great surge of pride and affection and sympathy and pity for the ship herself. It was she who had been matched against hopeless odds, and it was she who had lived and struggled home.

In spite of the emotion my thoughts, as I stood with the S.B.A by the 12 pounder, were still on what help would be awaiting us, for although there was a crowd on Parkeston Quay where we would berth, there was no sign of any ambulances.

As we swung to come alongside and the distance between the ship and the quay gradually narrowed, we could make out who was there, and in the forefront was our leading steward with Mick barking frantically and almost mad with delight, in his arms, Poor Mick! He had been left behind often enough before and was used to sleeping in strange places, but all through the night he had been awake, whimpering and shivering. Soon the mooring lines were passed, and then the best sight of all, a fleet of ambulances trundled into view. The Surgeon Commander from the base came on board, and at long last I felt that my troubles were over, for he had a party of sick berth ratings with stretchers, and at one they set about getting my men ashore.

I posted my own S.B.A. at the brow to note their names as they were landed and I saw all of them loaded into the ambulances until the last had gone. Then I went with the Captain and the other Officers to Captain 'D's office, where we spent a long time trying to piece together what had happened and going through the list of the ship's company to account for everybody and prepare a list of killed, wounded and missing.

It must have been nearly noon by the time that job was finished. Accommodation had been arranged for us in the Railway Hotel in the quay, and I went back to the ship to collect my things. There were Royal Marine sentry's posted, and a salvage tug alongside was pumping hard, so that already the list was corrected, and already too, there were dockyard matey's working on the damage.

The sick bay was in a sorry mess, but in spite of the damage, my clothes were all right so I put together what I needed. I noticed that two of the lower buttons had gone from my jacket, and catching sight of the battered face of one of them lying on the deck, picked it up and slipped it into my pocket. Then I went up to the Hotel, and how wonderful were the softness of the carpet and the quietness. The tops of my sea-boot stockings, and the knees of my trousers were soaked with blood, as were the cuffs of my torn jacket, but it was when I was lying in the luxury of a hot bath that the full significance of that battered button dawned on me, for there in a corresponding position was a perfectly circular bruise about two inches across, cheery red at the centre with a nasty blue-green outer ring.

Two anxious hours to contemplate death
At thirty knots consuming cold grey seas.
Action Stations, duffel coats, tin hats -
Below, a throbbing engine reprise.

Junkers aircraft bombing from the clouds
Brought urgency, the 'Enemy In Sight!'
The forward four point seven bellowed out
Their challenge to the battle cruisers might.
Tall shell spouts cased her as she turned to fire

Torpedoes, as they leapt, cacophony
Erupted, brute bombardment wrenched apart
The bridge, chewed steel in vicious gluttony.

Five minutes devastation. Suddenly peace,
Uncanny as she wallowed without power
Miraculously the lower hull survived
But Gibbon, Dow and Grant, and twenty more

Lay dead. Doc Jackson's needle eased the pain
For others. Pom-poms warned the RAF away
Bizarrely, Jumkers recognition flares
Confirmed the wild confusion of that day.

So. Vulnerable, rolling helplessly
She lay for seeming hours. The nervous ears
Rejoiced at turning screws. By fits and starts
She staggered home, a frozen fifteen hours

John Wedge

The following received gallantry awards for this action

Lieutenant Commander E. Coats was awarded the D.S.O
Cdr Eng. H. Griffiths the D.S.C.
Surg/Lt. R.N.V.R David Jackson the D.S.C.
Lt, A. Taudevin the D.S.C.
Lt. F. Winterbottom was Metioned In Despatches

Sub Lt, G.D. Agard-Butler was Mentioned In Despatches
C.E.R.A. G.M. Angus the D.S.M.
P.O. Steward S. Carter the D.S.M
Stoker H. Christopher. Mentioned In Despatches
Stoker P.O. N. Dawson. D.S.M.
Ldg Tel H. Dell. Mentioned In Destpatches
P.O. H. Hallett the D.S.M
A.B. G.Grant Mentioned In Despatches *
E.R.A. R. Hayhoe Mentioned In Despatches
A.B. W. Hill Mentioned In Despatches *
C.P.O. A. Hutchings Mentioned In Despatches
Chief Stoker A. Lawrence D.S.M
P.O. Stoker C. Norris Mentioned In Despatches
A.B. A.S Shelley Mentioned in Despatches
Stoker B. Walls D.S.M.
Gnr 'T' L. Wellman Mentioned in Despatches

* Indicates Posthumous award.

"ACTION STATIONS"

'Action stations'. Tin hats and apprehension
Rush to guns and hoses, engine room
And wireless office. Air of tension,
Eyes uplifted and some seawards gazing.,
Ears are straining for distant 'boom'
Or roar of engines. Lips are phrasing
Prayers, maybe, or curse upon the Hun.
Friendly aircraft in the distance loom
And are gone. Minutes pass. 'Carry on'

Midshipman
J.F.N. Wedge
H.M.S Worcester

Chapter 37

January 1942. H.M.S. Wallace. Known as 'One round Wallace' because her gunners brought down a German aircraft with their very first angry shot of the war. The shell case was kept as a souvenir aptly inscribed 'One round Wallace'. She was part of the Rosyth Escort Force, under the command of Lt Cdr E.G. Heywood Lonsdale had a new and young Sub Lieutenant, Philip Prince of Greece join who was later to marry Princess Elizabeth and to become Prince Philip, Duke of Edinburgh KG. KT. He remained on board the **Wallace** until November 1943 when he left to take a First Lieutenants course. **Wallace** was credited of having escorted over 200 most of which were up and down 'E-boat Alley' off the East Coast from Rosyth to Sheerness and visa - versa. During the scraps with the E-boats she severely damaged a number of them.
During 'Warship Week' in 1942 **Wallace** was adopted by the County of West Lothian.

* * * * *

The Early Days of an Ordinary Seaman
By the Duke of Buccleuch KT

On joining the Navy as an Ordinary Seaman (Hostilities Only). I took care to conceal my title, sticking to W.F.J. Dalkeith. I still have my pay-book and standard issue knife- a large blade and a marlin spike with my name stamped on it.
Like a great many others, I joined from university through the CW (Commissioned Worthy) scheme having done some cadet training at school and at university. CW candidates were usually dispersed among general entries at the rate of about two per forty, with the initial training at H.M.S. Collingwood, near Fareham, being the same for all. It consisted mainly of square bashing and classroom work that included general rules on seamanship and knot tying.
Sub Lieutenant Adams, a former school teacher, was in command of our class of between 30 and 40 with Chief Petty Officer (Retired) Tony Hammond was our immediate boss. Both were excellent.
Most of us fumbled our knots laboriously, until it was pointed out that if one was torpedoed and swimming in rough oil coated sea the bowline was the one knot that would save ones life when a lifeline was thrown, the pace of learning accelerated.

Many nights were spent in an air-raid shelter which was only marginally less comfortable than our Nissen hut. However, far more frightening than the prospect of air-raids was the great mast that towered above the parade ground. Climbing up its great height was bad enough, but walking along the yardarm was petrifying. One or two of our group virtually passed out at the thought of it.

Our group could hardly have been a more varied cross section of society from all parts of the British Isles. There was Bayliss, a plumber, Willie Cadden a Glasgow tram driver, Copley who had worked in a condom factory, Chapman an aggressive red-haired Yorkshire man, and Fred Delany from Cork, he confessed to being part of a gang who had burned down the home of the Grandfather of the friend with whom I had joined the Navy, John M. Synge. This did not bode well for Harmonious relationships, but Hitler was fortunately, perceived as the common enemy.

At the end of some eight weeks training, we were considered fit to go to sea and were sent as a batch to Portsmouth Royal Naval Barracks for a week or more square bashing and being taught how to sling a hammock, which was provided with one's name marked on it in large letters.

A particularly ferocious Chief Petty Officer was in charge of us and I well remember his stentorian voice when we fell in for parade in the morning, aimed mainly at the CW candidates. "Then as is keen gets fell in previous", One felt one's chance s of ever getting a commission were doomed if one did not.

It was an exciting day when the orders for our seagoing postings arrived. Now friends one had made were now being sent to all ends of the earth. How many survived and where they ended up is a mystery one can sadly never solve. My own posting, together with my friend John Singe, was to Rosyth where we would learn the name and type of ship in which we were to serve. The night train from Kings Cross to Waverly Station in Edinburgh was crammed with all three services. My rolled up hammock in the corridor was hardly a first class sleeper but I remember sleeping very well. There was just time for a wonderful breakfast in the canteen beyond Edinburgh's main Post Office, before a truck took us over the ferry to Rosyth.

HMS Cochrane was the name given to Rosyth Naval Base and it was with trepidation that we set off there to face the unknown. A surprisingly friendly atmosphere greeted us and were told that we would be joining H.M.S, **Viceroy** when she returned from Sheerness in two day's time. Cochrane was spacious enough to enable me to sling my hammock as I had been taught, but those two nights were the last I would know of luxury for several months to come. It was here that I learned the silly trick of washing one's collar in bleach so as to give a faded look that you saw when worn by proper old salts who were wont to jeer one as ‘Hello Rookie”.

H.M.S. Viceroy. I was able to watch the sleek and slender destroyer slicing through the Firth of Fourth under the great railway bridge. A shiver of excitement ran through me on seeing what was to be my home for the next three months at least. The October air was already warning that winter gales were not far away. Much of the ship’s company were lined up on the forecastle and quarterdeck, ready to man the steel berthing wires and I was already imagining myself as one of them.

There were three or four others I had only recently met whilst in Cochrane being drafted in at the same time, a Stoker P.O., a W/T operator and an Able Seaman, besides John Synge and myself. We crossed the gangway, were signed in by the Coxswain and then taken by and Able Seaman to our respective mess decks. The inside of the ship was like the inside of an ants nest, seething with activity, some men cleaning up to go on shore leave, others cleaning up the mess deck, others preparing for general duties around the ship. The air in the cramped spaces, holding a crew of 240 (never known a V&W to hold that many ed.) Having been designed for 140, was as thick as a plum duff that was the first odour to hit us as we passed the galley. It became thicker still as we penetrated further inside a series of steel boxes, a mixture of cigarette smoke, steamy oil from the capstan engine in the centre of the mess deck and vomit.

A charming, tall Leading Seaman greeted us and immediately made us feel one of them. He laughed when he saw our hammocks, saying we would not be seeing them again as the number of hammock billets was sufficient for only about half the more senior ratings. We were allocated lockers, the tops of which served as a wooden seat running along the ship’s side. When we asked where we would sleep, he gestured at the lockers, and the deck and lose planks which lay on top of the capstan engine. This is where I picked my berth, because as I discovered later it was at least dry compared with the deck which was swimming with water, oil, spilt cocoa and vomit.

Having parked our gear we were taken off to meet the Officer Of the Day, a friendly, heavily built red haired Sub Lieutenant. (‘Jimmy’ or number one). A Scotsman, Lieutenant MacAlister, RNVR whom I discovered came from Melrose. A little later we met the Captain, whose hostile glare and thick lips, that seemed to form the word ‘scum’, filled me with foreboding. He was Lieutenant Halifax R.N. And at the time it did not occur to me that someone in his position of responsibility must have been under considerable strain after long nights and days on the bridge escorting a twenty mile long convoy of straggling merchant ships creeping along the coast at 10 knots, everyone a sitting target for the E-boats at almost any point along the 400 mile route

from the Thames estuary. The forenoon was spent learning the way round the ship and meeting my companions in the mess to which I had been assigned. The ship's company was divided into two watches - Red and Blue. I was to be in Red and my friend John in Blue, so we seldom met after that.
As the air was already filled with cigarette smoke while lunch was being prepared in the galley following the rum issue, which burnt my throat like a rasp. I lit up a cigarette myself. After only a few puffs a voice cried out "What f****er is burning string?". The aim of the question left me in no doubt that my Balkan Sobranis Turkish cigarette was not appreciated. From then on it was 'Players please' from the canteen.
After the first meal, which wasn't at all bad. I was given my first duty, it was to paint the funnel! It was still quite hot as we had to keep up steam in case of a sudden crisis at sea. Another and more experienced seaman and I struggled with ropes and stage and pulleys, and eventually paint and a brush. Whilst we sloshed the paint on in a most inartistic fashion he told me about the **Viceroy**, how she was built in 1917 and in 1920 was 'mothballed' into reserve, and parked on a sand bank somewhere.
Miraculously her engines were still in fine fettle and able to produce 32 knots for which she had been designed. Her single 4.7 inch guns were replaced with two twin 4 inch high angle guns, useful for anti-aircraft as well as anti-U-boat fire. The only worrying signs of decrepitude was the rust that was barely concealed by more and more coats of paint.
The ships side was only one eighth of an inch thick steel plate to start with and I was to discover later when painting it, instead of the funnel, one was quite concerned that one might put a toe through it.
The next day I was introduced to my action station. This was a loading number of the left gun in 'A' turret on the fore deck. The combined shell and charge was nearly three feet long and fairly heavy. Pushing it into the breach when the gun was pointing towards the horizon was quite easy, but when the gun was elevated to a high angle, I simply didn't have the strength.
This I was to discover on our first day at sea when doing gun drill, but I was thankful to find that there were very few who could manage it. We did not fire many rounds that day and I never discovered what the target was. All I do remember was the really deafening blast on my ears for which we were given no protection whatever. Like so many others no doubt my present deafness probably owes much to those practice shoots. Happily during my time in **Viceroy,** we never needed to fire the guns in anger.
My first day at sea I was on duty watch 0800-1200 as starboard lookout on the bridge. This meant I covered the sector from straight ahead to Green 90 (right angles to the right side) It was a wonderful sensation sailing under the Forth Rail Bridge, with what looked like a toy train puffing along towards

Edinburgh. Soon we passed familiar land marks, such as North Berewick Law and the Bass Rock which I remembered as a child.
All kinds of incomprehensible things were happening on the bridge; the Captain and Navigator were taking endless bearings on certain landmarks with the compass mounted on the binnacle in the centre of the bridge; signal lamps were flashing and R.T (radio telephone) messages were crackling through discordant loudspeakers.
It was not difficult to settle into the ship's routine, there was simply no alternative and I was quite overwhelmed by the kindness of older hands helping me to adapt. In the course of it, I made many friends and I was quite surprised to find how frank and open people were about their backgrounds and their family life. This may be partly due to the ever present thought that at any moment one might be torpedoed or hit a mine and that would be that. It was a great comfort to me to feel accepted, they knew nothing of my background or title. This was fine and I continued in the routine, most night I slept on the deck beside 'A' gun. My first night I settled in the shelter provided by the base of the gun mounting until the Gun layer pointed out if he had to rotate the turret in a hurry, I would be turned into strawberry jam. After that I managed to get hold of a mail bag- (sleeping bags had not been invented in those days) and using my inflatable life belt as a pillow, I slept marvellously well.
It was then pointed out to me in the middle of E-boat Alley, a life belt round one's chest would be more useful than one under one's ear.
Washing, etc; presented difficulties as the facilities were provided for half the number using them. One longed for a proper bath and finding one in the YMCA in Sheerness was one of the great treats of my life.
When up at Rosyth, I occasionally made it to the Caledonian Hotel. Once I ventured into the New Club in Princess Street to rendezvous with my Father. The hall ported was most disconcerted at finding very ordinary seaman wandering about in such a hallowed place and politely asked if I was looking for the NAAFI Canteen! His composure was quite unchanged when I told him who I was meeting and why.
On board ship I was like any other CW candidate, with a lot of special instruction on practical navigation, cleaning the wardroom silver and polishing the brass name plate on the quarter deck - the only piece of brass allowed in the ship to avoid giving our presence away through moonlight reflecting off a shiny surface.
One day however the Captain received a signal as we approached Rosyth, saying that HRH Duchess of Gloucester wished to see me. He sent for me and demanded to know why on earth she would want to see me, in a voice of

fury and contempt. When I said it was probably because she was my aunt and Godmother, he snapped "You had better go and get yourself cleaned up then".

When I returned from my afternoon out. I found John Synge doing sentry duty on the gangway. He warned me about jolly jokes of putting a red carpet out for me on the gangway and to expect much ridicule. I was in two minds whether I should turn and make a run for it, but with a heavy heart I carried on to my normal quarters and not once did anyone of my fellow seamen give any indication that my status had changed. My faith in human nature was sealed.

My appointment to **Viceroy** ended a week sooner than expected. Thick January fog enveloped E-boat Alley and the convoy merchantmen were desperately trying to keep in contact with a variety of fog horns, hooters, sirens, and whistles. We had been ordered to move to the head of the convoy, so were proceeding a good deal faster than was wise. From my position near 'A' gun on the forecastle, I saw a stationary ship ahead a second or two before the eyes on the bridge. My warning cry was duly heard and although the Captain ordered full astern 1700 tons of destroyer could not be possibly stopped in time. Our bows rode up over a surprised Escort Trawler, which appeared to keel right over with the mast level with the sea, gradually we slid back and up she came with hardly a scratch and no casualties. When we examined our bows, the reason was plain to see. Everything had crumpled in as if made of tissue paper and I realised then how valuable was my paint in keeping the ship afloat. A spell in dry dock triggered the CW Candidates move to HMS King Alfred.

The cleaning of the quarter deck name plate had a happy sequel. In 1948, while I was the Director responsible for the management of Granton Harbour which my family had built 110 years before, I saw the superstructure of an unusually large ship in Malcolm Brechins ship breaker's yard. It normally took nothing bigger than a trawler, but when I approached closer. I was astounded to recognise my own paint work. It was **Viceroy** herself and Mr Brechin very kindly presented me with this nostalgic souvenir, now proudly displayed in an exhibition room at Drumlantig Castle.

Chapter 38

THE WARTIME SHOTLEY SHORE LEAVE RUN

Ships of the 16th destroyer flotilla (V&Ws and Hunts), when in Harwich harbour, would be either alongside Parkeston Quay for repairs, boiler cleaning, replenishing stores etc; or moored to buoys fore and aft in mid stream.
When shore leave ws given, the destroyers in mid stream would be visited by a large liberty boat (The Brightlingsea Ed) despatched from Parkeston Quay by the Harbour Master, this save the use of individual ships boats.
There were two points for landing liberty men, either Parkeston Quay, where one would have to go through customs with its restrictions. After passing through, on to Harwich Town or a train to London.
The other point on the opposite of the harbour was Shotley Pier, No Customs, or any kind of check here, a bus would be waiting to take you to Ipswich Town. A natural place for avoiding customs.
The liberty boat made a round trip to the destroyers giving leave, after collecting the liberty men, proceeded first to Shotley Pier and then to Parkeston Quay with the remainder and to wait further orders.
On board the destroyers a form of canteen messing was operated, this enabled each mess-deck to purchase some of it's own food requirements on a daily cost basis. However some basic foodstuffs, (eg; bread, meat, vegetables etc;) were provided from the ships own stores when able, and the remaining requirements were chiefly purchased from the N.A.A,F.I., hence 'canteen messing'.
This system often provided surpluses, especially tea, sugar, etc; and of course tobacco which was plentiful, duty free and cheap. The sailors of the 16th D.F. who wished to pass on their surpluses to their loved ones at home would make up parcels to post to them, as the general public were strictly rationed.
It can readily be seen that landing at Shotley Pier provided a safe and convenient way of avoiding custom duties.
H.M.S. Walpole's Duty Officer kindly or wisely turned a 'Nelsons blind eye' to the packages when the men paraded for shore leave and before embarking on the liberty boat.
As the wisdom and profit of landing at Shotley Pier spread through the remainder of the flotilla, so did the number of men and packages increased. No doubt the customs at Parkeston were alerted at this surge of activity at Shotley, and drew their own conclusions.

One day we were happily making our way to Shotley, complete with parcels securely wrapped and addressed ready for posting in Ipswich, when the inevitable happened. As we left the last destroyer and headed for Shotley the customs boat left Parkeston Quay at the same time. The warning cry of 'Customs' went up when it could be seen that the boat was heading straight for us. In a flash there were over thirty packages floating down stream on an ebb tide, the majority were light weight and floated for some time.
As previously mentioned some were addressed ready for posting and this enabled the customs to trace some of them back to the senders after retrieving them from the water. I cannot remember the ultimate outcome as my parcel vanished with the tide. Some admonishments were made and the number making runs ashore to Shotley were quite reduced. However the run was continued by the brave, or desperate, but the parcels were not addressed until safely reaching Ipswich and a very keen lookout kept for Customs.
The Customs as far as I know, never directly interfered again. I think that they considered a point had been made, and provided that we did not over do it, allowed us to continue. How we avoided Customs at Chatham Dockyard is another story.

THE MASK

I know how it will be sailor,
How gay and sweet and short
How you will swear 'Forever'
As long as your in port;
But when your back at sea sailor,
Why, once across the line,
The hair of any sweetheart
Will seem as gold as mine
My kisses may be sweet sailor,
My laughter may be gay;
I'll be the fairest ever
Until you sail away
Until you land again sailor
In other ports of call,
And find another sweetheart,
The fairest of them all.

And so I'll speed you sailor,
As you yourself would choose,
Unquestioning, unclinging,

Without a tear to lose.
And how are you to know sailor,
As you go down the line,
That I could kill the next girl
With hair as gold as mine!

* * * * * *

H.M.S. Verdun's Chef

Den Lynch

I was the Officers cook. The wardroom; great guys all, but they also silly buggers. For instance, they pinched the starter cannon from the Admirals garden, loaded it on the Verdun and took it on a trip. 'Chef' said the Gunner, "Have you got any spare potatoes, brussel sprouts, or anything in that line?" I said that I had. They were then loaded into the brass cannon, primed with explosives and fired!

When we got back to Rosyth a police officer was waiting and came aboard with a request that 'Jimmy' attend the big chief. All would be forgiven as long as Verdun held a reception. However it was my watch ashore that day. It wasn't my bloody idea after all.

The Gunners pennant was another daft idea. The officers of our wardroom raided another escort vessel to win back the prized flag. Our lot didn't win it back, but there were very subdued lot of my officers that sat down to breakfast the next day, including the 'Doc'a rugby player. The skipper was not pleased so I heard.

Prince Philip's birthday, and his wedding day is very much like my own. As an experienced chef who had worked at the posh Carlton and Ritz hotels and the fabulous restaurant Frascat, and had roughed it a lot with the boy scouts. The Verdun's officers could not believe their luck that they had a cook who could rise to any emergency when on convoy.

The Petty Officer Steward had been a valet in hotels, the rest of the gang were all great to work with. Most of our food came from the Elgin Farms on the Firth of Forth, so rationing was virtually non-existent.

That is where Lieutenant Prince Philip comes in. He was on the **Wallace** at Rosyth in Scotland. The Coxswain warned me that the 'Jimmy' from the Wallace wanted me to change ships because of the extra functions held on the Wallace. The First Lieutenant put it to me that if I did not volunteer. I could be officially 'Shanghaied'. I assured him that, in that case I would lose all my inbred skill and become an embarrassment.

He got the point, the decision was relayed immediately to the worried wardroom and the skipper, who could, until further notice enjoy his huge 'Convoy' breakfasts and the very best of the 'West End' catering. Afternoon teacakes, were tentatively suggested, but, please no 'fairy cakes', wouldn't go down well if the rest of the escort found out.

As Captains Chef on the Implacable I should have provided with a Xmas lunch. However he had been invited to the Lord Mayor of Sydney's function, so I got ready nothing at all. At five o'clock the Captain's secretary sent for me. Evidently the Mayor, evidently a few pints abaft the beam, had in the skippers words, insulted the King, the whole British Pacific Fleet and himself. He was returning to the ship post haste and required a proper Naval Christmas Dinner, but, I was warned, he particularly wanted his Xmas pudding. Now on being on very good terms with the ship's cook's for'd, they managed they managed to get me a good meal together, soup, turkey with the trimmings, lovely veg etc; but the only Christmas pudding they could get me was a hard round ball that had left in the heater for hours. I feared the worst.

My watch lined up with heads bowed, when the Captain, after the meal, sent for me. I knocked on his state room door. "Enter" he said. I stood reverently to attention, "Good afternoon" I ventured. He slowly looked up. "Lynch" he said, "It is not a very good afternoon, neither was it a very good morning, as you have been told. I walked out leaving behind a very good meal. However I must say that I enjoyed your presentation. I will not ask where you got it from. But! Where the hell was my Christmas pudding/ I had especially requested some. I was aware, he continued. That Nelson had lost one eye and one arm, what I had on my plate, disguised with rum sauce, was something a bit more personnel and delicate. If he had lost the other one, Lady Hamilton would not have been privy to his peccadillo's. And history would have been different".

I apologised and said something about one could always learn a lot from one's mistakes.

"And that goes for Nelson and that bloody Mayor of Sidney" the Skipper said. He thanked for my effort, and to the relief of my watch, wasn't keel hauled.

Such happening usually go unrecorded in the annuls of Naval History.

* * * * *

Requiem for a Fleet

Can you recall ere memory fades,
From '39 through two decades
The names of ships that we knew,
Tragically now famous names are few.
Though our fleet is now depleted,
At least some great name have been repeated
* *
First, let us think of ships who made
The supreme sacrifice and paid
The price of freedom, bought at such cost.
Every day we heard with sadness
Of more victims of that madness
And every day we mourned some mate we'd lost.
* *
The "Mighty Hood" - just three men saved,
Her name in history forever engraved,
But how could this happen to this titan of our ships?
We couldn't apprehend
How she quickly met her end,
And worried questions issued from very worried lips!
* *
In whispers seamen spoke
Of "Barham" and "Royal Oak."
Of "Repulse", "Prince of Wales" and their catastrophic loss.
"Hermes and "Courageous",
"Dorset" and Cornwall" all were nailed from the cross.
* *
"Southampton," "Fiji," "Gloucester"
All listed in the roster.
But there are many more whose names we have to put down here,
"Calypso," "Curacao",
"Coventry" and "Cairo"
"Curlew" and "Calcutta" and the tragic "Galatea"

The victor of the River Plate
Brave "Exeter" who met her fate
Along with "Encounter" and USS "Pope"
For these men there was not much hope
And now they lie beneath the Java Seas.

As the spirits of these seamen hover in the breeze

* *

"York" and "Neptune" in the Med,
Add their numbers to the dead,
"Edinburgh" "Trinidad"
"Manchester and "Naiad,"
"Hermione, "Bonaventure" and "Charybdis" had to go,
The waters of an English harbour left so long ago.

* *

Remember the Destroyer and Corvette
The "Whirlwind," "Wessex" and the "Wren."
The "Wryneck" and the "Waterhen."
Convoys relied on this gallant lot,
At least a few survived with the "Westcott."

* *

Scores of small ships perished in the fight,
This tragic list with no end in sight.
The names of these are remembered in our heart,
As we sadly had to part.
Surely as these names unfold, Many great stories can be told.

* *

How can we pay our debts,
To the overworked Corvettes,
The Landing Craft, the Sweepers, MTB's and small fry?
Some didn't have a name,
But they are on the Roll of Fame,
Recalled by their crews as the years roll by

* *

"Begonia" and "Bluebell,"
"Snapdragon," "Asphodel."
These vessels had no warlike names, and U-boat crews may mock,
But in their iron tomb,
As they sank to their doom
Would they still be mocking ships with names like "Rose" and "Hollyhock"?

* *

We turn now to the "Blanche" and the "B's"
To the "Dainty," "Daring" and the "D's"
"Fearless" and the "F's" Gallant "Gypsy" and the "G's"
"Exmouth," "Hyperion,"
"Inglefield" and "Imogen,"
And the names still go on.

The tales of "Laforey," "Lance" and the "Larne,"
Their stories told would make a good yarn.
In the Med these ships did roam,
But only "Lookout" managed to get home
The loss continued, would it never cease?
Only four Tribals saw the peace.
* *
There are still many more,
Who fell victims of the war.
As we travel through the list of ship's it's hard to see
How England could exist
With this casualty list
Yet still the list grew longer in that fight for victory.
* *
"Warspite" and "Malaya"
Whose names always portray a
Vision of the mighty ships and their heroic deeds.
"Ajax" and "Ahilles"
"Resolution," "Ramillies,"
Ships that man had ceased to build, and man no longer needs.
* *
These ships have now all gone,
But their memory lingers on,
Whilst ageing seamen swing the lamp, and talk of days gone by!
Of happy days and runs ashore
In Hong Kong and Singapore,
And thoughts of far horizons bring a glisten to the eye!
* *
In Nelson's day,
They used to say
That men were made of iron and their ships were built of wood,
But in the days of which I speak,
Men and ships attained their peak.
Men of steel in ships of steel, though not better but just as good.
Sailors of today
* *
Are more technical they say,
Pressing buttons, turning valves and flicking switches on a panel,
But sailors never change,
And to landlubbers may seem strange,
With his special sense of humour, and his aptitude for flannel!

But should the call for men
Be sent out once again
If our way of life is threatened by some mad, ambitious nations
We've seen it all before
And we've never wanted war;
They should know our skills have been handed down, through many generations.

* *

"Nelson," "Rodney," "Anson," "Howe."
All are just a memory now.
With "K.G.V" and "Duke of York," "Valiant" and "Renown."
"Venerable," "Theseus"
"Pioneer," "Perseus,"
Regal ships with regal names, all worthy of a crown.

* *

And the gallant band
Of men who manned
These ships whose names have made their mark, and passed upon their way
Will sometimes shed a little tear,
AS they gather every year,
To pay homage at the Cenotaph on each Remembrance day

* *

And for a little while
Their lips will wear a smile
As they think of ships and shipmates, and the days of fighting men.
Their deeds will not diminish,
Though this era had to finish,
And this land will never see a mighty fleet like that again!

Anon

Chapter 39

E-Boat Alley March, 1942

H.M.S. **Wolsey** was escorting a South bound convoy, when she developed an 'echo' and attacked with depth charges. Unfortunately one of the depth charges malfunctioned and exploded on making contact with the water instead of the depth setting. The damage caused entailed the Wolsey being towed back to Leith Dockyard for repairs. H.M.S. **Vortigern** was sent to take over the Wolsey's duties. During the night whilst the convoy was off the coast of Great Yarmouth it was attacked by a number of E-boats. During the scrap that ensued the **Vortigern** was torpedoed with the loss of 110 men. Because of the action that was going on the other escorts were unable to go to her assistance. It was not until daybreak that the "Guillemot" returned to the scene and found that the stern of the Vortigern was perturbing above the water with two seamen clinging to it. She proceeded to pick up 14 of the crew and returned them to Harwich.
The R.N.L.I lifeboat "H.F. Bailey", skippered by the renowned Joe Bloggs, was also in attendance recovering bodies. Another body, that of Petty Officer George Blundell was washed up on to the beach at Cromer.

* * * * * *

Windsor and Walpole attack an escorted enemy merchant ship

0552.. Altered course in succession to 135, and received 'Enemy in sight to Starboard".
0553.. Received "Stand by to turn to Starboard to fire torpedoes" Tubes were brought to the ready Port
0554.. Received "Enemy in sight to Port" While altering back in succession to 100 degrees, tubes were trained for and aft, as it was not clear at this stage on which side the torpedo target lay.
Fire was opened on a destroyer bearing 130. 'B' gun illuminated with star shell. Short range weapons opened fire on destroyer and E-boats.
0555.. **Walpole** was observed to turn away to Port. At the same moment a merchant ship was sighted bearing approximately 100, range 4000, approximate course 230.
Tubes were brought to the ready Starboard. Enemy sped was estimated at 15 knots. Speed was increased to 25 knots.
0557.. **Windsor** turned to Port and fired torpedoes at an estimated range of 2,500 yards and enemy inclination m090 right.

0559.. Ship was steadied up on a retiring course 315, with **Walpole** on the Starboard beam, distance 2 cables.
0600.. A large explosion was seen amidships in the merchant ship. Fire was ceased after torpedoes had been fired at Calpe and Fernie were by this time somewhere between **Windsor** and the enemy, and a large amount of smoke made it impossible to select targets.
0605.. **Windsor** took station astern of **Walpole.**
Windsor was under erratic fire from 0554 to 0559 a number of shells fell close, at 0556 she received a direct hit, a shell estimated as 3 or 4inch calibre demolished the motor boat and caused superficial damage.

* * * *

THE DESTROYER ON A VOYAGE OF BLUSHES
BY LUCAS GARNER. H.M.S. VIMY

Contrary to popular opinion, when a warship encounters the enemy, all is not a well disciplined calm.
The story commences in Freetown, West Africa. H.M.S. **Vimy,** launched in 1917 and maintained at sea after 1930 by the sweat and colourful language of the engine room staff, was ordered to escort, with two other destroyers, the battleship Queen Elizabeth to the U.S.A. For repairs.
The voyage was uneventful until a short distance from the West Indies. The going alongside the battleship for fresh bread etc; we came a little too close, and riding up her anti torpedo bulges, tore open our forecastle like a tin can on her armoured side.
This caused great annoyance to the watch below, who were enjoying the traditional Naval custom of an afternoon siesta.
We retired blushing, followed by the caustic comments of Queen Elizabeth's ship's company.
The same evening at dusk a torpedo attack was made on one of the escorts. The three destroyers dropped a considerable number of depth charges with no apparent effect and the search for the U-boat was spread over a wide area. Night had fallen and we had lost sight of the other ships. Suddenly a submarine surface on a parallel course to the **Vimy** and only a short distance on our beam. In a matter of seconds 'A' gun opened fire, the submarine fired a red Very signal, which was the correct recognition signal of the day, and both submarine altered course towards each other.
In our minds, there was some doubt, due to the fact that we were close to the U.S. Naval base in Trinidad and she could have been an Allied submarine. During this moment of indecision the order to cease fire was given. Not that

this made much difference, our gunners speed was efficient but their aim was notorious, having once bracketed a tug very nicely but missing the towed target by about a half a mile.
However instead of adopting the usual roles when a destroyer and U-boat meet, the submarine proceeded to ram us!
During the ensuing confusion someone fired a snowflake rocket which illuminated the scene to the great satisfaction of all those present. The U-boat bounced and scraped down our port side, inflicting a certain amount of damage to both parties.
Our crew were gazing curiously at the astonishing sight of what seemed hordes of the enemy, clad in the unwarlike uniform of little black bathing drawers and rope soled shoes, busily engaged in throwing themselves into the sea.
Our Port propellor chewed into the Submarines hull as she slid astern and not being built to withstand such maltreatment, she gracefully subsided into the depths.
After collecting the crew of the U 162, who incidentally only lost one of their number, we learnt that she had been seriously damaged by the depth charge attacks and would have probably sunk anyway.
We limped into the Port of Spain where at the U.S. Naval Base we were patched up and were regaled by the Americans with ice cream and the latest Hollywood epics.
During this brief interlude I celebrated my 21st birthday with the delectable produce of the West Indies so dear to the heart of every matelot - rum!!
Orders the arrived for us to escort a small convoy to Gibraltar, with the assistance of one Corvette.
On the very first day of the voyage we spotted what seemed to be a periscope and after closing to 'Action Stations', opened fire on the object, But on approaching closer, how glad we were of the gunners notorious marksmanship. What we had mistaken for a periscope was the mast of a crude raft, crowded with pathetic survivors of a torpedoed ship. Among them were one woman and three small children. They had been adrift for some considerable time and although the men on the raft had rigged a small piece of canvas to protect the children from the fierce tropical sun, the effects of the heat and the lack of drinking water left them in a pitiable condition. Our Doctor and S.B.A. Tended to their needs and they were later transferred to a tanker that was calling at the nearby island of Tabago. We resumed our duties and continued the voyage without further incident.
After leaving Gibraltar we made our way to Portsmouth and from there the **Vimy** continued her work in the North Atlantic, taking part in other actions

including the Normandy Landing. In 1945 she was retired and like the rest of the V&Ws retired and scrapped after having played a gallant part in two wars.

BELIEVE IT OR NOT

Tommy Vann H.M.S. **Windsor.**

Whilst in convoy in the Channel during 1942, a thick fog descended upon us. We were therefore making our way slowly when there was a tremendous crash, one of the merchant ships that we were escorting the Methol Hill had collided with us and made a fourteen hole in the side of us. Fortunately the water tight doors were closed so only the store room was flooded.
Our nearest port was Hull so we made our way there as fast as possible. While underway Chief E. R.A. Standing DSM went down to retrieve the rum, he was heard to say "Sod the rest of the stores".
On arrival in Hull, the only dock that could possibly accommodate us was a large Arctic trawler dock, we managed to get in with approximately a foot to spare each end.
Half the ships company was sent on fourteen days leave subject to recall. I had the second leave, that is if the ship would be in that long. Being an engine room rating I had to turn to and clean ship. All damaged stores were to be put on the jetty. When going ashore one night I noticed four tea chests drying out on the jetty with the rest of the stores. I said to my 'oppo' (mate), Chopper Charman, (you've probably guessed why he was called 'Chopper', need I say more) "I'm going to play a little joke". So I put my mother's name and address on the chest. Low and behold, I received a letter telling me that it had arrived by an R.N. Truck that had been to our Naval Stores in town, (Leicester). I just could not believe it. Anyway the tea was shared with the neighbours in the street and sometime later I received a letter from one of those neighbours, thanking me for the tea, they enjoyed it very much, even if it did taste a bit salty, One dear old lady said that it must have been the sea air that had made it taste like that. I of course knew better.

* * * * * *

H.M.S. Walpole

Without wishing to appear too dramatic, we have managed to survive up to now, and as you will see 1942 is quite an eventful year for H.M.S. **Walpole.**

From the 1st of January to the 11th saw continuous convoy escort duties and further E-boat patrols, if the weather was too rough the patrols would be cancelled, E-boats did not sail if the sea was at all turbulent.

Walpole left Sheerness on the 11th to escort convoy FN88, this time all the way to Rosyth, then on the 14th escorted the county class cruiser H.M.S. Suffolk to Aberdeen. The next day we joined convoy FS100 to act as close escort with the hunt class destroyer H.M.S. Waddon.

17th January FS 100 and escorts approached the Thames Estuary in the late afternoon and the merchant ships prepared to anchor. At this time convoys were not allowed to trade up the estuary during the hours of darkness on account of enemy mine laying. As **Walpole** slowed down at the rear of the convoy to protect stragglers and to advise on anchoring, a Dornier 217 bomber attempted to strafe and bomb **Walpole** - possibly a dummy run?

Each individual convoy is given a code name as well as a number. In the event of imminent danger to a convoy as assessed by shore radar a plain language message is flashed by ship-shore radio to the convoy escorts. For possible air attacks the word 'Blue' followed by the convoy code name is given. At this time I was on ship-shore frequency watch and knowing the FS100 code word I was able to pass the 'Blue' warning to the bridge immediately minutes I received it. This gave the Captain and the crew a few vital to be fully prepared, as they would normally be at stand by action stations, Our Captain Lt Cmdr J.H. Eaden exercised great skill and coolness in these moments. The Dornier made another passing run, machine gunning **Walpole** and making several holes in the funnel, as well as shooting away one of our W/T aerials.

Walpole had by now almost stopped at the rear of the convoy and the enemy must have mistaken us for a merchantman. The Dornier made a low level run from astern, and when the bomb doors opened, our Captain ordered, 'Full ahead both', to the engine room. As we picked up speed quite quickly the bombs exploded in our wake. After releasing her bombs the enemy aircraft turned away and presented a complete and perfect target. Excellent shooting from our gunners made sure that the enemy did not escape. The plane crashed in flames, there were no survivors.

Lt Cmdr Eaden was mentioned in despatches and one of our gunners received the D.S.M... A wonderful start to 1942!

* * * * * *

H.M.S. WITCH

H.M.S. **Witch** was my home for three and a half years. I was an H.O. (Hostilities only) Telegraphist and although my seamanship was not brilliant, I could read Morse at 22 words per minute - that was my job.
The following is a report of the rescue of 24 survivors from the American Steamship Independence.
The boats crew in the rescue were mainly Officers and men of the seaman branch. The only way that I could assist was (with others) in the lowering and hightening of the rescue boats.
I was able to witness most of the operation and I was in awe of those brave men of the boats crews who risked their lives to save others.
The sea was heavy and very, very cold.
I and others were so proud of the rescuers who did their job with the minimum of fuss in difficult conditions.

Ray Hodgson

COMMUNIQUÉ

From;- W. J. Lee, surviving third officer, steamship Independence Hall.
To- The Honourable The First Sea Lord of the Admiralty.
Subject- H.M.S. **Witch.** Commendations of Officers and crew.
1) As a private citizen of the U.S.A. I feel it my duty to bring to the attention of the Admiralty the heroic efforts of the Commander, Officers and the crew of H.M.S. **Witch.**
Lieut, Cdr Holmes in Command.
2) At about 1430, 7th March 1942, with the wind at gale force and seas mountainous, the American steamship Independence was broken in half and grounded on a shoal off Sable Island.
Tremendous seas destroyed all lifeboats. At about noon 8th March, three units of the Royal Canadian Navy arrived on the scene and launched lifeboats which made valiant but unsuccessful efforts to reach the wreckage. At 1700 that day H.M.S. **Witch** approached and laid his ship close to the shoal.
Through his tenacity and seamanship and the ability and courage of the pulling boat officers and crew, four trips were made through extremely high surf which was now doubly dangerous due to cross tide and wind. Thirty -seven survivors, all remaining on the wreckage were taken off, the last after nightfall. One crew member of H.M.S. **Witch**, the Boatswain, was lost during the rescue attempts.

3) Sub Lieut. Fothergill, who was in charge of the first two rescue attempts, was responsible for the removal of 24 Survivors. His seamanship is deserving of the highest praise. While seas were running most dangerously, he brought his boat back and forth through white water, a distance of about a mile each way. At times his boat actually stood on end, yet he and his crew maintained stroke and control.
4) Lieut. Eric Peterson, of the Royal Canadian Navy, who made the final two trips, removed a total of 14 survivors. He too is deserving of praise for bringing his boat through safely after nightfall.
5) After arrival on board, the survivors were taken in hand by Officers and crew and every attention and courtesy was shown us.
6) Lest it may not be brought to your attention by official report. I should tell you that when the **Witch's** boatswain was lost, Lieut. Janion went overboard in an endeavour to rescue him, risking his life in extremely high seas.
7) I append a list of those, by no means complete, who did their utmost for our comfort and arrival ashore.
8) I trust that you will regard this as an expression or our sincere gratitude and admiration for the splendid seamanship and high courage of these men of His Majesty's Navy. Their actions were indeed in keeping with the highest traditions of the Royal Navy.

New York
March 18th 1942.

Signed Walter J. Lee
Sole surviving deck Officer.
Steamship Independence Hall

Personnel of **H.M.S, Witch** referred to in para 7.
Lieut. Commodore Holes R.N.
Lieut. Janion. R.N.V.R
Lieut. Souter R.N.V.R.
Surgeon Lieut. Gates R.N.
Sub-Lieut Fothergill R.N.V.R.
Commissioned Engineer Saunders R.N.
Sub- Lieut. Breckell, R.N.V.R.
Midshipman Bickett, R.N.V.R.
Those manning the rescue boats;-
Sailing whaler.
Lieut. Terence, Lieut. Janion. Gunner (T) B.C. Kavanaugh
P.O. W. Trick, Yeo' Sigs C. Johnson. L/Sea J Witley.
A/B S. Welch 1st Whaler
S/Lt Fothergill

P.O. J. Taylor Ldg/Sea F. Hardman, A/B H. Dalby, A/B J. Dodd, A/B H Bannister.
2nd Whaler;-
S/Lt Fothergill,
P.O. C. Dean, A/B S. Hale, A/B H Duncan, and one R.C.N. Rating
The two Canadian ships in attendance;-
H.M.C.S. Niagara, Chedabucto also launched boats.
Petty Officer Jan Trick lost his life in the rescue attempt.

From Philip F. Gresser,
Palm Beach,
Florida, U.S.A
I enrolled in the apprentice seaman's programme Of the U.S. Maritime Service in July 1941. I was eighteen years old and the U.S. Had not yet entered the second world war.
My Father was second engineer on a Moore McCormack vessel 'Independence Hall' a world war one Hod Islander. He telephoned me in New York where we lived and advised me that there was a fireman/water tenders job open on the ship which was then loading cargo at Philadelphia.
So I reported to the seaman's union hall and was assigned to the vessel. On arrival I noticed that she was loading a complete cargo of war materials. Barbed wire, munitions and finally 13 tanks on the deck, six forward and seven aft of the midship house.
We sailed unescorted to New York, Boston and finally Halifax, Nova Scotia where we were to become part of the convoy SC73 to sail first to Scotland, then on to Murmansk.
We sailed from Halifax on March 6th 1942 in single file, we were to form a convoy either some hours later or the following day. We were the third ship from last, the last two, one of which was torpedoed and sunk. During the day the weather worsened and by the following morning it was horrible.
On the morning of March the 7th, the Bosun and other crew members were either trying to swing out or swing in the two lifeboats on the lee side of the mid ships house when the Bosun was gashed in the head by one of the round bars. The third mate, Mr Lee, came back from the bridge with the medical kit to stitch the Bosun's wound, and ultimately this is what saved Mr Lee's life.
Suddenly there was a tremendous bang and the fire room bilge started filling with water, when the bang happened the engine room telegraph went full astern and the engine was so set.
The oiler started the bilge pump to drain number three hold, but the fire room continued to fill with water (none of us in the machinery space knew that we had broken in two). By noon when I was supposed to be relieved, the fire

room floor plates were already starting to float around and I was probably smoking two cigarettes at the same time and already thinking that I would be dead before the day was over. My relief was standing at the top of the boiler room yelling at me that he was afraid to come down. The third engineer tied a rope round me so that I could be pulled out of the fire room in the event that I was injured or completely flooded out.

Sometime later someone came down (it may have been my Father) and told me to come up on deck via the engine room ladders. I went topside and out on deck, the first thing I noticed was what appeared to be another vessel a few hundred yards away from us. I asked what ship it was and was told, the other half of our ship.

About an hour later, the third officer, Mr Lee, told us to prepare to abandon ship. We were told to get into the lifeboats on the weather side, this we did, but as soon as we started to lower them it became obvious that if we touched water we would be slammed into the side of the ship and probably killed. We pulled the boats back up on deck and went into one of the rooms. The house had rooms on both port and starboard sides with two open passage ways running through from for to aft. We all went into the crews mess rooms where there was some food, and after we had broken into the slop chest. Those of us who were wet were able to get some dry clothes, cigarettes and boots.

We had just settled into the mess room when some lube oil drums on the upper deck us broke loose and as we rolled over from side to side, so did the oil drums. Eventually they began to break through the overhead. We decided to abandon the mess room for the top of the engine room. This was not as easy as it sounds because great waves were coming through both the midships passage ways and any movement had to be carefully timed and quickly done between the waves. We made these moves one at a time until most of us were inside the engine room fidley. The wiper, Richard Nathan (known to us as 'Shorty') made his move, his timing was off and a wave caught him and carried him through the passage way and over the rail. He managed to grasp on of the cargo masts and hold on for about half a minute, screaming 'Help me, help me' but all we could do was to stand there and watch him being swept away by a wave. Those few minutes haunted me for a long time afterwards and it was a long time before I stopped dreaming about the whole incident.

The weather was still bad and we were all cold and wet some of us hugged each other to try and get warm. There were now known to be seven dead. By now we had no food or water and many of us were thirsty. We dare not smoke because of the lube oil and kerosene which we afraid might catch fire.

The radio operator thought that he had got out an S.O.S. before the ship broke and the antenna parted.
We were aground off Sable Island and sinking slowly, all we could do was to stay where we were and hope and pray that our plight was known. We remained like this all night.
In the morning we heard an aircraft flying nearby, and as it had calmed down slightly we all went to the top deck of the house and waved whatever we could lay pour hands on to attract the planes attention. It flew overhead and banked to let us know that he had seen us and then flew off. We hoped that whoever he notified would be there soon because the weather was still bad and we were still slowly sinking.
A couple of hours later a Canadian corvette showed up and came as close as it could and proceeded to try and launch a boat. Almost immediately the boat capsized but luckily all the men were able to get back on board the corvette.
Signals were exchanged and they advised us that they would try again later when the weather subsided. An hour or so later a British destroyer, H.M.S. **Witch** approached, again as close as it could in the very shallow water and proceeded to launch one of it's boats. This boat also capsized and one man was lost in the effort. When we heard this we really began to give up hope. We thought that no one would do anything until the weather had calmed down, we did not think that we could last much longer.
The **"Witch"** launched another boat, this one made it to us and proceeded to remove us, several at a time. At this point there were 38 of us. The chief cook and the oiler had died during the night. The cook by his own hand and the oiler had gone crazy. A total of ten were now dead.
Witch's boat made several trips back and forth, using oars only, until we were all safely on board. We were taken below, our clothes dried out for us, given food and water and made to feel comfortable. I was given a hammock to sleep in.
The next morning we arrived in Halifax where we were met by people of the Canadian Red Cross.

Chapter 40

TO RUSSIA WITHOUT LOVE

1st March 1942 H.M.S. **Verdun** and H.M.S. **Woolston** were called upon to strengthen the escort of convoy PQ12 to the Northern Russian Port of Murmansk. These convoys were described by Winston Churchill as 'The worst journey in the world'. And although these ships had been designed and built for the main purpose of working the English Channel and the North Sea. The dire need for extra escorts ships entailed as always calling upon the trustworthy old V&W destroyers.

This convoy was to really put them to the test, for although until then there had been very little enemy activity in attacking the Russian convoys so far, the weather, as always, was to prove the worst enemy, this can be well illustrated by the fact that on that convoy one of the rescue whalers iced up and capsized in the rough seas.

On the 5th March the convoy was sighted by a German reconnaissance aircraft. This was reported to the German High Command in Norway upon which the mighty German battleship, the most modern, largest, and heavily armed battleship in the world at that time accompanied by her screening destroyers set forth to intercept. Due to the atrocious weather and a bad sighting report however, they failed to make contact with the convoy and it arrived in the Kola Inlet and with the exception of the rescue whaler, without loss although some of the ships incurred ice damage.

What the crews of the two old V&Ws endured during that convoy is hard to imagine, for, with the exception of a duffle coat they had not been issued with any extra warm clothing. They sailed for the return journey from the Kola Inlet on the 23rd March, during the journey one U-boat was rammed and sunk by the minesweeper Sharpshooter they all arrived at Reykjavik on the 3rd April, very glad to be home.

Once again the V&Ws having proved their strength and worth and were to be engaged in many more of those awful convoys, in fact in all 17 V&Ws took part in 59 Russian convoys (including return convoys).

The Russian Convoys

Seventeen of the V&Ws were involved in 59 of those convoys, and although the following does not mention any V&Ws in particular it may give the reader an insight of what did occur in that particular sphere of the sea war.

The first convoy to Russia, code name 'Dervish' sailed from Loch Ewe calling at Iceland and arrived in Archangel on the 21st August 1941.
Throughout the winter of 1941-42 the convoys continued without being attacked or even detected. The greatest problem was that of the ice. It was necessary for the seamen to chip the ice off the superstructure, lest the ship became top heavy and thereby turn turtle in the rough seas.
It was not until the 5th March that a lone German aircraft spotted P.Q.12. It was of course immediately reported and the mighty German Battleship Tirpitz and a flotilla of destroyers set out to intercept, but due to the bad weather and a bad sighting report, they never made contact, once again the convoy arrived intact with the exception of the rescue ship Shera which had iced up and capsized.
This of course alerted the Germans, They were soon to amass 300 aircraft on the air fields along the Norwegian coast. U-boats from other parts of the ocean were called up.
So it was that PQ13 was sighted and attacked by JU88 aircraft, one of their first victims was the SS Ballot who was bombed and damaged, so much so that there was a possibility of her sinking, so a lifeboat was lowered with sixteen men in it.
A flotilla of German destroyers then attacked the convoy. The atrocious weather had scattered the convoy over a huge area. They came across the cruiser HMS Trinidad who engaged them, Trinidad then found one of the destroyers which had been abandoned after being in action with British destroyers. Trinidad fired a torpedo in order to finish off this German destroyer, but for some unknown reason the torpedo did a 180 degree turn and crashed into her bows, fortunately all water tight doors had been closed and she was able, by going astern at about three knots reach Murmansk.
Meanwhile the rescue ship Silja who had picked up the sixteen men from the Ballot was herself running very short of fuel, she had already burnt everything possible, so she made for the ice. When she went into the ice she found the SS Induna already there. Those who had been taken off the Ballot decided that it would be much more comfortable to be aboard the Induna, so they walked across the ice and boarded her.

Austin Byrne's story is entitled
"We made it Kid"

These were the words said to me be a very remarkable man, after we had spent four days in an open boat in the Arctic after the Submarine U-376 had torpedoes the SS Induna on the 30th March 1942.
He was not a crew member of the Induna, but like others was from the SS Ballot which had been torpedoed earlier had been taken aboard by the rescue ship Silja. As it was thought that the Ballot was about to sink after suffering a bombing attack, sixteen members of the crew took to a lifeboat and were picked up by the Silja.
The Induna like others went into the ice to escape being torpedoed by U-boats, she was soon joined by Silja who had run out of fuel, the Ballot crew members walked across the ice and boarded the Induna, which would be more comfortable.
The Induna then took the Silja in tow and set off for Murmansk but in the heavy seas the tow broke at about 10pm and despite looking for two and a half hours, she had no success, until 4am the Induna had to set a course and proceed to Murmansk.
At about 7.30 the next morning the Induna was torpedoed in number five hold right under the aviation spirit this caught fire and the ensuing explosion threw barbed wire on to the deck where large drums of petrol turning them into a burning mass.
We were sent to our lifeboat stations, a few people started to run through the fire, others on the stern jumped into the freezing sea out of the way of the heat and flames, the last man through was the man from the Ballot came running barefooted through the fire leaving bloody footprints on the ice from his badly cut feet, the boat had been lowered to deck level, we were ordered into the boat when this man came running through the flames his hair had been burnt off, his face ears and hands were badly burnt, his jacket and trousers were still burning as he rolled into the boat as the occupants beat out the flames that were engulfing him.
The boat was lowered, with eight of us including a seventeen year old steward boy by the name of Anderson aboard. The mate ordered us to row round to the other side, the lee side, to take off those that were remaining on the deck because the boat would have been smashed up. Before we could go alongside the submarine fired another torpedo, the Induna sank quickly taking those that had still been aboard.
The man that had been badly burnt sat on the taught with the seas breaking over him, he was covered with a blanket and a spare coat. After a while he became encased in ice, which got thicker as time went on, we tried chatting

to him, but he could hardly talk, but not once did he moan. The other gunner and I did all the bailing.

After four days of this hell they sighted land just at dusk, when we told the badly burnt man he said "Gunners will you turn the boat so that I might see. This we did, he then said "Put an oar in my hands, I can rock my body to help, by this time his hands were twice as thick as they should be, his fingers were drawn bent with the cold, his knuckles had burst and covered with scabs, the whole of them was black, and yet he still wanted to help. It was then that we also saw boats which turned out to be Russian fishing vessels. They were hauled aboard, some had to have ropes tied round them, for they were frozen stiff. Once aboard we were given warm drinks to help defrost our stomachs. One of the Russian crew called me, I am not certain but I think it was a woman, they were having difficulty with the cabin boy Anderson, she could not get him down, I think he ws frozen bent. I helped her to get his jacket off by cutting it up the back, he was black up to above his waist, when she saw this she said "Leave him".

I was then called to have a drink of Vodka, when you have not eaten for four days it goes right down to your feet, then another, and another, I do not know how many I had, I sang for them, believe me I cannot sing. I was called by one of the Russian crew and taken to a bunk. This man got up as far as he could, put out his hand for me to hold and he said as best he could "We made it kid", words that I shall never forget. I was led away from him. His face I can never forget, burnt and frozen, he had lines where he had opened his mouth, his eyes, the whites looked as they had frozen lumps in them, how much pain he must have suffered during those four days cannot be imagined. His head was one big mass of burn flesh, his ears were just big sore things. But he had willed himself to live through all the pain of his burns. The freezing winds, the ice that had formed over him, what his legs and feet were like after being burnt and in the water for four days I cannot imagine.

We were hastened to Murmansk and taken to a makeshift hospital. I went to sleep, when I woke up I was told "Kid, the cabin boy has died", when I woke again I was told "Kid, your Yank has died". The man who told me this was in the next bed to me. So, did he ask for me before he died? I don't know, but looking back I would like to have been with him when he went to meet his maker. Of the other six, only one, Austin Byrne, (who is the author of this narrative) did not have any amputations, but was told that he would never be able to father children. Some years later he proved them wrong.

* * * * *

Bill Short paying homage at the grave of seventeen year old boy J. Anderson who died after four days in an open boat in the Arctic.
The British Cemetery Murmansk 2001

In the other lifeboat, Bill Short recalls;-

The other lifeboat was damaged during launching and Bill Short, who should have been in the other lifeboat found that the lifeboat had already been launched and had a full compliment, however they shouted for Bill to jump. There was little alternative. The water in the Arctic at that time of the year is mighty cold, he managed somehow to be hauled aboard the already overcrowded lifeboat. It was actually designed to carry 25 persons, there were now 34, packed like sardines in that boat. However hopes were high that we would soon be picked up. As night fell we realised that it was to be a bitterly cold night with snow, sleet and forty foot waves battering the lifeboat.
Whisky was found on board, and there had always been the thought that alcohol of any kind would keep out the cold, this fallacy was proved wrong, because, those who indulged and drank too much fell asleep, never to wake again. No matter how much the others shook them, they did not stir, they had died from hypothermia. Sadly that first night six died and their bodies were committed to the deep, which lightened the already flooding boat slightly out of the water. The water was creeping higher and higher, the pump was useless having frozen solid.
In this boat too was another badly burnt seaman who was lying in the boat where he died, frozen to the bottom of the boat, it was impossible to move him.
All the rations that were supposed to sustain us were frozen solid as was the water keg so we were reduced to licking ice. Water in the boat was now up to our knees. The weather never abated, gale force winds, snow and sleet and the waves were frightening. This continued for four days by then it was only the buoyancy tanks that were keeping us afloat. One man went mad, sea spray was freezing on the gunwale and he started to lick the ice, his tongue became swollen and he died.
Then at last we were sighted by a Hurricane piloted by a Russian.
We had given up all hope of being rescued, from time to time we sighted land through the whiteout, but it seemed so far away. When we were torpedoed we were 175 miles from Murmansk, when we were picked up we were a scant 25 miles from Murmansk.
We were finally rescued by a Russian Minesweeper, of the original 34 there were now only 17, including a 15 year old cabin boy, all were so weak that we had to be hauled aboard by ropes. I tried to walk to get the circulation going in my legs, but it was impossible, they just would not support me. We were all taken to the Hospital, I was covered in goose grease and bandaged

from head to toe in an attempt to warm me up. A tube was put down into my stomach and tepid water was poured into my stomach to clear the ice.

When the bandages were removed, it was found that gangrene had set in in both my legs. I was then taken down to the makeshift theatre which was in fact a school classroom where six operation were being carried out at the same time.

I was placed on a school table, a white sheet erected in front of me so that I could not see what was being done, and then told in broken English "We are going to cut your legs off". There had been no preparation, no anaesthetic, medical supplies were nil.

All that I can remember before passing out was the excruciating pain. When I regained consciousness I was told that I had been delirious for three days. Both my legs had been 'chopped off' one above, the other below the knee.

Screens were around me and no one was allowed to come near me.

It was rather ironic, in that 'hospital' the conditions were unbelievable. The school had huge windows. The German bombers came over every hour on the hour. All the windows were boarded up because they had all been blown in, so, consequently there was no air circulation, the stench from gangrene wounds was awful. (One was not aware of the smell after a time). The room was jammed solid with beds, all filled with the wounded, with the wounds all spewing out gangrene. The room had been the schools assembly hall.

When I became aware of my surroundings, I discovered that both of my legs had been literally chopped off, one above the other below the knee, and there were great incisions to the stumps in order to drain away the gangrene, it just flowed on to the bed. Infection was never thought about occurring. My legs had been chopped of as a butcher would chop a piece of meat, the bones were sticking out, the nerve ends exposed, so, when anyone came near me the nerves reacted. Crude surgery I admit, but I survived.

The dressings were pure hell, gangrene causing the dressing to stick, torn of like paper off raw meat. I did Yell!! They sprayed hydrogen peroxide on to the raw flesh, as in the Murmansk winter, wounds did not heal quickly, in fact only after five months did a slight skin start to form.

Conditions were mind boggling, if frost bite was in the fingers or toes, they let them go black and then chop them off. Food was not nourishing, for five months we had rice stewed, fried, boiled, a little meat which was supposed to be Yak. We joked when we got it by saying "There must have been another amputation today. That was the only way we could keep our spirits up, each in his own way, but crude humour seemed to work. In fairness to the Russians, they had little or no food themselves.

Consequently my weight went down to six stone (normally I was twelve). I was like someone from Belsen with bones sticking out all over and my close cropped hair.

Toilet facilities just did not exist and with no legs, my bowels etc; were evacuated directly on to the bed (to keep the gangrene company) I do not remember a sheet being changed, only wiped. There were very few nurses trying to attend to too many patients. A very upsetting situation, but we were so weak, we could do nothing else. I had no bowel control.

It was comedy again when I received my blood transfusion. I was so thin that the doctors had five attempts on each arm to find a vein, a fruitless effort. A senior doctor was then called, he just stuck the needle into my arm, the needle had been used so many times, that was my transfusion, four months too late.

Five months passed, my wounds were never stitched and the bones still stuck out, nerves exposed. Naval ships were having a hard time getting through.

Eventually we were put aboard the US ship Tuscaloosa, it was pure heaven, comfy beds etc; In the sick bay I was very well looked after on the trip home.

When we arrived at Greenock I was interviewed by customs officials who asked. "What nationality are you?" I thought this strange, but said "Scottish". I then realised that with shaven head and weighing about six stone and dressed in Russian clothes that they had found for us, no wonder they thought that we were foreigners!

******

Jim Campbell

15 year old cabin boy SS Induna

We sailed from Gourock on ¾ March 1942 for the tail 'o the bank, we joined a few other ships and set sail for Iceland.
We sat off the capital Reykjavik, waiting for the other ships to arrive from the United States, we were there for about a week, no shore leave, we just sat night after night watching the lights in the city and wishing that we were among them, anything just for a break. We took off for points unknown, at that time everything was pure guess work and conjecture, we had only been travelling about six or seven hours, when we did an about face, and went back to Reykjavik. We were told that the Tirpitz was on the prowl, hence the about turn. The information must have been false because we left again the next afternoon.
The weather at this time was quite pleasant, the second day out we found ourselves in the middle of a minefield, rumour was that it was ours. I think we were fortunate, that the weather was as good as it was, because the mines could be seen quite clearly, everyone who was not on duty was required on deck for mine spotting. At this time the Royal Naval Escort was still with us, and they had marksmen firing away, but with no success that I was aware of.
During the night or early morning the Navy disappeared. We heard that the Tirpitz was again on the move, so to protect the convoy, they headed off to it's projected course.
Later the same day the weather deteriorated, the wind got up, a swell developed, and it began to get very cold, during the night and next morning it was obvious it was going to be a nasty day. To make it even worse we were suddenly attacked by a small force of German bombers, they played havoc with us, sinking at least two ships that I personally saw being hit. I must confess that this to me as a young whipper snapper was very exciting, actually being in the thick of things. A few hours after the bombers had left there appeared a lone plane just going round the horizon, out of range, no doubt keeping his H.Q up to date on our position.
Our convoy was spread out over a considerable distance, and it was certain that other ships were being sunk by U-boats. We could hear explosions, and sometimes see plumes of smoke in the distance, of course there were all sorts of theories being espoused by the know it all's, ie; U-boat packs waiting behind every large wave, or just over the horizon. In retrospect, I'm sure that most of the talk was to keep their spirits up, except of course the doom and gloom merchants, of which every ship had one or two.

The weather really took a nose dive, winds hard, rain and wave size rapidly increasing. I saw waves of at least thirty or forty feet high, looking across at the other ships in the vicinity, I saw one, to use the modern idiom actually surfing, both bow and stern out of the water, propeller just turning. The ship being carried along on the crest of the wave, then suddenly sliding down the wave, disappearing for a short time, then popping back up like a cork out of a bottle, and again being carried along on a wave, mark you we were not faring very much better.

Everyone was at one time or another feeding the fish (being seasick) yours truly included I must admit that this was a very frightening time, no one knew whether or not the next wave would hold us down, the storm raged all day and night and when it finally abated, we were at the edge of the ice field, together with a couple of other ships, we were told later that the convoy had been scattered all over the ocean. Whilst the Skipper was making preparation to reverse out, a small trawler by the name of Silja caught up with us. She was to be a present to the Russian Government. Unfortunately she had run out of fuel and had to rip up all the ship's furniture and most of the decking to keep going. The Silja had picked up some of the survivors from an American ship the SS Ballot, which had been bombed by German aircraft. They were transferred to our ship by walking across the ice, quite a novel experience.

We reversed out of the ice field and took the Silja in tow, During the night the weather again roughed up and the tow rope parted. We searched around for her for some considerable time without success.

At this time we were approximately 80 miles from Murmansk.

Early next morning I was in the salon. I had prepared things for breakfast, and was just going to sit down when we were struck by a torpedo. I was thrown forward and struck my head on the bulkhead between the pantry and the salon. I must have been knocked out, because the next thing I remember is Jerry Lanning the Chief Steward telling me to go and get my life belt from the pantry. I went for it, but some one had beat me to it. He sent me to the Skippers cabin and told me to get a spare. I went for it but unfortunately or fortunately, as the case may be, because someone grabbed me and put me in the lifeboat. Whilst in the lifeboat I saw some of the firemen bring up from the engine room one of the crew who was badly burnt almost black, unfortunately he was dead.

The torpedo had struck aft of the engine room and stern. We were carrying ammunition below decks, and high octane Benzine in forty gallon drums on deck.

The explosion of the torpedo caused a fire which triggered off the ammunition, fortunately, only one lot at a time blew or we would have all

gone for a burton. It was the same with the drums of Benzine, they went off spasmodically. The fire aft of the bridge prevented many of the crew and DEMS ratings from getting in the lifeboats.
My boat was lowered into the water, the torpedo had struck during a bad rain squall, the sea was very rough. I was told to grab an oar and use it to prevent the lifeboat being smashed against the ships side, I did and was pushing the oar against my stomach to exert more pressure, when I was smacked on the back of my head and told to push from the side, as I did so the lifeboat smashed against the side of the ship and my oar was propelled backwards into the sea. The person who smacked me was Sam Carpenter, the Bosun of the SS Ballot, this man was extraordinary to say the least. He took charge of the lifeboat and tried to sort out the survival foodstuffs, they were frozen solid, the water and oil we were supposed to cover our exposed parts with to prevent frostbite etc; Pemmican, a type of dried meat was frozen solid, we couldn't dent it with an axe, so we had nothing to eat or drink.
Now this man, Sam Carpenter, sat and rowed the boat for days, if he hadn't kept the boat on an even keel, we would not be here today. I honestly don't know where he got the strength or single mindedness to keep going.
I remember the 2nd mate sitting under a blanket/tarpaulin? At the stern, he never moved or said anything that I can remember to anyone. I do remember a chap named Noble, one of the DEMS rating asking us all to sing hymns and other songs to try and cheer us up, and keep going. I thought he died in the lifeboat, but I have since learned that he survived, if he is still alive now (1994) he will be 93 because he was 41 when we were sunk.
It was a very traumatic time for every one in the lifeboat, most of us had never met during the voyage as we all had various duties to perform in different parts of the ship, and of course there were the survivors from SS Ballot.
I honestly don't think that many in the lifeboat, after the first day actually remember clearly what went on, so intense was the cold, I was told at the time that we were sunk that the temperature was 45 degrees below zero, and a maximum life expectancy if you were unfortunate enough to be in the water was 12 minutes.
I was sitting on the port side of the lifeboat facing aft. There was of course the usual cheerful comments being shunted about, eg; "Gee could I go a feed of fish and chips", or steak, or for that matter anything. "Boy could I murder a pint etc: I also have a vivd recollection of some saying he was going to the pub to meet his mates and he stepped off the lifeboat.
After a couple of days there was a succession of bodies going over the side, as one after another succumbed to the intense cold and to the pressure of the situation that we were in.

I must say that I cannot remember the number of hours or days I spent in the lifeboat. However I do remember hearing a plane circling over us just before we were picked up by a Russian ship. I was sitting with my left hand on the gunwale to prevent being thrown all over the place. When I was lifted from the lifeboat, four fingers of my hand stayed attached to the gunwale, my thumb was so damaged that I have never been able to bend it. The four fingers of my right hand were all split open to the second knuckle, as a result of this I have not been able to straighten the second, third or fourth fingers, or bend the first, my right thumb is the only digit undamaged. All five toes of my left foot were so bad that they had to be amputated, my right foot was taken off above the ankle, Later back in hospital back in Scotland, it was re-amputated because I forgot that it had gone, Crazy eh? It happened quite easily. I was sitting on the edge of a table in the ward kitchen, when a nurse called me, without thinking I jumped down to go to her, landed on my stump, bursting it wide open, so I have finished with a stump six inches below the knee.

The last time I remember walking on my own two feet was on the ship that picked us up. I wanted to go to the toilet, and someone helped me to get there, actually this is the last thing that I remember for some time. The next thing that I remember was waking up in hospital in Murmansk. I later found out that it was a school that had been converted. It was situated atop a hill directly above the docks. I have no idea how long I was out. All I can remember was the intense pain, and being given morphine to deaden the pain, I'm sure that if we had not been given these injections, many of us would not have survived, or would have, to put it mildly, crazy, (some say we still are). There were many incidents in the hospital, both humorous and sad. We had very little food, and the Russian people were in the same situation. However there were time when we received some tins of food from ships which had been fortunate to get through. The contents were varied, however we did get a few tins of beans and pork, just I think momentary escape from boredom and pain.

There were some British Naval Surgeons in the hospital. They were under the command of Lt Commander H.S. Millar, a great guy, nothing was too much trouble for him. He was tremendous in procuring food for us from the ships in the harbour. He wrote to me a couple of time after I got home. The address was, Royal Naval Station c/o Naval Party 200 GPO London. We also had a very good interpreter, she was a Russian girl named Shura, again nothing was a trouble to her, a real nice lassie.

One of the bitterest memories of this time were the incessant air raids, they hardly ever stopped, night and day. The bloody Stuka's got right over the top of the hospital and started towards the docks below, and of course letting their bombs go, obviously not all the bombs were on target, many fell on the hillside, and on occasions appeared to be coming up the hill towards us. There were no windows left, all had been shattered and broken by blasts, the openings had been shuttered up by old pieces of timber and anything else laying around the hospital which was crowded with survivors and locals who had been injured in the air raids. I would add that there were also casualties from the front line, which was only about fifteen miles away.

I don't think that I can do justice to the events that were taking place at this time, primarily because I was suffering like everybody else. The pain and suffering had to be seen to be believed. I saw grown men leap into the air from the prone position. No one who has not experienced the excruciating pain when the circulation is returning to the frost bitten limbs, or for that matter any part of the body, can under any circumstances, comprehend the mental anguish or terror felt, whilst waiting for the next part of the body to defrost. Screams, moans and groans were all part of the every day noise. No one took any notice or made any comment, only to offer sympathy or encouragement.

There was however for a short time one who was exempt from sympathy or encouragement. He was one of the Lasca seamen. He kept repeating the same word over and over, Pain, pain, pain endlessly on and on, so much so that a chap named Ernie Carr, a seaman from HMS Forrester, he a very smashed left arm. He warned the Lascar that if he did not shut up, he would shut him up. I'm sure that Ali didn't understand what Ernie had said, but I know he felt what Ernie meant, because he smacked him on the chin, knocking him cold. Everyone cheered. It was not vindictive cheering, more the type for a laugh to relieve the monotony and pain than anything else. Similar to the pork and beans episode, unfortunately poor Ali copped it both times. There were two events which afforded some pleasure during the three months in Murmansk. The first was a movie called "The Great Waltz". The music, scenery, and costumes were beautiful. The second was a concert given by the Russian sailors from one of their fleets, Red, White, or black sea, I cannot remember which, the dancing and singing were of a very high standard.

During the time spent in Murmansk hospital it became obvious to all who suffered from exposure, that we were lucky to be under the care of doctors and nurses who were experts in the handling and treatment of frostbite and exposure cases.

After I had been there for about nine or ten weeks, they thought that it would be a good idea to give me a bath, provided that I kept my hands and feet out of the water, (they were both heavily bandaged). I was taken down to this big ablution block, stripped and put into a beautiful hot bath. I was lying there with my mind miles away when I became aware of a lot of giggling, and nurses talking to someone behind me, she must have been telling them who I was, and why I was there, because the next minute I was surrounded by about twenty naked women! I was only fifteen and had never seen a naked woman, my eyes were popping out of my head, because of my bandages which I must not get wet, I was unable to cover myself. The girls obviously noticed because they started laughing and giggling and talking twenty to the dozen. My nurses said something to them and they all returned to their showers. I was dried and taken back to the ward. The nurse must have told the rest of the staff, because they kept smiling and giving me little waves as they went about their duties. The interpreter told me that they were Red Army girls attached to the Ack, ack batteries around the area. They must have been as strong as horses, because when the heavy ack, ack guns sounded off, they sounded like machine guns they were so rapid.

We had been told on a couple of occasions that we would be going home shortly. However there was always an explanation of some sort as to why we would not be going this time. The last being that the liner coming to take us had been diverted to another theatre of war. Nevertheless we tried to keep in good spirits.

After being in Murmansk for three months they told us that we were going to be moved, they didn't say where to. Any way the great day did arrive, we were prepared and made ready. Towards the evening we were moved from our ward downstairs ready to be put into whatever vehicles we were to be transported in.

As usual the air raid sirens sounded, we were told to sit quietly, for sound travelled a great distances at night, (that order still puzzles me, how did they expect the bomber pilots to hear any noise made on the ground) any way we did sit quiet, more from fright than any other reason. A nurse walking past with a tray full of dishes dropped it. You wouldn't believe it, everyone either screamed, cried out or yelled in sheer terror. Just then the ack, ack guns started banging out. Bombs started dropping all over, you would have thought that the nurse had deliberately set the whole thing going, it was unbelievable. We sat around for some time. Then the casualties from the bombing started coming in, the most poignant being two young kids, a girl and a boy bringing in a woman who I took to be their mother, they were supporting her, one under either shoulder. Both her legs seemed to be hanging on by two pieces of skin and were dragging along the ground. Of all the people that I saw with injuries, this is the one I remember most vividly.

The all clear eventually sounded, and we were put into vehicles and taken to a rail yard and put into cattle trucks filled with stretchers, after travelling for some time in what was I must admit the most comfortable mode of travel I had ever experienced, to the contrary, I'm sure the trucks had square wheels,

no joking. After a few hours, during which we had only one stop to empty the slop bucket, and take on food and water. I must say that the Russian people were really marvellous, they had very little of anything, yet had no hesitation in giving what they had to us. Some of the black bread was so hard it was impossible to break it, a bit like the survival food in the lifeboat. In no way am I criticising, These poor people had to try and eat it, hard as it was.
After travelling for some time we eventually arrived at a small port (I have no idea where) and put aboard a Russian hospital ship. What a change! It was so white and clean, lovely beds or bunks in small cabins which held four people. This was heaven after what we had been used to. We still had no idea where we were going, I don't think we cared, it was so peaceful, no air raids, no bombing. We had as escort several British minesweepers, the Leda, Bramble and Salamander. I was told later how wounded survivors were carried aboard these ships. We the arrived at our destination, Archangel, surprise, surprise we were met with the sound of sirens, of course what else? A bloody air raid. They were not as frequent as those in Murmansk, however they were enough to keep your nerves on edge. The weather had shown a marked improvement, we actually had a window that we could see through, a little bit of sunshine, no heavy field artillery firing in the distance, so on the whole things were looking up.
We had been at Archangel for a few weeks when we were visited by some R. N. top brass, they were accompanied by Godfrey Winn, the author of the book on Russian convoy PQ17, a very nice chap. He sent me an autographed copy of the book. A year before he died he wrote to me and said that he was coming to New Zealand and that he was looking forward to seeing me again.
With fewer air raids and good weather we were beginning to feel a bit better in ourselves. I was getting a bit of special attention from a Russian doctor named Onmoprienko, he told me he was like his son. I discovered later from the staff that his son had been killed during an air raid. He would come and sit with me and tell me what was happening in the various theatres of the war. He was a very lonely and sad man. His son had been his only child.
There was great excitement throughout the hospital on the day of the first thousand bomber raid on Cologne. You would have thought the war had ended, everyone going around with big grins on their faces. Needless to say the comments being bandied about were not complimentary to the Germans. I don't think that anyone would have had any objections, or would have been sorry if every city in Germany had been subjected to the same treatment. In fact we were all hoping it would happen. Revenge is a terrible weapon. At that time the situation that we were in, revenge was a motivating factor in keeping us all going. Thank God time mellows us or it would be a horrible

world to live in, even more than it is now.
Just to make sure that I did not get too comfortable, my appendix started playing me up, and I was told it would have to come out.
There was a lovely young lass by the name of Tanya. I don't know if she had been told by the doctor to look after me, but look after me she did. When I had to be taken to the theatre to have my appendix removed, she actually carried me down, and when I awoke several hours later, she was still sitting by me bed, with a big smile on her face, she was a real tonic to everyone, every time she came into the ward she had a beautiful smile all over her face, she was like a breath of fresh air.
Rumours started going around again that we were going home, but as usual they were just rumours. It was heart breaking. After the pain had subsided a bit, we all began to sit up and take notice of what was going on, unfortunately, nothing.
While the staff were very good and could not do enough for us, we were hardly in a position to do the Highland Fling or such like with feet and hands bandaged there was nothing very much that any of us could do.
To add to our enjoyment, the air raids started to be a bit more frequent, and sad to say, it got a bit too much for me and I started yelling and screaming so much that they had to sedate me. The surprising thing about this is, this is the first time I have remembered it since then. I had blotted it out. I remember being carried down to the air raid shelter and was screaming like a banshee. It is amazing to remember it after all those years.
At last the rumours were true. We were prepared and made ready to be transported to the Kola Inlet, the other side of Murmansk. Arrangements had been made to ship us home from there. Before leaving, some of the staff came round the wards giving gifts. I received a beautiful four stringed mandolin and an embroidered skull cap. As I have said, the Russian people were extremely kind hearted.
I was taken from the hospital and put aboard the minesweeper Salamander. During the trip my left hand became extremely painful. Where the second finger had been was open and there were a few pieces of broken bone floating around. One of them was hitting a nerve and sending me crazy. Unfortunately there were no facilities aboard to do anything about it. No anaesthetics etc; The only thing that deadened the pain was pint size mugs of Navy rum. I have to admit, the ship was not the only thing that was floating.
On arrival at the Kola Inlet were told, as usual, that the ship that was to take us home had not arrived. Surprise!, surprise! We were then transferred to waiting ambulances to take us to hospital. I was actually in an ambulance ready to take off, when someone shouted for us to stay where we were. They

took us from the ambulance and put us on board an American Naval ship that was along side a wharf. The ship was the USS Tuscaloosa, a heavy battle cruiser. (It was the American Flag Ship during 'D' day) We were told that the Captain saw from the bridge what he thought were Russian wounded. WE looked like it, because most of us had had our hair removed because it was falling out in handfuls, due no doubt to the scalp being frozen during out time in the lifeboat. However someone told him who we were and why we were being taken to the hospital. He gave instructions to get as many as possible aboard as he was leaving for the U.K that afternoon.

I cannot say how many were loaded, but there were stretchers and bodies (live) in every little space they could find. I was one of the lucky ones, because I was put in the sick bay. I was still having a lot of pain in my hand, so after an examination by the doctor, he said he would remove the loose pieces of bone. Not long after we sailed, I was taken to the theatre and given an injection of Sodium Pentothal. This drug was the latest on the market. (What a difference from the old Ether) I remember the doctor telling me to count to forty, the last number I got to was five. This same drug was later used as a truth drug.

I woke later in the day with a painful hand, but glad to say a bearable pain. I also noticed some new faces in the sick bay and was told that they were from the German raider 'Ulm'. 53 had been picked up. I never found out if they had been adrift or if we had sunk their ship.

The officers and crew aboard the Tuscaloosa were a great bunch of guys, almost on a par with the Russians who had looked after us in both hospitals. The reason I make distinction is simple. The Americans had all the latest drugs and equipment, which they gave unstintingly, but the Russians worked miracles with almost nothing.

We arrived in Scotland, there was a tremendous hype. We were hounded by news media from the ship until we were placed in ambulances and taken to Hirmyars hospital. Unfortunately, somehow in all the excitement between the time I left the ship and arrived at the hospital, I lost the mandolin, a pearl handled.45 automatic pistol which had been given to me by an American seaman in Murmansk and some Hersheys chocolate bars given to me by the sick bay crew. Welcome Home!

There isn't very much more that I can say about the voyage, ships, or crews, obviously there is a lot more, but, I can only say what I saw and felt. I realise that most of this is self orientated, and some of it in retrospect, because of it abbreviated.

Jim Campbell.

The ironical thing about all this is, had the SS Ballot crew remained on board, they would have survived, for a Russian tug went to her aid and towed her into Murmansk!

* * * * * *

Some years after the war, a lifeboat, containing the bodies of four British Merchant seamen, floated in the Gulf Stream into the Kola Inlet, which had been their original destination. The Russians buried those bodies on the shore and erected a stone monument where the boat landed. The boat had obviously been caught up in the ice, and after some years, when the ice melted enough for the boat to be released and float away.

Granite monument erected by the Russians to the memory of the four British seamen washed up on the shores of the Kola inlet some years after the war

Chapter 41

TO SAVE A MANS LIFE

When a merchant seaman in a ship in convoy was taken ill with acute peritonitis he was give only twelve hours to live if an operation was not done. When the signal was received the ships doctor was rowed over in the whaler. The seaman was then put on a stretcher loaded into the whaler and rowed back to the destroyer.
It was 100 miles to port and a gale was increasing in fury, Across the heavy seas the seaman was transferred to H.M.S. **Verdun** which then headed into the gale towards the harbour. With the sea sometimes sweeping the bridge and at times reduced to half speed.
That was at eight bells of the morning watch. Eight and a half hours later, at one bell of the first dog watch, two hours behind schedule because of the heavy going, the **Verdun** steamed at twenty knots past the breakwater to the quayside in the harbour.
Arrangements had been made for an ambulance to be at the quay side, even in the harbour the weather was so bad that the patient could not be transferred to a tender. So the Captain decided to go right alongside the quay. In normal circumstances the destroyer would never have entered the harbour in such weather.
Within six minutes of going alongside the quay **Verdun** was off again to rejoin the convoy.
The operation on the patient was performed immediately and was expected to make a full recovery.

Bob Charles.

H.M.S **Verdun**.

* * * *

H.M.S. WANDERER

As experienced by Alf Floyd

In the Navy one rarely leaves a ship for another without going through barracks. During the war I never spent more than three weeks in barracks, after getting leave entitlements. This time was to be no exception, but it did not worry me for I was never enamoured with the place (Chatham Barracks).

It was usually overcrowded and run by those men that we called 'barrack stantions', this because for the duration of the war, they had nice office jobs and were able each night to go to their homes in the area. At this time it was probably the most unpleasant. There were air - raids and all personnel had to go underground into the 'tunnel'. Sleeping in the tunnel was most uncomfortable to say the least, it was smelly due to bad ventilation. At first I decided to take my chance and sleep in the barrack room where there was plenty of room, given that most had billets in the tunnel. On one occasion the raids came too close for comfort, and I did spend some time in the tunnel. It seems in retrospect that I had become more conditioned to air raids and the events of war. Nevertheless, I still get funny feelings in my stomach when I hear a siren. This is because, out here in the hills overlooking Melbourne the siren is used to call the volunteer fire fighters when there is a bush fire.

This time I managed to get a weekend leave pass and decided to go to Edinburgh. Rail travel in those days was tiresome due to the air-raid warnings and the like. I was returning to Chatham, the train was held up several times. This meant that I arrived in London too late to get my connection to Chatham. I had to spend time in the centre of London to await the first train out, which was the paper train. What to do? I went to the canteen that I had often used at London Bridge. It was non-existent having been the subject of many air-raids. However I decided to cross London Bridge to find somewhere to stop. There was a raid on and the searchlights were sweeping the sky. I got half way across London Bridge when the bombs came down rather close. I retreated to the London Bridge Station to the drone of the bombers. The station was full and the steps leading down to the platform were covered with human beings of all sizes. I reached the platform to find that people of both sexes and all ages were sleeping up to within twelve inches of the platforms edge. The canvas toilet facilities were inadequate by far for so many people and the smell was obnoxious. I only had to spend one night there. I pitied all those who were spending night after night during the Blitz. I eventually reached Chatham in the early hours. I was to again experience air-raids when I reached Liverpool, for that is where I was about to go.

In a few days, I was posted on the drafting board to go to a Flower Class Corvette. They had been introduced to act as convoy escorts and equipped with depth charges. They were rather small an saucer shaped, so they rolled quite a bit. I understood that there was no Engineer Officer on the one I was to go to and I would be the senior engine room rating.

I went off to the drafting office to explain that I was to get a posting nearer to home. There was a huddle in the back room, and eventually the draft to the

Corvette was cancelled and in it's place I was to go to Liverpool to join H.M.S. **Wanderer**.
On arrival at Liverpool, **Wanderer** was at sea and I had to spend some time ashore in the building that used to house Vernon's football pools. There were many of us staying there and the night was spent sleeping on the floor. Lying there I was not too happy as the roof was made of glass. It recalled the story that I had heard of Chatham Barracks in WW1 when survivors were sleeping under the drill shed glass roof.
Wanderer returned to Liverpool on the first of May and I joined her at Gladstone dock. She was due for a boiler clean and each watch had a few day's leave. I didn't get any as it was thought that I had had enough before joining ship. During those eight days Liverpool was heavily bombed, and whilst ashore I witnessed many homeless children and young adults, unwashed, following water tankers to catch a few drops of water from the tankers dripping taps. So many homes had been demolished and many had lost their parents. They lived in air-raid shelters. The worst hit area was Bootle and the dock area where most of the working class lived.
At the time, the aircraft carrier Furious was lying in Gladstone dock, lying at right angles with her were nine destroyers in rows of three. We were the outside of the last three.
The worst night of the bombing was when an ammunition train and Bryant & Mays match factory were hit and set ablaze. I stayed in my hammock trying to remain calm until the shrapnel was rattling on the ships side. I went up top and saw the outside ship of the first three sinking, she had been hit below the water line. The next stick of bombs missed us, but the ship next to us had a fire in the ready use ammunition magazine. I doubt there was any ammunition there as the fire was soon put out. The bombs that missed us went on and hit the dock gate, so we were imprisoned in the dock until a tug came and pulled the gate open. H.M.S. Furious, the main target, remained untouched. She was one of the pre-war carriers and I believe she survived the war.
Eventually we were able to get free and put out to sea, leaving the raging fires of Liverpool in our wake. I was glad to get away, Feeling much safer at sea.
My first trip in **Wanderer** was not to be a happy one, the old V&Ws were never intended for the job in the North Atlantic. Toilets were few and very basic, water for washing had to be pumped from a tank on the upper deck by a semi-rotary pump. Sometimes the sea was coming over the deck and getting a bucket of water was hazardous.
Convoys were usually in three groups, slow, medium, and fast. Fast was best for us as the speed was about fifteen knots. We had quite a few of those,

which were mostly troop convoys going South. Most though would be slow, where we would go to 20 degrees West and then return with another home bound convoy.
With all the additions of war aboard this ship. Radar Degaussing and the Acoustic hammer, meant that the space for living (which had never been a priority in the V&Ws) had been reduced even further. It was not unusual to have a foot descend on to the mess table whilst having a morning cup of tea. Once a foot landed alongside my cup of tea followed by the rest of the body, he immediately grabbed some bread and started to eat it, not the done thing in the peace time navy, then we were very fussy about cleanliness and no one would handle food without visiting the bathroom. I remonstrated with this stoker, but he just ignored me. So I said "Get your cap and be outside the office" this was normally sufficient to make the point and then the incident is then usually forgotten, but not this stoker, he grabbed his hat and went to the office. I got a dressing down from the Warrant Officer for being too particular. I learned that I was looked upon as and interloper, as most of those on the mess deck had been together for a long time. Even though I was senior rating on the mess I kept to myself and vowed to never again discipline a rating. That was my first and my last.
At this time the U-boats were hunting in 'Wolf Packs'. They would follow the convoy until there was a break in the escorts pattern, then at night they would surface and sink a ship before diving and scampering away. We were powerless in that situation, as depth charging endangered those survivors in the water.
The convoy screen was really insufficient. We being Senior Officer Zig Zagged ahead of the convoy whilst another did the same astern.
On each flank were corvettes or the American four stackers. These U.S. destroyers were too heavy and rolled badly in heavy seas. We received fifty of them in exchange for bases in the Indies and other places. The best use for one of them was at St Nazaire where Cambeltown breached the lock and was blown up.
On one of these trips we received a 'hurry up' signal to go to the assistance of one of theses American destroyers, which had a Dutch crew. It had been hit and was sinking. She actually sank as we came up from astern. It was dark and we could hear the cries of those in the water. We did rescue some of them but many were lost. It was after that event that we were issued with battery operated red lights which clipped to our life belts.
One of my earlier trips in **Wanderer** was to the North where we expected to go to Iceland. We left Liverpool and steamed between the islands of the coast of Scotland to Loch Ewe where we anchored for the night and refuelled. We

left Loch Ewe and steamed out into the Atlantic though the Faroe's and on to Iceland escorting an outward bound convoy. Somewhere around the Denmark Straights we took over a homeward bound convoy designated SC31 The position of this convoy was just South of where the Hood was sunk, which put us in the path of the Bismarck which was making South after sinking the Hood.
Hood and the Prince of Wales were patrolling South when H.M.S. Suffolk and Norfolk sighted the Bismarck. The Hood, Prince of Wales accompanied by six destroyers steamed to intercept.
On that fateful day I had the first watch in the engine room. As I came off watch at 0400, the torpedo men were lowering the guard rails and getting the torpedo tubes ready I asked what was up and was told that we were in the path of the Bismarck. I did not worry as we knew that the Hood was on her way to intercept, we all felt that nothing could stop the Hood. I turned in, and during the middle watch, at 0600 I awakened and everyone was saying that the Hood had gone. It was unbelievable that our great unsinkable ship had in fact been sunk. So it was that Hood had intercepted and opened fire at 0540 and by 0600 she was no more. Actually when I came off watch and we were getting ready to have a go, the Hood was still in the game and Bismarck was trying to shake off the two cruisers that had been shadowing her though out the night. By 0800 we were only about 100 miles from the Bismarck.
On our way back to the UK we passed the force on its way back to Scapa Flow after Bismarck had also been sunk. We received a signal from the carrier Victorious in reply to our congratulatory signal saying how lucky we had been. It was pinned on the notice board for all to see. I was devastated when I learned that there had been only three survivors, and my brother was not one of them. 94 Officers and 1321 ratings had perished.
It had taken the entire Home Fleet, plus Force H from Gibraltar, the Fleet Air Arm together with Catalina's from Coastal Command to finally find, and sink the Bismarck. Her accompanying ship the Prinz Eugen managed to get clear and returned to Brest unscathed. Personally I think that was a great fete of seamanship. Bismark had sunk in flames, the crew fought to the last singing Sieg Heils. Survivors were few. So, Hood was lost, Prince of Wales damaged, H.M.S. Mashona was sunk on the return journey. The position of the graves of those who went down with the Hood is 63.20 degrees North 31.50 degrees West.
On a convoy returning from Freetown, Sierra Leone, I was asleep in my hammock when there was an enormous crash and the ship shook. I was out of my hammock and half way up the ladder before I had time to think, this was it, I thought, we have been hit. To get out of our lower mess deck we had to go through a manhole just wide enough for one man at a time. Despite the

swiftness with which I had got to the ladder I was not the first. In fact we had not been hit, when I got up on deck I found that we were on the top of a U-boat, sending it to the bottom. We had torn our Asdic dome in doing so and were lucky not to have taken in water. We were credited with the sinking and the Skipper received the D.S.O.

Nearly every convoy during 1941-42 was fraught with danger. In most cases the sea was the next big worry for the Atlantic is more often rough than it is calm. From the time we left Liverpool Bay and caught up with the convoy, we were on the alert. I rarely changed clothing until we left the outward bound and raced to rendezvous with the returning convoy. It always seemed safer then to change clothing. Life belts were our constant companions.

All the glamour of the M.T.B's was gone and in its stead was the misery of a small ship in stormy waters. The food was kept in wire cages on the upper deck and was usually covered in salt spray. Cooking was difficult to say the least, tinned meat and vegetables were the norm with corned beef as an alternative. Little wonder that I made a bee-line to an eating place that I got to know in Lime Street, to taste real food without the sea spray.

On our return I was able to get home to see my distraught parents. My Father could not believe that my Brother Charlie had gone, and when an impostor claiming to be a survivor, Dad went off to meet him. Of course we knew that there was no chance of anyone surviving in those bitterly cold and rough waters.

The sinking of our merchant ships were far too frequent, the U-boats were having a 'Happy Time' sinking so many of our ships that Britain was on the verge of running out of food.

It was vital to find a way of protecting our convoys against the U-boats or Britain would starve, long range German bombers and Focke Wolf Condors were able to give the precise position of the convoy's to the Wolf Packs. It was necessary to have air protection. One day I witnessed the first flight of Sea Hurricanes being catapulted from the foc'sle of a merchant ship. I thought it was Audacity, but later found out that it was in fact 'Maplin' I remember the pilot's name Lt, Everett. He had to ditch his plane and did so alongside us. He was quickly picked up. That was the beginning of the escort carrier, of which the Audacity was one. Sadly she was sunk in December of that year.

The rescue of survivors and ship's boats and the pitiful state that some of them were in when we reached them, some had been adrift in open boats for as many as ten days made me feel then, and still do, that the Merchant Service never received the recognition that they deserved. Some of their ships had been retrieved from the scrap heaps and should never had been at sea. A six inch gun mounted on their deck made them prey for the U-boats.

My last trip on **Wanderer** was tricky, the constant dropping of depth charges had shook the condensers badly, so much so that the tubes were leaking, so that the salt water was contaminating the fresh water in the boilers. To correct this we had to get away from the convoy routs and shut down. We had a flower class corvette circling round us while we in the engine room took the inspection plates off the condenser and the E.R.A. Plugged the leaks. It was only a temporary repair. When we got nearer home we did a few ahead and astern movements, only to find that we still had problems. It was then decided that we would have to go to Chatham for a major refit. It was to be a long job, so, I, and most of the ships company returned to Barracks.

May 1942.

H.M.S. Worcester was in East India Dock, Poplar, London where she had been repaired after the 'Channel Dash'.

On leaving Poplar Docks she headed for Scapa Flow for trails etc; In August **Worcester** received orders to rendezvous with H.M. Ships Ashanti, Victorious and Rodney and escort them back to Scapa. It was during this voyage to rendezvous we sailed through the Minches in a howling gale, pitching, rolling, corkscrewing and hitting a milestone every inch of the way. Off the North West coast of Ireland, the sea was so rough that a member of the crew was washed overboard. Lifeboats were manned, but we were unable to rescue our shipmate. **Worcester** soon rendezvoused with her charges, it was then that the Victorious decided to do flying exercises. 'Curses' **Worcester** was detailed 'Crash Boat'.

Back to Scapa from where we carried out U-boat sweeps and patrols after which we then headed for Iceland with a passenger on board. A regulating P.O. (Crusher) bound for H.M.S. Norfolk. Our crew were at day defence stations and this 'crusher' went round the ship shouting "Put that cigarette out". It was not long before he was missing. - On the mess deck with his head over a bucket.

On arrival at Hafnarfjordhur we were alongside the Duke of York, Whilst alongside the D.O.Y. No;2 Boiler flashed up and a pall of black smoke blew across the D.O.Y's superstructure. **Worcester** soon received a signal from the Admiral stating that if there was a repeat performance, the **Worcester** crew would have to scrub down the superstructure.

A large number of the Home Fleet were also in the fjord, K.G.V., Norfolk, Cumberland, plus a number of destroyers. The Norfolk incidentally challenged the **Worcester** to a game of darts. Three legs of 1001. A team was hurriedly recruited and went aboard the Norfolk. Our team beat them!

Liberty men had a few hours in Reykjavik, made a few purchases and drunk a few bottles of beer. One per cent alcohol. Iceland was a prohibition country.
Worcester left the fjord and dropped anchor in Seydhisfjordhur on the East Coast, this was for the purpose of taking on fresh food. All that came aboard was crates of tinned potatoes - two crates per mess. Quite a number of these tins were rancid and there must be a trail of tins from Seydhisfjordhur to Spitzbergen.
Worcester rendezvoused with two oil tankers and joined the 'Home Fleet' escorting the Russian Convoy QP14. This convoy was bringing home survivors of that disastrous convoy PQ17 and had sailed from Murmansk on the 13th September. On the 20th the minesweeper 'Leda' was torpedoed and sunk, later that day H.M.S. Somali was also torpedoed, she however did not sink immediately, and was taken in tow by H.M.S. Ashanti. However she broke in two during rough weather and sunk after four days of being towed.
The **Worcester** was ordered to sink a merchantman whose bows and stern had been blown off, this vessel was carrying a cargo of timber which was preventing her from sinking, thus the **Worcester** had to sink her by gunfire. This ship was the Grey Ranger which had been torpedoed by U-435 which had penetrated the screen and sank two other ships on the 22nd September. On the 23rd a Liberator of Coastal Command found and sank the U-253. The convoy arrived at Loch Ewe on the 26th.
Next a signal was received saying that the enemy, in the shape of the Von Hipper was out from her Norwegian fjord. I thought 'Here we go again, if it is not the Scharnhorst and Co; It's the Von Hipper.
December 1942 Worcester, was in action again in the English Channel against two German supply ships, plus escorts. This was to be my last spell of action in the **Worcester.** I left her in Pompey harbour. I was on a stretcher. A fine S.B.A. I turned out to be, knocked out in the first round.
There was a rating who lived in the city of Worcester, he was severely wounded in, I believe, the right arm.

H.L.T. Davis. S.B.A.

* * * * *

JUMPING JACK SKEATS
H.M.S. WILD SWAN

Boats, (destroyers to the ill informed) whilst being the eyes of the Fleet at sea, ranging far ahead of the lumbering battlewaggons, they lose their glory in harbour and get relegated to far away berths where no one can see them, or are directed to the buoys - hence my tale.

Tying up to a buoy can be a simple matter in fair weather with a good coxswain and some helpful forecastle men, but can be rather traumatic when conditions are not favourable or when the skipper has decided to give some junior officer some experience, as well he might, so here goes.

Jack wearing the same overalls and plimsolls, joined the motor boat via the boom and Jacob's ladder with a Bosun's bag hitched around his waist and is taken to the buoy. This is a spinning top shaped chunk of metal with a large heavy ring in the middle supporting a cable which disappears down a hole leading to three or so spread anchors. So far so good, but it is not generally known that the dock yard matey's are prone to making a boob, by letting the buoys to seagulls for their daily conferences, and there has been a very long conference this day which had left the surface rather sticky. Gingerly Jack holds on to the ring waiting for the boat to approach and the heaving line to be thrown at him, it is always thrown at him to make sure it gets there. Meanwhile a fair old chop builds up and the water is slopping everywhere making a foothold pretty difficult. Here comes the Monkey Fist, the line is caught and held, now the picking up rope which is secured to the ring of the buoy by shackling it back on itself. Life now gets interesting as the Captain takes up the slack and feels the weight of the boat which has drifted away on the tide and causes the buoy to tilt with one side a foot or so under water. Jack slithers to the other side, one arm up in the air and hold on to a passing cloud. The Captain turns slowly to bring the boat up to the buoy, an event which annoys the picking up rope and makes it heated. It grinds, it thumps, the strands begin to strengthen, the jute heart is forced out and begins to smoke, Jack dreams of a wire necklace. Gently she comes up until the hawse pipe is overhead and then the fun really starts as the buoy, freed of part of the weight of the ring and cable, begins to spin. Have you ever felt like a mouse on a treadmill? I have and was forced to say uncharitable things about seagulls. Anyway down comes the anchor cable, shackled on, with pin and pellet in pace, exchanged for the picking up rope and away we go, mission completed - nearly.

Sadly the skipper has pulled rank on me and gone ashore with the motor boat, the men on the forecastle have vanished, it is now beginning to rain and seagulls are dive bombing me in an unfriendly manner - they want their conference table back. I shout, I scream, but all to no avail, one moment it all depends on me, the next I am the forgotten man suffering from BO Nothing for it but to laboriously drag my little self up the cable, link, by link, slide under the guard rail and drip my way back to the mess deck.

Hello! Jack they say, where have you been? We thought you had gone ashore so we didn't save you any tea... Roll on my twelve PLEASE roll on my twelve, this buoy jumping is ageing me beyond my twenty years.

* * * * * *

H.M.S. Wild Swan
Or
The Frantic Duck
As she was so affectionately known.
* *

Wild Swan had finished her escort duty with a convoy on the afternoon of the 17th June 1942. Late that evening she was steaming at 15 knots through the Bay of Biscay on their way home. The crew were looking forward to some shore leave, when suddenly one of the lookouts shouted 'Aircraft'. A German Focke Wolf was heading for them, **Wild Swan** immediately went to action stations and the gunners opened fire with their twelve pounder and Pom poms. Their fire was so accurate that the aircraft turned and made off. The crew remained at action stations knowing that their position will have been relayed to the Luftwaffe. It was not to be long before twelve JU88's were sighted. **Wild Swan** was just passing a flotilla of Spanish fishing vessels and as the JU88's came into attack she opened fire with such devastating effect that two of the JU88's collided and burst into flames, one crashed into the sea but the other crashed into one of the Spanish trawlers. The remaining aircraft continued the attack and the first bombs straddled the unfortunate **Wild Swan**.

The little ship jumped and heaved, and then slowly steadied. The violence of the explosion had brought down the mast, flooded the engine room and the after boiler room, and jammed the helm hard over. Although the engines had stopped, the ship carried way and turned in a great circle. Helpless she drifted on to one of the Spanish trawlers and sank it.

Helpless as she was the **Wild Swan** was far from finished and the twelve pounder guns crew kept up a devastating barrage and brought two more of the German aircraft crashing into the sea.

By now the German aircraft had become very wary of their gallant little opponent, but the ship was in a very bad way, decks were littered with debris, and she was listing heavily to port. Worse still, the crew could hear an ominous creaking and cracking that could only mean one thing, that their ship was breaking up, disregarding this, they still fought on, when another aircraft came sweeping in to the attack they opened up simultaneously with the twelve pounder and the Pom-poms and the Lewis guns, the bombs burst just off the starboard quarter. However the bomber had been hit and just scraped over the ship and crashed into the sea near to another of the Spanish fishing vessels on the port quarter.

The last stick of bombs had done more underwater damage, and the ship started to crack in half. Members of the crew worked frantically among the wreckage, rigging up a jury aerial in order to send out a distress signal. It was beginning to get dark so the Captain realising that they could not hold on much longer gave the order to abandon ship.

The Spanish trawlers had disappeared, so the destroyers crew and the Spanish fishermen they had rescued from the rammed trawler, launched the whaler and motor boat and filled them to capacity. The remainder took to the Carley floats. They pulled away from the ship and watched her slowly sink. **Wild Swan** although mortally wounded had fought off her attackers and inflicted destruction on half their number. The survivors were picked up by another of the same class of destroyer, H.M.S. **Vansittart.**

Chapter 42

Convoy Maniac - RB 1

By James H. Reed

H.M.S. Vanoc

This story covers just a few days, a little more than a week, but the events of that short period late in September 1942 and the start of an early winter in the North Atlantic must forever be remembered by those who survived the crossing, and were extremely lucky to do so. At the same time we remember those who paid the supreme price.

As far as the escorts are concerned, the events started at Halifax, Nova Scotia.

Most of the escorts operating on these convoys would escort the convoy to mid Atlantic where they would pass the responsibility to other escorts operating from the shores of the U.K. Because very few of the escorts had the fuel capacity to round up stragglers, hunt for U-boats and dash to the rescue of those whose ships had been sunk.

The Atlantic at this time of the year there could be gales and the ensuing very rough seas or fog and all these ships wore the well worked look that comes only from days, and weeks of continual fighting against these elements. Paint would be worn off, and the grey paint nearly white from the salt.

Two such ships that day were the old V&W class destroyers **Vanoc** and **Veteran** both about 25 years old, but still very sound and ideal efficient ships for the job.

There was always good comradeship between these ship's crews when on shore leave or alongside, sometimes sharing sessions of tombola or just a smoke and a yarn.

The crew of the **Vanoc**, cleaning up after a spell of convoying, watched as the 'Old Man', Commander Churchill crossed one or two ships to come back on board after a visit to Naval H.Q. Ashore. Needless to say a few good natured remarks passed round the lads "What's he volunteers for now" and so on. Of course these remarks were always made discreetly but enough for the 'Old Man' to hear every word, but he never let on, although he must have chuckled inwardly. Every man respected him. He was one of the old breed of no nonsense Naval Commanders and was old enough to be the father of most of us. Also he would suffer sea sickness with the best of us.

Shortly after the Captains arrival on board, the Bosun's mate piped 'clear lower deck, fall in aft', an order reserved for very rare and special occasions. The response was immediate, and in no time a tightly packed circle was formed around the Captain who was standing on a hatch. No dock workers were allowed on board, just the crew.

The Captain then proceeded, in as few words as possible to tell us that the **Veteran** and ourselves, **Vanoc**, were to go back home to the U.K., that a few hours shore leave would be taken in two watches for shopping purposes and above all, not to mention anything to anyone ashore. Secrecy was an accepted fact throughout the war, but we always were reminded that 'Careless Talk Cost Lives'.

One serious and main factor to be considered by these escorts crossing the North Atlantic was the need for maximum oil fuel. The water tank that was used for washing, cleaning etc; had to be sacrificed for fuel to give extra endurance. This left just one small tank of about 1500 gallons for food and drinking only. No luxuries like washing and shaving or cleaning. The only access to this water was a small tank in the galley which was restricted to meal times, at other times the stop cock was locked.

Needless to say similar preparations were going on in the **Veteran.** It must be remembered that the complement of these very overcrowded ships could be up to 170 officers and men, which gave no leeway in the efforts to conserve fresh water and indeed fuel oil, over several days of appalling weather.

The convoy, at that time called 'Honeymoon'- remembering the thousands of American honeymoon couples who had sailed in these ships in peace time, left Halifax at 1100 on Wednesday September 16th 1942, bound for St Johns Newfoundland. The convoy consisted of eight ships, the original convoy was to be of eleven ships. However one was totally destroyed by fire the other two were found to be unsuitable for a deep sea crossing.

At the given sailing time **Vanoc** and **Veteran** slipped their moorings and with screw turning got under way with the usual good hearted remarks from our sister escorts ringing in our ears. As we cleared harbour and approached the open sea we saw for the first time the convoy we were to escort home to the U.K.

Prior to departure to St Johns, the escort commanders and ships captains attended a briefing at Naval H.Q. At this meeting the official name of the convoy became R.B.1. The previous name 'Honeymoon' became obsolete. The code name became 'Maniac'. At that time Captain Beckett said that although the code word was very appropriate, he considered it should be in the plural. One can only wonder who could sardonically and cynically suggest such a name.

The convoy departed from St Johns at 1400 on the 21st September and formed into three columns, a total of eight ships with two destroyer escort. To the seasoned crews of convoy escorts of all types of cargo and troop transports, the eight ships of RB1 presented something we had not seen before, not cargo ships, but ships of high superstructure, two with twin funnels and the others with high single funnels. From a distance, in a haze or at night or a U-boats periscope just above sea level could quite easily recognise these ships as large troopships, some resembling our more famous liners. This illusion was soon shattered as we came closer and saw that they were in fact coastal or river pleasure boats. By no stretch of the imagination would ant seafarer consider them to be suitable for an Atlantic crossing near winter. However someone had, and all the ships had undergone considerable work to 'whaleback' with heavy timbers and the most vulnerable parts of the superstructure. These ships carried no cargo, no passengers, in ballast, to reduce the top hamper and it later emerged that they were manned entirely by volunteers from Coastlines Shipping, Liverpool who had come over on the Queen Mary, 500 officers and men.

Within 36 hours of sailing the convoy was in the area of the German wolf packs. Between the 22nd and the 26th September **Vanoc** received at least 29 U-boat sighting reports and there were 10 reports of U-boats making sighting reports of a convoy.

RB1 was sighted and reported by U-404 who was accompanied by U-380 and U-91 who were on patrol in the area. The report indicated that the convoy was a fast troop transport convoy. The German U-boat Command instructed the Vorwarts group of 10 U-boats to close and engage, also group Pfiel of seven U-boats to proceed to the scene on completion of operations against convoy SC100.

The Germans were completely fooled by the ship's profile, and considered the convoy so important that the high command sent 17 U-boats to attack. In fact the Germans identified the ships to be of the Queen Mary Class. **Vanoc's** Commander Churchill, sent the following signal to C in C Western Atlantic. 'RB1 was shadowed from ahead all last night and suspect shadowing continues today Thursday 24th. Escorts have in sufficient fuel to carry out putting down sweep. Evasive tactics proved useless in extreme visibility with full moon. Air cover would be appreciated as soon as possible'.

Friday 25th. Fourteen U-boats had reported as being in contact with the convoy and at 1337 local time U-216 attacked and sank the twin funnelled ship SS, Boston, some of the survivors were picked up by **Veteran**, and others by the rescue ship New Bedford an unconfirmed report gave the **Veteran** as having saved 48 survivors.

The two escorts were kept busy trying to keep the U-boats at bay and keeping the convoy together, this was not helped by one of the merchant ships breaking down and going round in circles when it eventually rejoined the convoy at about 1830, the convoy was reformed with seven ships in line abreast with **Veteran** to port and **Vanoc** to starboard. Later **Veteran** signalled to **Vanoc**. 'Suggest we change stations, as you seem to be getting all the action and getting short of depth charges. **Vanoc** agreed, I am short of fuel, I will take station ahead and you astern.

The next attack came at 2057 when U-96 attacked the second of the two funnelled ships, SS New York, the torpedoes caused a heavy explosion which started fires, she remained afloat for some time, but was attacked again. The convoy became disorganised and scattered. The escorts fired flares to force the U-boats to submerge out of sight. **Veteran** again stood by to take on survivors, whilst **Vanoc** proceeded to attempt to reform and protect the convoy in the darkness **Veteran** reported that she was proceeding to rejoin the convoy and that she had 28 survivors aboard. The lookouts on both of the escorts were continuously searching for the tell tale signs of periscopes. The U-boats were blatantly signalling to each other information to attack, four more attacks were made but all were unsuccessful.

At 0736 the next morning U-404 (Von Bulow) fired a spread of three torpedoes. Two found their target **Veteran** blew up and must have sunk within seconds for there were no survivors. Vanoc was at this time was far over the horizon, trying to reform the convoy. H.M.S. **Veteran** Lieutenant Commander T.H. Garwood had a complement of Nine officers and 150 men and was believed to be carrying 28 survivors from the New York and 48 from the Boston.

C in C Western Atlantic has sent a signal to HMS Sabre, HMS Scimitar and HMS Saladin which read "If you have completed refuelling, proceed to reinforce convoy RB1, giving the position of the now depleted convoy.

On 1000 hours on Saturday 26th September **Vanoc** sighted a single ship ahead and identified her as the President Warfield and at the same Saladin and Scimitar were sighted and proceeded to escort her, they were joined by the **Vanoc**. A coastal command aircraft came into sight and was asked to carry out a search for the **Veteran** without success. All W/T signals to the stricken ship also failed.

To the crew of the **Vanoc** coming out of the night action, all that was seen of the convoy was this single funnel ship and many thought that the two of us were the only survivors. However, the Germans had not given up yet, although many of the U-boats had been outpaced and left behind. The Yorktown had decided to leave the convoy and sail independently. At 2025 on September 26th she was sighted by U-619. The U-boat attacked, obtaining a torpedo hit on the port side immediately beneath the bridge. This caused a complete collapse of all the superstructure of the wooden bridge and everything forward, the engines stopped and the ship tore itself apart and sank within three minutes. The survivors in the water in extremely difficult conditions managed to man four rafts and a waterlogged boat they had managed to right and bale out. These survivors had to endure this ordeal from 2025 on Saturday 26th until 1900 on Monday 28th of September when they were picked up by the destroyer Sardonix after being sighted by probably a Very Long Range Liberator. However of the complement of 62, 18 men lost their lives.

So with hindsight and completely unknown at the time, the state of Convoy 'Maniac' on the night of Saturday September 26th was;- One destroyer H.M.S. **Vanoc,** five river boats, Northland, Southland, President Warfield, New Bedford and Naushan. The losses were H.M.S. **Veteran**, SS Boston, New York, and Yorktown. With the loss of life of 302 souls.

Jim Reeds opinion of the 'Maniac' convoy;-

I was there at the time on the only surviving escort, H.M.S. **Vanoc**. I have always had misgivings about the true reason for this convoy and am in disagreement with what has been accepted of its story.

First, you must remember that the year was 1942 and the month of September, the start of the season of equinoctial gales. What was more important, it was in 1942 and the latter months that the North Atlantic convoy system was at its most grave time, and only a whisker away from total collapse and destruction. Over 1000 merchant ships had been sunk and the German U-boat command had withdrawn U-boats from other areas to concentrate on the destruction of the North Atlantic convoy system. Over 160 U-boats were operating in the Atlantic.

Two more set backs must also be considered: The Black Hole, an area of over 300 square miles of the convoy routes, had no air cover and gave the U-boats an enormous advantage of being able to press home their attacks. The other set back was the fact that in about April 1942 the first German milch - cows entered the Atlantic. These oil tanker U-boats lying some 500 miles north-west of Bermuda, could refuel many U-boats, avoiding their return to their bases in France or Germany.

Convoy 'Maniac' was indeed a decoy convoy which invited destruction in the Atlantic to safeguard another great convoy of vessels laden with munitions of war which were desperately wanted during World War Two. The eight ships engaged in trading on the Great Lakes sailed in convoy intended to decoy enemy U-boats away from another great munitions and troop convoy which set sail from America at the same time. The plan succeeded and the latter got through without loss.

* * * *

HMS Veteran
Sunk with total loss of life, including over eighty survivors, whilst escorting the decoy convoy 'Maniac' RB1 torpedoed by U-404 on 26th September 1942

*We did not always get the U-boat,
but we did get some 'big eats'*

The sinking of H.M.S. Veteran, by Admiral Von Bulow Commander of U- 404

You will be interested to hear something about the convoy, now known to be designated as RB1.
On 21st September 1942 order to U-404 of which I was in command, and six other U-boats received orders to dispose in line north to south to intercept an east going convoy. The knowledge of this departure may have come out of secret channels and the observation of British and American wireless traffic.
On the 13th September first contact was made by one of the U-boats in a northern position of the line, but because of weather conditions and skilful manoeuvring of the convoy, contact was often lost. No attacks could be launched before the 25th when during the day and night the British steamers Boston and New York were torpedoed and sunk by two U-boats, whilst U-404 was handicapped with temporary breakdown of one of the diesel engines. The two big steamers I was attacking on the 26th were likely stragglers of the convoy shepherded by this destroyer. I fired three torpedoes but as I did so **Veteran** ran across my sight. Having fired I immediately submerged and heard two explosions and noise indicating the break up of a ship. I did not know it was the destroyer and only learnt this later, and also was not aware until recently that there were no survivors.
One incident you might like to hear, was when at daybreak on the 1st June, some 300 miles off the coast of Bermuda; U-404 Attacked the American freighter West Notus by gunfire. The risk to meet an adversary much superior in artillery had to be taken because the shortage of fuel, which would have needed to take up a position ahead. Opening fire the U-404 torpedo launching had the good fortune to obtain a hit on the bridge by one of the fist shells and flames spread out. Very effective fire by their 5inch calibre gun was returned with some near misses and splinters which caused some damage to us, as we were running away and zig zagging. The suddenly the ship was abandoned and the boats were lowered. Two of the boats got away in good order, the third was sucked with water and motionless. One of theses men was ordered to come aboard (he was the chief mate). I welcomed him with a handshake and the words' I am sorry but this is war. I hope it will soon be over and I am sure we will be very good friends' We had a long conversation about the ship, the cargo and the gunfight whilst we were towing the damaged lifeboat to the other boats that were now under sail. Returning to the burning ship was found another man in a life jacket, picked him up and took care of his wounded leg and delivered him to the other life boats.

The enclosed copies of cuttings from Ohio newspaper dated about the end of July 1942 was sent to me by a Mr Ritzenthaler who later with a Mr Sherlock visited me in Germany. This rescue work was a matter of course and very simple humanity, but it may be of interest in the light of propaganda against the Germans during the war years. I have never heard a 'Hurrah' by the crew when a ship had been torpedoed and sunk.

*****

When I received the news that my old ship was lost at sea, I was shattered. I could hardly believe that the ship on which I had served for almost two years was no more. I was even more shattered when I learnt that there were no survivors.
I had left the **Veteran** in March 1942, when I was drafted to the gunnery school at Royal Naval Barracks Chatham to qualify as G.I.
Shortly after I heard of her loss, I received a letter from the wife of one of my **Veteran** shipmates, asking if I could find out whether her husband, Yeoman of signals Berie Wiltshire was on board and therefore one of the casualties. She told me that she had received a letter from him saying that he was in hospital in Halifax (where the ship was based) and that he had heard that the ship was returning to the U.K. Shortly and that he would do his damnedest to get aboard again before she sailed. Regrettably my enquiries revealed that he did.
It was then that I learnt that there were no survivors, and addition to the ship's company there was a large number of Merchant Navy survivors also on board. **Veteran** had been engaged in picking up survivors when she was torpedoed. Something we had done countless times during my time on her.
You will realise that I had a number of friends on the ship, but my thoughts went out to two in particular, Jock Falconer and Jimmy Mavir, both A.B,'s
My gunlayer and trainer on 'A' gun The former was a three badged AB. Jimmy Mavir was from Carlisle and joined the ship when I did, he was a one badged AB, but like Jock, not interested in further advancement. His main ambition in life was women, and according to his own stories, was very successful.
So ended a story of a ship that I did not want to join, Horrified at what I found when I first went aboard, but which will forever be remembered by me.
On Remembrance Sunday, the old ship **Veteran** is always foremost in my thoughts.

Jack Stokes.

Chapter 43

How Many Lumps of Sugar?

After completing my training at the new barracks at Gosport and also at St Vincent I was drafted to H.M.S. **Windsor.**
She was laying alongside at Parkestone quay near Harwich.
We soon set sail for Rosyth, it was a fairly rough passage, any way I felt rough, so much so that I gave my packet of 20 'Players', with 19 still in it away, That was the end of smoking for me. I found drinking much better. 'An eighteen year old trying to grow up'.
Later we found ourselves in Scapa and preparing to escort two tankers to Spitzbergen in order to fuel North bound convoys to Russia.
Shortly after sailing one of the generators packed up, so there was no heating on the mess decks. As we approached the Arctic circle and among the ice, the ship of course went stone cold and never seemed to warm up.
We (we had **Worcester** in company) took the tankers up the fjord to Spitzbergen where we lowered the whaler and a party went ashore.
They came back with various articles, including boxes of lump sugar. One 'Jolly Jack' had a fur coat and a spear. What he hoped to do with the spear, heaven only knows.
On the way back we met up with a south bound convoy (QP14). The **Worcester** lost a man overboard, also a Tribal class destroyer was sunk (Somali). The sugar was divided among the lads when we got back to Chatham. Unfortunately some of the lads in my mess lost out when the dock yard matey's loosened the pipe gland leading to the 'heads' (toilets) and sprayed the sugar that was left in the box!

* * * * *

November 1942

On the 6th November 1942 **Westcott** along with Boadicea, Hartland and Walney were detailed to enter Oran Harbour, with Hartland and Walney to break through the boom, and discharge troops to take over Oran. **Westcott** had been ordered to remove all confidential material in Gibraltar, and take over the role of Hartland or Walney should one of these fail to make the journey, as one of them was having bother with her engines.
On entering Oran Bay, all was quiet with town lights on and car headlights moving around the roads. When Hartland and Walney crashed through the boom, things changed somewhat, and apart from tracers everywhere, the

Vichy forces on the hill set searchlights swinging around the bay, and opened fire on us with machine gun and heavy guns. Thankfully they missed us but hit the Boadicea with heavy guns, some of the crew were killed and injured, we opened fire on the searchlights, dousing them all. We stayed in the Bay until dawn in case we were needed, but by then both Hartland and Walney had been sunk, but had landed the troops who had taken all the harbour.
Westcott and Boadicea then left for the open sea and were engaged as an escort to a flat top utility carrier, possibly the Argus. Boadicea left us to go to Gibraltar for repairs and land the injured. **Westcott** then joined another destroyer, the Partridge. The carrier was flying off Spitfires and Hurricanes in support of the troops.
8th November we contacted a submarine with our Asdic and followed up with depth charge attacks, after a few minutes, oil and other material floated to the surface. After ensuring that there were no more engine noises or movement of the Ping' for some time, we were awarded the kill, which was later confirmed as the Vichy submarine Actaeon in a position 36 degrees. 48' North and 00 degrees 59' West.
Further duties in the Mediterranean saw us off Oran again, on 8th December 1942, when with Achates, we detected another submarine. This time depth charging brought the sub to the surface. I was with P.O. Jarvis AA 2. I, being a leading Seaman AA 3 on the two pounder Pom-Pom amidships, was the gun layer, he being the trainer and in charge of the gun with the trigger for firing at his discretion. This was the Arginaute, another Vichy submarine. We saw the crew running towards their twelve pounder and trying to get it ready for firing. P.O. Jarvis told A.B. Frame, the loader, to ring the bridge to get the O.K. to open fire. This was given. I was aiming at the base of the conning tower, and many of the crew were in the water calling out. P.O. Jarvis opened fire with about fifteen rounds, this caused the whole crew to jump into the sea. At the same time the Chief Engineer who had been opening the vents to scuttle the boat, appeared at the top of the conning tower. As the shots hit he dived over the opposite side, and I heard that he had broken his neck and died. All the crew were Italian and we kept them in the stoker's mess under armed guard until we arrived back in Gibraltar.
After this we left Gibraltar in December and went to Portsmouth dockyard. I was promoted to Petty Officer during the journey. I had passed in June 1942 with P.O. Jarvis, but he had two badges, and I had only been in the R.N for two years and five months, and was told I was a bit young and would have to wait six months.

Ronald Blacker

THE OLD V&W

The warm sunshine bathed the rock and the harbour below. Occasionally a golden gleam, coming from the face of the rock, marked the windscreen of a turning car climbing the twisting road. Gibraltar seemed to be more crowded with warships than usual, while the commercial harbour contained a vast array of vessels of all kinds. It was **November 1942** and the great battle that had been raging for a fortnight in the Western Desert was over, and Rommel was in full retreat. It did seem that someone at last had beaten Rommel, and looking around the harbour at the Naval might assembled there, we wondered what was to be the next move.

During the first dog watch our sailing orders came aboard. "Being in all respects ready for sea, H.M.S. **Venomous** will proceed at 2300hrs" went the familiar Naval prose. As soon as we cleared the harbour, with the light of Algeciras twinkling on our starboard beam, the Captain spoke to the ships company over the internal relay system. We were about to take part in operation 'Torch', which called for simultaneous Anglo-American landings in French North Africa on the morning of November the 8th. A prerequisite for the success of the operation was the quick capture of the three large ports. Algiers, Oran and Casablanca. Our part in the 'Torch' operation was to meet at sea two large depot ships, H.M.S. Hecla and H.M.S. Vindictive which were to be the base ships at Algiers and Oran and, in company with another destroyer, H.M.S Marne, to escort them safely to their respective ports. Obviously this was a important if not spectacular role in 'Torch' and quite likely to be uneventful. But the Captain warned us that after the initial landings on November the 8th, every U-boat in the Mediterranean and Eastern Atlantic would be whistled up to attack our convoy.

The two depot ships had already sailed from Cape Town a week previously and we were to rendezvous with them near the Canaries.

On November the 8th in the forenoon we met the depot ships coming from the South. The two destroyers then turned about, stationed themselves one on either side and proceeded Northwards towards the Strait of Gibraltar.

The large convoy and its heavy escort (of which the two depot ships had been a part) soon drew ahead of us and disappeared. We continued our more leisurely course, the two big ships with their escorts. The Hecla we knew from earlier days of the war in the North Atlantic, when she had been the depot ship in Hvalfjord, Iceland. We had often gone alongside Hecla and she had provided us with fresh provisions, deliciously white bread, cinema shows and skilled technicians to deal with our engine room defects. H.M.S. Marne

was a brand new destroyer that we had not encountered previously, and we in **Venomous** felt rather shabby and outdated in or 24 year old ship.
Later that day we listened to the first B.B.C news of the landings. The British landings at Algiers and Oran had succeeded after initial setbacks, but the Americans seemed to be making slower progress at Casablanca. Meanwhile, we moved northwards at a moderate speed as we were timed to arrive about five days after the first landings. We felt comfortably detached from the sterner business going on at the ports, but were very much on our guard. Obviously two destroyers provided a very incomplete antisubmarine screen and the enemy had been attacking in 'Wolf Packs'.
By November the 11th we were level with Casablanca, about 40 miles out. We wondered how the American landing was going on. The news that day had mentioned that a French battleship in the dockyard was offering strenuous resistance to the Americans. We were too far away to see anything.
At about 2330hrs there were two bright flashes from the Hecla followed by a heavy explosion. Almost simultaneously the radar and asdic cabinets were calling the bridge. Radar reported the decreasing size of the echo from Hecla and the Asdic reported a submerged echo at about 2,000 yards on out port bow. Immediately we altered course to intercept what was almost certainly a U-boat. Within a minute we were steaming at full speed, thanks to our close feed system. Radar then reported a surface target dead ahead. Evidently the enemy had surfaced. When the range had closed sufficiently we fired a star shell. Up went the binoculars on the bridge. The flare burned brightly, and almost under our bows it seemed, was the U-boat, like a monstrous black whale, its wet side glistening in the yellow light.
"Stand by to Ram!!". Everyone on the bridge held tightly to some firm object and braced for the shock. The U-boat however could turn in a tighter circle and was too quick for us. She was clear with ten yards to spare, and her gun crews were already training their 5-inch gun on us. Neither of our 4.7's could bear as we reeled to port under full helm. A quick witted seaman on our starboard Oerlikon opened fire and the enemy gun crew melted under the murderous hail. Still reeling crazily to port, we came round again for another run in and the U-boat was diving at panic speed. Once again she managed to evade our cleaving bows, but as we raced by we fired a pattern of depth charges, one actually striking the submerging conning tower.
Astern the sea shuddered, boiled and upheaved itself into a gigantic water spout. Bt the light of our ten inch searchlight we saw a huge, black, cigar shape appear, to break slowly into two, both parts disappearing almost immediately.

Meanwhile the other destroyer had stopped to pick up survivors from the Hecla. There were about 800 men in the oil covered water. With scrambling nets down and all hands manning the sides Marne had picked up about 100 men when her stern was completely blown off by a torpedo. But miraculously her water tight bulkheads held and she remained afloat, a helpless hulk waiting for the next crashing blow which would send her to the bottom of the Atlantic.
The old **Venomous** was now left with the triple task of protecting the helpless Marne, picking up about 700 men and at the same time fighting of a wolf pack already closing in for the kill. Each one of these tasks clashed with the other two. We no longer had the freedom of dashing after radar and asdic contacts, for this would leave the Marne unprotected, and we could not depth charge freely because of our men in the water. Somehow we had to pick these men up out of the sea, that would mean stopping and presenting ourselves as an easy target for the U-boats. The other depot ship meantime had relieved us of yet a fourth task by quitting the scene at high speed, this was no place for a large vessel to dally.
Having completed a half dozen sweeps around the crippled destroyer, **Venomous** made for the men in the water, whose position was revealed by hundreds of minute, bobbling life belt lights. Soon we had our scrambling nets down, and all men who could be spared were manning the sides. As we wallowed in the heavy swell, over the side they came, black and slippery with oil, half lifted and dragged often by their hair, vomiting and coughing up the filthy oil. Most were hurried to the warmth of the mess deck, while those suffering acutely from exposure were taken to the blazing heat of the ships galley.
Reports were now coming from the Asdic and radar of suspicious contacts, but the floating wreckage from the Hecla had been confusing the operators. Now the radar reported a definite contact slowly closing us. Our Captain had the awful decision to make, either to remain stationary and perhaps save another 100 men, or get under way and attack the stalking U-boat. If we delayed too long we should certainly be torpedoed and all would be lost, but if we started turning our screws we would certainly kill many men.
We continued picking up men for another five minutes, allowing the U-boat to close to within 1,000 yards.
Then seizing the microphone of the loud hailer, the Captain warned the men in the water. "Keep clear of the screws! I must go ahead to investigate a contact! I will come back for you! I will come back for you!. Seeing their last chance apparently slipping away from them, several of the men tried to cling to the ship and to the scrambling net, with disastrous results.

We had soon worked up to top speed and an audible sigh of relief went through the ship after the terrible twenty minutes of waiting for torpedoes out of the darkness.

The Asdic echo was now loud and clear and our quarry dived. Judging ourselves to be at least a mile from the men in the water, the Captain ordered a heavy pattern of depth charges to be dropped. The ship shuddered violently as eight charges erupted a couple of hundred yards astern. Tilting over dangerously at full helm, we swept the area with our searchlight. A mass of oil spread like a dark stain over the surface. Asdic reported a lost contact, but to make absolutely sure we made another run over the target and dropped another pattern. No submarine could have possibly lived through that.

When we returned to the crippled Marne and the men in the water, we noticed that their lights were getting more dispersed. This would make our task more difficult and after circling the Marne several times to conduct a thorough antisubmarine sweep, we again stopped to pick up survivors. Many of them were now numbed with cold and needed a great deal of help to climb the scrambling nets. On the bridge they could do little but wait, expecting any second to feel the crashing blow which would end all our anxieties. We were only too painfully aware of the easy target we presented to the enemy. It was a wonderful relief to feel the ship get underway as once again we went to investigate a dangerous echo. Altogether we made four depth charge attacks that night but with inconclusive results, between these attacks we would make periodic sweeps around Marne then stop and pick up more men.

When dawn finally came we had nearly 600 survivors from the stricken Hecla in the **Venomous**, and, the Marne was still there. We continued sweeping around the Marne and picking up what few men were left alive in the water until late afternoon, when two destroyers and a tug from Gibraltar arrived to take charge of the Marne.

Now after nearly twelve hours at full power, our reserves of oil fuel were about exhausted. The **Venomous**, and old V&W Destroyer had been built in 1918 fro the shorted ranges in the North Sea. It was obvious that we had insufficient oil to reach Gibraltar. We had tried unsuccessfully to go alongside Marne for her oil, but the ships were crashing heavily together in the swell. The Captain then decided to make for Casablanca, about thirty miles to the Eastward.

Arriving off the port at about 1700 hours, we were challenged by the American cruiser Augusta, who started swinging her huge turrets on us in a distinctly unfriendly way. We speedily identified ourselves and went into the harbour, going alongside an American 'Woolworth' carrier, to which we transferred the Hecla survivors.

About two hours later a few hundred of the survivors, dressed in U.S. Navy working uniforms, were able to leave us, after a bath and a good meal. As we looked around the harbour, it was evident that Casablanca had only been taken that very morning.
The French Battleship Jean Bart was lying on her side with smoke and flames pouring out from an enormous gash. Meanwhile our sailors had taken full advantage of the American's greenness by trading the famous **Venomous** cap ribbons for cartons of cigarettes. The young American sailors, fresh from the peace of the Unites States, stared in shocked silence upon the ninety pitiful forms laid out under hammocks on our forecastle.
Having topped up with oil from the carrier, we slipped and proceeded out of harbour and kept up a steady twenty knots to Gibraltar. On the way we performed the melancholy task of burying at sea all those who had died after being picked up. On arrival at Gibraltar, all the Hecla survivors wen to ashore to the base, and we set to cleaning ship. To the great disgust of everyone, we discovered that **Venomous** was duty ship that night for the Strait U-boat patrol, this meant another sleepless night chasing radar echo's, which usually turned out to be unlit Moorish fishing vessels.
At about 0900 next morning, bleary eyed and very sorry for ourselves, we entered harbour just as the huge battle ship King George V was leaving for the United Kingdom. A significant line of sailors stood to attention on the forecastle and a superb Royal Marine band played on the quarter deck of the great ship as she made her way towards the harbour entrance.
Coming abreast of the great flagship, shabby little **Venomous** had just made her salute and received the condescending reply, when the perfect symmetry of the ranks standing to attention was rudely broken by a large number of American sailors, who should have been decently tucked out of sight, rushing to the guard-rail in the waist of the great ship, and waving their hands excitedly. Clear across the water came their shout, **"Good Old Venomous!!"**.

F.N.G (Fredo) Thomas.

Chapter 44

"COOKS TO THE GALLEY"

The standards of catering in a wartime V&W could sometimes be found wanting. I know that there were probably several boats where the food was excellent. Some individual messes possessed matelot's who were potential chefs and enthusiastic amateur cooks. We certainly had one coder, 'Dougie' who could make excellent pastry. For Christmas he made a dozen Christmas puddings and dozens of mince pies. His ordinary meals were so good that you forgot about them. Whereas in other messes the standard was so dreadful that you would remember the meals forever after. Each and everyone of our cooks in the galley was a memorable one off. At one time we had a P.O. Cook and things were not too bad. He was a survivor from another destroyer torpedoed by an East Coast E-boat. The result was that as the watch filed passed the steel door galley it became a custom to beat on the loose fitting doors. It was supposed to be gratifying to see the glibbering P.O. Come flying out of the galley on the lee side, making for the iron deck and the open air, his life jacket inflated to hot air balloon dimensions.
When he had his inevitable breakdown, he was replaced by a teenager H.O. Rating. Despite the fact that all his aptitude tests suggested that he would make a cook, he was adamantly against the idea. To this end he fought against a hundred and twenty matelot's daily. This was in the days of the coal fired galley stoves. In the unlikely event that he could get it going, he would let it go out, when the cooks reported to the galley to collect food for their mess at dinner time they would find the food in the same condition as it had been delivered for cooking.
In the days of counselling and caring it is rather sad to recall the kindly chats with sexagenarian old stripey's failed to improve his efforts, nor did a discreet beating up behind galley doors. For his own bodily safety he was returned to barracks.
He was followed by a petty officer who specialised in baking white bread, a rare commodity in wartime. His care of the dishes left in his charge was of a high order and we embarked on a period of at least one good meal a day. For the rest, breakfast was largely an individual effort, although unlimited supplies of fried bread was available from the galley. Tins of baked beans were obtained from the telephone kiosk sized NAAFI. Also a magnificent mature old English Cheddar that I wish we could get these days. After the first bite it bit you back. Seven pound jars of mustard pickle and huge tins of Argentinean bully beef was available for the evening meal. Not exactly the

basis if cordon bleu cooking, but devoured with enthusiasm by hungry teen age matelot's.

The pipe "Clear lower deck, up whaler" at 0500 in Sheerness harbour on a dark, wet and cold morning in mid winter always made me think that I'd never make twenty five and that T.B. would probably carry me off prematurely. Fifty odd years later I realised that my foreboding were unfounded. The whaler safely up and the ton of water pouring from the plug hole, we would repair to the mess deck and a welcome breakfast of beans on fried bread, This would be followed by the unforgettable mug of char made with carnation milk and demerara sugar. Even today I have a neighbour who still serves up tea in this fashion, an ex-stoker, he is probably the only matelot to serve his time in the Shetlands and made several trips to Norway in the Shetland bus, and then, drafted back to barracks, volunteered to return to Shetland for another stint.

Meanwhile, down aft, I imagine the officers, despite also having a coal fired kitchen range, probably did somewhat better. The chief idiosyncrasy there was the galley chimney, a delightful rustic affair, 'H' shaped and standing about six or seven feet above the quarter deck stood right in the line of fire of X gun. On going to action stations one rating was detailed off to remove the chimney and lay it on the deck, this prevented it being shot away and possibly encourage a four inch shell explosion.

Deryk Wakeham

Chapter 45

H.M.S. Verity

And the sinking of S.S. Strathallan

December 1942

After about eighteen months of Atlantic convoys, using Halifax, Nova Scotia, Boston. Massachusetts, St Johns Newfoundland as our bases H.M.S.**Verity** was ordered to take part in the North African invasion, so that brought us to the Mediterranean where we did a spell with 'H' Force.
Of course during this time we were involved with other activities, the most memorable being when we were part of the escort of a convoy which included the troopship S.S. Strathallan. This ship was making its way to Oran, loaded with supplies and transporting nurses and their medical equipment together with army and R.A.F. Personnel. They were destined to join up with the First Army who were in North Africa.
We were ordered to leave the convoy but why, or where we were heading for is unknown to me. Some time later we were ordered to return to the convoy as the S.S. Strathallen was in trouble.
I had the morning watch and when I went to the mess to grab a cup of tea, it was piped over the ship "Stand by to pick up survivors". So I gulped my tea down and hurried to the upper deck.
Arriving on the upper deck there was room for me on the starboard side scrambling net. Being left handed as an asset as I could hold on with my right hand and with my left, help the survivors out of the water. The Captain could not of course, delay the safe passage of the ship, so we were only able to pick up a few men and women. This procedure went on all day long during which time we managed to pick up 1,007 survivors. So many in fact that the ship was 'listing' so we had to move around to remedy this.
It was getting dusk by the time we reached Oran where we landed these survivors, who 'fell in' on the jetty in their respective groups. Amongst these survivors were many nurses as well as Army and R.A.F. Personnel.
The order came to 'Clean Ship' before we set sail, no one knew where to. We finally realised when we arrived in Iceland! This was Christmas Day 1942 as we tied up alongside H.M.S. Renown. We then had 'Big Eats'.

S/M Bone
(From the neck up!)

Survivors coming alongside.
Fortunately it was calm weather

Torpedoed

1943

Cooks To The Galley Again!

Being my turn for cook of the mess, my oppo (friend) and I decided to treat the lads to something different that would make a change from Chinese wedding cake.
My oppo said he would leave it to me. So I though that I would try and make a currant caked, (never done before). I gathered all the ingredients, mixed the cake mixture and placed it in a tin, ready to take to the galley.
At that moment the O.O.D (officer of the day) came into the mess and asked me what I was doing. "I'm baking a currant cake sir". "Very good " said the O.O.D. "But when are you going to put the currants in?" As they were on the table next to the tin. "Oh!" I said "That's torn it" After a few moments I said, "Problem solved Sir" I picked up a pencil and started pushing the currants into the mix, (with the blunt end of course). I got six or seven currants in and then gave up. At that point the O.O.D. Said "You can hardly call that a currant cake". "No sir you couldn't't" after a few moments hesitation I said "When I have baked the cake I will convert the cake by cutting it horizontally, and spread jam between the two layers and rename the cake a jam sponge sir" "God bless it and all who eat it" is all he said.

Albert Irlam

*****

Verdun Characters Remembered
By Derek Wakem

"Harry Ram", Barely five feet tall, with a chest like a barrel the Quartermaster would shake his fist at the bridge voice pipe when at the wheel and reprimanded for yawning. Everybody took a perverse pleasure in pulling his leg.
One evening he was bet that he could not get himself through the handle of one of those five gallon "Fannies" He began well and got his feet through. The he wiggled the steel handle up about his hips. The just as he stood there getting his breath the alarm bell rang and 'Action Stations' Sounded. Harry took off with everybody else on the mess deck, except that he was wearing a large aluminium protuberance on the back, unable to remove it. Arriving at the wheel house he spent the next hour or so aiding the coxswain and trying to look nonchalant.

Harry was small and ape like and could be prevailed to sit on some large, hairy three badged A/B's lap. Then with hand up his jumper, he became a ventriloquist dummy.
Ordinary Seaman Karlsson of East London. A very example of "Essex Man" probably from the Romford area. At least six feet tall and plump. His speciality was female impersonations and transvestite acts for our entertainment. His stripper act, down to the buff was a wonder of concealment of his equipment.
"Guns" who famously sat heavily on a full bottle of whisky. The Glaswegian's description of the removal of glass particles from "Guns" bottom made for great entertainment.
The infamous misfire on 'A' gun during a shoot off May Island. Whilst sorting out a possible hang fire the guns came down and trained around to port. At that moment the shell went of and we all watched as the projectile took off towards a small gaggle of Scottish M.F.V's going about their business. Luckily it was an air burst above and to the right of the innocent fishermen.
The previously mentioned Glaswegian S.B.A (sick bay attendant). His ambition was to perform an amputation. Luckily he only got as far as a finger although he did attend the Doctor for the amputation of the arm of a maritime gunner who had been caught in a barrage balloon winch in the dark.
As you may deduce from the foregoing, not a lot that was funny occurred in the Rosyth Escort Force.
I was a lowly O.D. (ordinary seaman) preparing the ship for docking at Rosyth and had applied to be up rated to Able Seaman.
Having diligently practised heaving the line. I was quite proud and confident as I watched my shipmates unsuccessful attempts to reach the waiting dock yard matey's. I heaved my line - and beamed with delight as I saw it land at the feet of one of them.
Unfortunately he fumbled it at the same time as I let the end slip out of my hand. There was my heaving line floating in the water!
With my shipmates grinning with glee the officer roared "Sidey, you're a very ordinary seaman!!"
I still blush at the thought to this day!

Eric Sidey
HMS Viceroy

H.M.S. WANDERER

Courses finished at the end of April 1943 and we all said farewell to our term mates and went off on fourteen days leave before joining our next ships. Mine was to be the WW1, V&W destroyer **Wanderer**, just completing her conversion into a long range escort for the North Atlantic convoys. I joined her in Devonport on 11th May in a state of some euphoria having just got engaged.

Wanderer was due for recommission the day after I joined her and to be ready for sea by the end of the month. This appeared to be an impossible task as she was still in a state of chaos, red lead paint everywhere, a tangle of wires, leads and pipes, a gaping hole where the funnel was to be and much equipment yet to be fitted, a depressing sight. She had two of her 4.72 guns removed and replaced by the latest A/S weapon forward, the Hedgehog, and lots more depth charges aft. One boiler and its funnel gone to make way for extra fuel tanks and another mess deck for radar and asdic operators. She also had one of the new warning radars fitted to detect submarines attacking on the surface at night and an air warning radar.

My job were to be Gunnery and Radar Officer and Forecastle officer. Although gunnery would have been my last choice, it turned out to be quite fun. There was a 4.7" BL Mark 1 at each end of the ship and four twin 20mm anti aircraft Oerlikon guns. The control system for the 4.7"'s was basic. It consisted of a sight on the bridge Pelorous compass to indicate target bearing to the guns, operated by me, ranges from the radar and a range/rate clock in a tiny TS to give predicted ranges based on enemy course and speed. But for a submarine at close quarters, all I had to do was to lean over the front of the bridge and order the Captain of the gun to open fire, he did the rest! For firing at shadows at 5-7 miles I devised a system using a sextant (to measure angle of sight), radar range, a stop watch and a series of trajectory graphs on a portable board to work out an angle and fuse setting for the guns. Sadly I never had the chance to use it in action, but my successor did against E-boats in the English Channel with good results. For firing practice we often used to drop a dan buoy and use it as a target 'periscope', and bang away at it, Up ladder, spread line shoots usually only sub calibre at 2-3,000 yards, but good fun.

Our Captain was Lt Cdr R.E. (Bob) Whinney, an anti submarine specialist, he was an enthusiastic and skilled submarine hunter. His First Lieut had a tough time under him and we had three in the first year. The Navigator was a tough and unflappable R.N.R Lieut'. The Second Lieut' was Jack Frost R.N.V.R who kept watch with the Gunner 'T'. the officer in charge of the depth charges. The Kindergarten watch consisted of two nineteen year olds, myself and the Asdic Officer, S/Lieut Derek Kidd R.N.V.R. A splendid fellow and good at his job, not an easy one with a specialist boss who knew it all. If a sudden emergency arose it always seemed to come in out watch. At sea Kidd and I did standing forenoon's, 8-12, the first dog watches 4-6 and the firsts 8-midnight, and the rest were done by the opposite watch led by Jack Frost, with whom I shared a cabin, so we only saw each other when we were turning over as Officer Of the Watch (OOW) on the bridge.

The approach to our cabin was directly from the 'Iron deck' down a vertical ladder, topped by a two foot high casing with a hatch on top.

Getting in and out in rough weather was exciting and often wetting. I had the top bunk and had to wear an oilskin coat in wet weather because the deck leaked. In very rough weather the upper deck was out of bounds and if we were marooned aft we slept in the wardroom, those on the bridge had to stay there until the weather moderated! Kidd and I always seemed to be the lucky ones aft.

Amazingly we managed to leave Devonport after a day's sea trials, on the 1st June for a rough passage to Greenock, escorting a submarine. It certainly shook us down and a lot of other things up! We then did our work up, one day in the Clyde and four day's off Londonderry, this was followed by two days at Larne leading our Escort Group in group exercises with the destroyer Inconstant, the frigate Glenarm and two others. We were now considered full operational and on the 1st July we sailed from the Clyde with our group as escort for a large fast convoy KMF19 with troop reinforcement for Sicily.

On the way the destroyers nipped into Gibraltar and Algiers for fuel and finally handed the convoy over off Bizerta on the day of the landings. We then had to search for a reported submarine off Galita Island and were passed by the Battle Fleet steaming at High Speed to carry out their bombardments for the landings. A fine sight.

On our return we escorted a liner from bone and took her to Algiers, off which our consort, the Inconstant made an Asdic contact which she reported as a confirmed submarine, as all her contacts had been so reported and had proved otherwise, we left her to it. This time she was proved right and was able later to claim the sinking of an Italian submarine, almost single handed after many hours and at great depth.

After calling at Algiers and Oran to collect a convoy for the UK We had to detach off Gibraltar and go into the dockyard for engine room repairs, as well as some welcome rest and relaxation in the sun.

On the 28th July we had to go to the assistance of a merchant ship off Cape St Vincent. She had been bombed and abandoned by her crew. We put a party on board her, led by the Midshipman and they were able to secure a tow to a tug which had arrived. We were escorting them back to Gib' when during my forenoon watch the merchant ship suddenly sank. One minute she was there and the next she had gone. Apparently her bulkhead had collapsed. Our Midshipman had just time to tell the tug to slip the tow before she went down like a stone. Fortunately the boarding party were soon picked up and back on board after their ducking.

We finally left Gib' with a homeward bound convoy on the 4th August and were back in Londonderry six day's later after a trouble free trip. But a week later we were off again for Gib' escorting a slow convoy KMS24. Our new group leader was the destroyer Hurricane.

On the 21st August we sank our first U-boat, U523 in the Bay of Biscay. At about 3.00 am the alarm bells rang and I was quickly up on the bridge, an unidentified radar contact had been made at about eight miles by our wizard operator A.B. Herbert, and we were racing towards it. I went into the radar cabinet to check it, and at just two miles it disappeared, it had to be a submarine and must have sighted our bow wave. We reduced speed and at once got asdic contact, two ten depth charge attacks quickly followed. Apparently these put all her lights out and drove her down to 600 feet. We then lost contact and there followed and anxious three hours as we carried out a square search, our patience was rewarded and contact was regained.

For the first time we carried out an attack with pour new weapon, the Hedgehog; this fired twenty four small bombs ahead of the ship and landed in a circle above the predicted future position of the submarine, they sank to arrive at the right depth and time as their target. The scientist had told us that, if one bomb hit a kill was guaranteed, so when a small rumble came up from the depths after seventeen seconds we felt sure of success. However to make absolutely sure, the Captain carried out another attack with twenty depth charges and was wheeling round for one more when the submarine rose dramatically to the surface in a flurry of foam only a 1000 yards on our port beam. At last the guns were able to take a hand in the action and shells were quickly on target. It's crew came tumbling up from below and threw themselves overboard. Initially the Captain had turned to ram, but this was not going to be necessary, the guns ceased fire and we stopped to pick up survivors. About twenty were hauled up the scrambling nets, and after being given survivors clothing, were bedded down in the tiller flat. After just a few minutes the submarine slid stern first back beneath the waves to the cheers from our ships company. Our prisoners were seen to be just a bunch of youngsters, scruffy, and unhealthy looking, and glad to be out of the war.

We then rejoined the convoy and received congratulations all round. Our passenger, and RAF Officer and four men, had something extra to talk about when we took them into Lisbon harbour two nights later. They were on some clandestine operation and were taken off into the night by a darkened boat.

The Skipper Lt Cmdr Bob Whinney on the bridge

The kindergarten watch

On the bridge in warmer and calmer climes

On the bridge in calm waters

Not so calm

Gun crew

We then left as silently as we had arrived thinking wistfully of the joys that lay behind all those bright lights we could see so near.
On arrive in Gib' the Army came aboard to escort our prisoners into captivity, Blindfolded. We then got down to the serious business of celebrating our first success. In due course both the Captain and Derek Kidd were awarded the D.S.C.
After five days in harbour we steamed back into the Atlantic to join a homeward bound slow convoy. This time we had no excitement and arrived back in Londonderry on the 15th September, now it was my turn for some home leave.
Ten days later we were of for some group exercises, with our new leader Commander Westmacott in the Hurricane, before a slow convoy across the Atlantic. We had one successful submarine attack on the convoy and arrived at Argentina in Newfoundland on the 9th October. Four days later we left St Johns to await our next convoy. On the way we tested our Hedgehog just off the coast with predictable success, the sea surface was quickly covered in stunned cod, our whaler was immediately lowered and filled with lovely fresh fish. The Newfoundlanders were quick to react too and several boats were on their way out from the shore, they were grateful for the unexpected bonanza!
On the 16th October we left with another slow convoy, SC144 homeward bound and we had a trouble free crossing. Back in 'Derry I was sent off on a gunnery course in Belfast, this was enlivened by Charles Crossley and Chris Eason who had recently arrived from the U.S.A. In their brand new American built Captain Class Frigate, a total contrast to my splendid old 'Hooker'.
Our next task was to escort yet another slow convoy to Gibraltar. This too was trouble free except for the attention of one Junkers 290, unfortunately this was only recognised as such too late for my A/A system to be brought into action. Very annoying!
On the 24th November we left Gib' to join a convoy coming up from Freetown, homeward bound. AS we approached it from astern we detected a shadowing U-boat on radar but we were unable to make Asdic contact when it dived. The Admiralty had assessed that there were twelve U-boats homing in on the convoy and had sent the crack 2nd Escort group to reinforce it. This was under the command of the legendary Captain Johnny Walker in the Starling. On the night of the 27/28th November the submarine pack made a mass attack from the port side of the convoy. Walker had anticipated this and his group were well placed to detect them from the out field, they were nearly all driven off or sunk, aided by Coastal Command aircraft fitted with the Leigh lights. We were part of the escort on the starboard side of the convoy so we had to watch it all going on and listening to the radio traffic between

the ships actually involved in the hunting, very frustrating! The sky was frequently lit up by star shells, flares and by the lights of the aircraft as they went into attack. The one submarine that did get through the convoy was sunk by the Corvette Dahlia before it could do any damage, two or three others were sunk without any losses on our side. This was one of the last convoy engagements of the war, at last we were beginning to win the Battle of the Atlantic. The weapons and tactics and more escorts together with the good intelligence from Bletchly were turning the tables on the U-boats just in time.

Next day brought a gale so there were no more attacks. One of the merchant ships reported a man overboard and we were detailed to search for him, a hopeless task in that weather. Added to which our Doctor, Sidney Fuller had to perform an operation, using the Captains cabin. It was virtually impossible to keep the ship steady for even a few minutes, but all was well and we arrived back at our base on the 5th December.

We were soon back at sea again in foul weather to support Transatlantic convoys, our sister ship **Watchman** soon lost her Asdic dome in the heavy seas and had to return to base. We then had condenseritis and had to return to 'Derry too. Our leader the Hurricane was then torpedoed by a 'Gnat' on Christmas Eve and, because of the impossibility of towing her to safety, she had to be abandoned and sunk by her consort, the Glenarm. We heard this sad news when we arrived when we arrived back in 'Derry on Christmas Day. Yet again Christmas had to be celebrated on a different day, this time on Boxing Day. After a short service on deck we repaired to the Wardroom with the Chiefs and Petty Officers as our guests for a 'dram' or two. We managed to sink fifteen bottles of spirits between twenty-five of us before sitting down to Christmas dinner at 2.30pm after which we slept well.

Repairs took a few days but at last we sailed down the twisty river Foyle only to hit an underwater obstruction and end up on the mud. We had to return for damage inspection, but fortunately there was none and we left the next day, 5th January 1944 in company with **Watchman** and Woodpecker to rejoin the poor Glenarm who had been at sea throughout Christmas and New Year and was not to get back until the 20th January, a total of thirty-four days continuously at sea in mostly foul weather.

After refuelling at Horta in the Azores we carried out a sweep towards Ireland. On the afternoon of the 17th we got an Asdic contact with a deep submarine in poor sea conditions and carried out a whole series of attacks, including a successful one with the Hedgehog and some slow creeping attacks with our consorts. Unfortunately the latter had difficulty in keeping in contact. After ten hours, contact was finally lost and we assumed that the

submarine had been sunk. This was confirmed sometime later by intelligence as the U-305. We then returned to 'Derry for another celebration.
As we never took our clothes off at sea and we did not have a bath on board, or indeed much fresh water to spare for washing, our first action on return to Harbour was to go ashore for a bath. The Northern Counties Country Club in the centre of Londonderry generously offered this facility to all visiting officers for a charge of one shilling! One of the best shillings worth I have ever had, particularly as it required two lots of bath water to get really clean and what bliss that was!
Two other features of the time spent in 'Derry were visits to the tactical trainer where we fought paper submarine battles assisted by a bunch of pretty Wrens and, at the opposite extreme, battles at the town hall called ship's company dances. These were just an excuse for letting off steam after a spell at sea.
We were off to sea again on the 2nd February for a patrol in a U-boat area with the **Watchman,** the new American built frigate the Byron and the river class frigate, the Strule. We detected one submarine and carried out an inconclusive hunt with the Byron. We then had to refuel at sea, this was from a tanker using the astern method, it occasioned much shouting between the bridge and forecastle as we manoeuvred to pick up the tow. After which we had to rejoin our group on our own. It was a dark and dirty night, the A/S speaker on the bridge suddenly began to emit a roar. Derek leapt to the Asdic direction indicator to check the bearing as we both knew it to be a torpedo fired at us from short range and urgent action was required. I ordered the wheel hard over to starboard and the engine to slow in case it was a 'Gnat'. The roaring increased the bearing of the torpedo drew all to slowly aft and we were convinced that we would be hit in the stern. Happily it just missed us. If we had been sunk on our own in bad weather, in mid winter and without getting a distress signal out, we would have a poor chance of rescue. Meanwhile we had sounded the alarm rattlers and called the Captain, so the bridge quickly filled with people and reports of crews closing up at their action stations. We carried out an Asdic search, but in bad weather conditions we never made contact and went on our way rejoicing not to be swimming.
Our search area took us further North, finally we were odered to return to Scapa Flow where we arrived on the 16th February. We went alongside the depot ship Tyne outboard of the brand new 'M' class destroyer Mahratta. We felt like an ugly duckling beside the immaculate swan. However we were made to feel very welcome and everything was done to prepare us for our next operation, to escort a convoy to Russia. Horror of horrors we were ill equipped, not arcticised, poor A/S armament and held together with rust.

Four days after a tremendous rush to fit an extra Oerlikon gun, get in specially warm clothing and make good all our defects, we sailed for the Faroes to top up with fuel. It also gave some of us the opportunity to go ashore for a rare leg stretch. Next morning at 3.30am on the 22nd February we left the shelter of the fjord for what was the most unpleasant days of my life. We caught up with the convoy JW57 during my forenoon watch, it was a cool calm and grey day when suddenly came the dreaded cry 'Man Overboard' from the starboard side, We quickly turned round, called away the lifeboat's crew and closed the man, now lying face down in the sea. The Doctor had managed to get away with the boat and started resuscitation as soon as he was pulled into the boat, alas it was to no avail. Although he was one of the strongest swimmers in the ship the shock of hitting the water at 30° F had killed him after just two strokes. It boded ill for any other unfortunates who might have to swim for it. The young man an ordinary seaman, had been cleaning his gun, lost his balance when the ship rolled and toppled over the guard rail. Two hours later we buried him in his hammock with full honours, the gloom on board deepened.

The threat became increasingly obvious as we steamed northwards, first of all Junkers 88's began to circle and report us and we could hear U-boats radioing their sighting reports. Destroyers dashed about to investigate the bearings of these but the Asdic conditions were notoriously bad in this area, a layer of cold water on top of a warm one deflected the sound beam upwards, the submarines just went below the water to escape detection.

The weather then deteriorated, snow storms, a biting wind and an increasingly rough sea combined to make the upper deck work almost impossible, at times spray froze on bare metal which entailed a continuous struggle to keep the guns from freezing up, while too much ice on the upper deck was a threat to the ship's stability, so the duty watch was kept busy chipping. Watch keeping on the bridge for four hours at a time was a wretched business and we considered reducing to two hour watches, but then of course we would virtually have no sleep, so we kept to four hours and many layers of clothing.

At about 10.00pm on the night of the 23rd, we heard a dull thud from the other side of the convoy, a red glow lit up the low cloud and almost at once Mahratta reported that she had been torpedoed. A couple of minutes later she was hit by a second torpedo and we knew that nothing could save her or most of her crew on a night like that. Her radio operator continued to report the hitting of the second torpedo over and over again, because his receiver had been put out of action, his voice rising to a pitch until finally there was

silence and we knew that the end had come. It was terrible to listen to him and imagine the scenes of distress. For just three days she had been our 'chummy' ship and they could not have been a more friendly crowd in a fine new ship. We felt so sad and hoped that at least a few would be saved, in fact less than a score were picked up, no officers despite the efforts of two consorts. (according to my records only two survived Ed).
Shortly after this our Asdic set broke down, without it we felt defenceless against a submarine, we could neither detect it or hear an approaching torpedo. We were then ordered to sweep down a bearing of a submarine's radio transmission. Our Asdic mechanic was hopeful that he could mend the set quickly and the Captain was reluctant to report the breakdown, so down the bearing we went, blind, and on our own. It was a wrong and dangerous decision. Midnight came and still no Asdic. Derek went down to the bottom of the ship to try and help the mechanic and I turned in. My bunk was on the ship's side and on the water line, the noise of the waves was clear and I was more conscious than usual that only a rusty thin sheet of steel was between me and a freezing cold sea. That was the night that I prayed my hardest, and then, in faith, read myself to sleep with my favourite childhood book 'The Wind In The Willows'.
Throughout the following day there were submarine alarms and many attacks were made on the submarines but none were reported as successful due to the difficult conditions. The convoy steamed steadily on, so far unscathed. That night the submarines attempted to attack on the surface and the order was given to illuminate with star shells. The ancient **Wanderer** was the only one able to comply, all the rest reported that their guns were frozen up. We felt proud that all our efforts had proved successful.
The next morning 27th February we reached the limit of our endurance 73. 30 North 26 Eats, and were ordered to return to the Faroes. We were glad to be off in company with our old friend **Watchman**, who almost immediately reported a contact with a 'confirmed submarine', probably a shadower astern of the convoy, we had a short hunt, but again we wee defeated by the layer.
We then ran into a force 11 North Westerly gale which quickly built up tremendous seas, we should have hove to, but were too short of fuel, so we corkscrewed along with the waves rushing at us on the starboard quarter, threatening to poop us or make us broach to and roll over. The Captain decided the only way to save the ship, now almost empty of fuel and lacking in stability, was to fill some of the fuel tanks with sea water, a desperate measure, but it worked.
At last we arrived off the fjord entrance at midnight on the 1st March, but our troubles were not yet over. There was a blinding snowstorm and the gale funnelled by the fjord seemed to have redoubled its strength. We found our

way through the boom entrance but then had to turn the ship to go alongside the oiler. She began to drift sideways, high out of the water and beam on to the gale, engines alone could not turn her in the narrow confines of the fjord, the lee shore was getting perilously close. The Captain ordered me to let go the anchor, but this would not hold her up into the wind. He then ordered me to slip the cable, but this was impossible, so I cleared the forecastle and waited for the cable to part as the Captain went full ahead on the engines in the last attempt to get clear. This we did. The cable parted round the stem but we managed to get round and alongside the tanker. We were thamkful people. **Watchman** was not so fortunate, she managed to crash through the boom and anchor with insufficient fuel to go any further.

The tanker had to go to her the next day when the weather had moderated.

Next morning we sailed for home at best speed. It was an exhilarating ride in bright sunshine and a huge quarter swell, but with full tanks, our worries behind us, we rolled merrily southwards with thankful hearts.

On return from leave there was a draft chit for me ordering me to the new 'W' Class destroyer Wessex, still building in Glasgow. The **Wanderer** was to go to Newport in Wales for a minor refit to prepare her for the 'D' day landings. Naturally I would have preferred to have stayed on my old ship for the greatest invasion in history, but it was not to be. I went with her to Newport and left her there on the 24th March for two weeks leave. My time in **Wanderer** had been a time of growing up fast, neither Derek or I had watch keeping certificates on arrival, we were the youngest officers on board and faced with many crisis whilst on watch together, we never had a cross word or disagreement. My only regret is that we never kept in touch with each other, but in war time one tended to make new friends and after the war, Derek became a Doctor and went to Canada, where he could not be traced. Bob Whinney got a second D.S.O. For sinking another submarine in the Channel during the invasion. Many years later he got in touch with me about the book he was writing. I lent him some sketches made at the time of the sinking of the first submarine, but they were not used. I would like to have seen his draft, but only saw it after it had been printed.

The old **Wanderer** finished her 25 year life on a high note, the sinking of a submarine in shallow waters in the Channel proved too much for her weakened hull. The explosion of the depth charges caused numerous leaks 76 and she had to go into dock. She was found to be too badly damaged to be worth repairing. Three submarine sunk in a year was a fine record to go out on.

Captain D. Foster.

H.M.S. **Wanderer.**

Depth charge party.
We did not get the U-boat.
but we got some 'big eats'

THE PYJAMA GAME

By Commander W. S. Donald D.S.C

HMS **Verdun**

One evening in March 1943 I berthed **Verdun** alongside **Wolsey** at Rosyth. We had spent the previous night anchored at Molhill on A/A duty. As usual I had slept in my sea cabin below the bridge in pyjama comfort, with full sea rig at hand in case of emergencies. After a 'Red Alert' I pulled this over my pyjamas and remained thus clad all day.
On reaching **Wolsey** my croney, Tim Taylor called me over from his bridge to join him for a drink in his cabin. We had conversed for some time when his First Lieutenant knocked on the door.
"We have some guest in the wardroom sir, will you two join us?"
I said to Tim "You carry on, I can't go down in this sea rig".
Tim said "Nobody will mind, I will explain that you have just come in from sea. Come on".
In a wardroom full of wives and Wrens I kept as still as I could, but a bit of pyjama trouser slipped into view on one leg. This was seen by one of the girls who squealed. "Look everyone Bill's got his pyjama's on!!
I never lived this down, at all subsequent parties I was always asked.
"Got you pyjama's on again Bill?"

* * * * * *

And From The Lower Deck;-

In 1943 I joined HMS **Verdun,** a member of the Rosyth Escort Force, engaged upon escorting East Coast convoys from Methil in the Firth of Forth down to Sheerness and the Thames Estuary.
Amongst the mass of warlike equipment carried on board, from four, four inch guns, sundry Oerlikon 20mm guns, almost a hundred depth charges and two radar sets, we carried a sophisticated radio receiver. This was dedicated to picking up intercom communications between E-boats. These German torpedo boats were much larger than our MTB's, almost a hundred feet long. Their main aim was to sink merchant ships in the convoy. They operated from a base in Holland at Ijmuiden. Twelve or fifteen E-boats made up each attacking force. We had two destroyers as escorts and a trawler to pick up survivors from torpedoed merchant ships.

From the spring onwards the attacking E-boats would set out from Holland in daylight. The RAF therefore could often relay the information to us. We could then know that we would be attacked around midnight. E-boat Alley being the channel around the 'Bulge' of East Anglia. This was swept free from mines at frequent intervals because both E-boats and German aircraft were known to sow new mines in the channels. The sweepers came out both the Humber Estuary and Harwich.
One 'secret weapon' that we possessed was a radio receiver that was dedicated to picking up the E-boat fleet's intercom conversations. For several years the E-boats were evidently unaware that their transmissions were being picked up - and acted upon.
We carried two ratings on board who were German Linguists. One was a 'real' German. Aged about twenty three, he was an Aryan and a former Berliner. His 'oppo' was a small, rotund, pear shaped Polish Jew aged in his late thirties. He looked exactly like Doberman used to look in the Sgt, Bilko programmes in later years.
At 'Stand to' at dawn and dusk and at 'action stations it was their job to don the headphones and listen in. When they received German transmissions they noted them down, translated them and passed the information to the bridge. To help them they had a very useful booklet in which all the German intercom codes were printed. There was also an accompanying book with the names and ranks of all the E-boat commanders, and their call sign code names. The code was very simple, akin to our RAF intercom talk. 'Roger', 'Wilco' etc:
The great usefulness of knowing what the opposition was saying lay in the fact that, with twelve or fifteen E-boats dashing around in the dark at close on fifty miles an hour. It was possible momentarily to lose a group, say, of three. These would then creep round to the other side of the column of merchant ships and then be among them with torpedoes.
Our two linguists had interesting histories, as previously mentioned the young, blond, 'real' German had been a member of the Hitler Youth. "Just like boy scouts" he told me. How he had arrived in the U.K. And convinced the navy that he was 'safe' I never liked to ask him. His 'Oppo', the Polish Jew, of course had found it easier to establish his bona fides. Both had naval pay books made out in their new names. Their service documents and records, likewise told the same story. They had 'families' ashore who wrote to them and they wrote back. The idea being that, if captured they would hopefully avoid serious interrogation by the Germans and no reprisals would be taken against them. At that time, of course, we were still unaware of the likely end of a captured Polish Jew.

They were both afforded Petty Officer status which gave them extra pay amongst other comforts. The navy rule stated that no rating could be promoted while suffering from venereal disease. The Pole, despite his uncharming exterior, was always either visiting a hospital when we were at home in Rosyth, undergoing a course of injections for V.D. Or else he had just been discharged and was about to travel over to Edinburgh, presumably to see the same girl, and be reinfected yet again. For the nine months we were together he seemed to spend most of the time being injected.

Every evening, at duck and then again at dawn, we all 'stood to' at our appointed action stations. The two linguists donned their headphones and move around the dial. I and another P.O. plotted the information on a large scale chart. I also made a written record of everything that was said over the ship's intercom. This information was used later to compile a written account of the action.

The linguist began to pick up the gossip amongst the boats. The long range radar then began to pick up echo's. Finally the Gunnery Radar would receive accurate ranges of individual craft. Ultimately with the aid of star shells and illuminating rockets, we could get sixteen parachute flares in the air at once. Whole sea areas were brighter than day. The E-boats with their light coloured camouflage stood out clear in detail. Anyone on their decks also stood out as black figures as contrast. Like on the boat discovered moored to a navigation buoy having a pee over the side.

Action would then ensue with the E-boats travelling in groups of three at some forty knots at times. They manoeuvred into a position where they could launch their torpedoes at the two lines of merchant ships. By now action had been joined by two Hunt Class destroyer escorts, not forgetting the tug at the rear, waiting to pick up survivors.

The moment the torpedoes were launched the Linguists would pick up the triumphant German report. This would soon be confirmed by the Asdic operator who could hear torpedoes clearly through his hydroplane beneath our hull. Sadistically he would amplify the sound over the ship's intercom so that we could all enjoy the eldritch noise of an approaching missile. In the main however, torpedoes were set to run deeper than our shallow draft. The heavily laden merchant ship's and tankers were the prime targets.

In the spring of 1944 two things happened. The Germans after five years, started to maintain radio silence throughout their journey over from Holland. No talk was allowed until it was obvious that we had spotted them. Then the noise over the air was chaotic. The second thing that happened was that both 'Headache Operator's' were drafted away to serve in larger, fleet destroyers in the Channel for the 'D' day landings. We never saw them again. Their

radio set they left behind and, as it was beside me when in action. I used to switch it on and wait for the E-boat traffic once they were detected.
So it was that one night we saw and heard a huge explosion as several hundred gallons of aircraft quality petrol exploded and blew an E-boat into small, blackened shards of timber. The agonising call signs to the disappeared boat gave the game away as to which craft we had destroyed. Who scored the vital hit was never known, however at least three destroyers were firing at it.
I saw one Hunt Class destroyer with a bow mounted Bofors gun firing downwards at a boat close under its bow. We however were still firing 2" illuminating rockets and star shell to light the scene.
The next morning we steamed slowly over the area but there was little evidence. One of the Hunt Class was reputed to have managed to salvage a Nazi naval ensign, a very prestigious souvenir if true. We saw nothing of value, or even recognisable.
E-boats, mines, glider bombs and German midget submarines were still sinking East Coast escorts right up until the last months of the war in Europe.

Deryk Wakem

Chapter 46

A ROUGH NIGHT

A harsh yellow sunset and a steeply falling glass gave warning that it was going to blow. By 200hrs when I took over the watch the storm approaching its full fury. The ships motion was wild and fantastic ship was shipping it green and bumping cruelly. The ship was practically hove to. With the wheel hard a starboard and the starboard engine going dead slow whilst the port engine was going half ahead, it was just possible to keep the ship under control.
The tremendous sea struck the ship rolling her over to a frightening angle and shattered the glass in the wheel house and hurling everybody on the bridge in a sprawling heap to leeward. The roar of the gale drowned the noise of the splintering glass, but not the language of the Gunner who had hit a tender portion of his anatomy on the engine room telegraph.
The Quartermaster, a young Devon man with just over a years service, was thrown clear of the wheel, but fought his way up the steep slope of the slippery bridge and again grabbed the spokes of the wheel. "Is she steering all right Quartermaster?" Bellowed the Captain in a voice which could just be heard faintly over the scream of the gale.
"Yes zur" yelled the Quartermaster " Everything in the garden's Lovely". An odd remark, but one which showed the right spirit.
A still bigger sea struck the ship. The ship was not so much rolled over as pressed down by hundreds of tons of water. The roll recorder registered 58 degrees. The old destroyer righted herself to an angle of 30 degrees and there she lay while the sea rained blow after blow. The fuse box was broken, and there was a firework display as the fuses blew. Below decks everything was in darkness since the blowing of the fuses, and the electricians were hard at it running extra leads and rigging emergency lighting. A heavy sea beat in the wardroom scuttle and bent the ships side, buckling several main frames and the deck. A torrent of water poured down the hatch into the fore mess deck.
At once men jumped to the bursting scuttles and held them down to stop the inrush of sea water, while seamen, stokers, cooks, and stewards set about shoring them up under the direction of the engineer nearly all the proper stores had been washed overboard, but with the mess tables, stools, a gun rammer and other odds and ends they made a workman like job of it.
A tour of inspection showed that most of that which was movable on deck had been swept overboard. The motor boat was gone. The searchlight tower was buckled and twisted and presented a ridiculous broken lopsided

Escorting a convoy in rough weather off Flamborough Head

Sunk in shallow waters off the East Coast. Note the lone figure standing on the superstructure

HMS Vimiera
Convoy escort duty before being mined on the 9th January 1942.
Photograph taken from HMS Vivien who survived the war and was scrapped in 1948

appearance. The engine room escape hatch, a strong steel cylinder riveted to the deck, had been torn off and lay in the lee scuppers.
The ship's cat, Minnie was missing for a time and there was great anxiety until a leading seaman discovered her crouching terrified in the seaman's bathroom. In some mysterious way she had made her way aft along the upper deck without being swept overboard. l The seaman put her down his oilskin trouser leg and carried her back to her terrified kittens. The cat family were then made comfortable in the engineers bunk.
With the coming of daylight the storm blew itself out and all hand s busied themselves clearing away the wreckage. Shortly after noon we sighted the coast. One more convoy was safely over.

* * * *

SEASICKNESS

A rise, a fall, a long suspense
A, word just spoken, in the air.
A reel, a swerve, a time intense
As eyes rest on uneaten fare.

A sigh, a gulp, a quick upheave,
A dash to parley with a wave.
Too late! The deck does now receive
What I had fondly hoped to save.

O God! O Christ! How I blaspheme!
Your sea, your waves, your windy sky!
O man of earth ! How I do scream
Oh let me be, Oh let me die.

Of steel, of men, of gun and shell
Seasick I care for no such strength.
Give me the earth, a cool green dell.
I'll give you all the ocean's length.

What man, can stand, the bile so vile
That slimy coming from inside?
It pains, it strains, Oh rasping file,
In regions of the unseen side!

I fling my soul to tide and wind,
God, do your worst with it, or give
Ease to my tummy full of wind;
Or let me die where fishes live.

A/B. R.B. Wright

Sent in by A Muir B.E.M

HMS **VIMY**

* * * * * *

H.M.S. Woolston
Celebrates her 25th Birthday

September 3rd 1943 **Woolston** was among the Naval vessels that took part in the invasion of Sicily, and celebrated her birthday by escorting a convoy towards the landing beaches. Once the ships were safely in, her job was to patrol fro lurking U-boats and stand by to give a blazing reception to enemy aircraft which might try to interfere with the convoy.
"We thought things were going to be a bit hot " said Lieut, E.C. Jones R.N.V.R, a chemist in peace time, who comes from Croydon "But the only thing that came up to expectations was the sun".
Altogether **Woolston** spent nine days off Sicily. She opened fire on enemy aircraft many times and her log book reports the crashing of one enemy plane crashing in flames. It was impossible to tell who had shot it down.
From the time she left Britain until a few days ago, the **Woolston** had steamed 7,000 miles and spent 60 out of 62 days at sea. It was not until the last lap that her Commanding Officer, Lieut, F.W. Hawkins R.N. Told the ships company where they were going. The over the loud speaker system he read an order of the day from Admiral Ramsey. "The capture of Sicily has been decided upon" he read. There was a cheer from the ship's company as he read on " You must continually bear in mind that the army is helpless and entirely dependant upon us until we establish them ashore. We did not let them down when they had to retreat from Dunkirk, Greece or Crete and we shall not let them down when they are advancing,". "We will not let them down ". The **Woolston** and the other ships of the Royal Navy made this their slogan. And they did not let the Army down, and look forward to further opportunity of showing their fighting Qualities.

H.M.S. Vimy

Shortly after conversion to a Long range Escort **Vimy** was steaming from Gib' en route to Freetown, West Africa when the Asdic made a positive contact.
With a new Skipper and a green, but enthusiastic crew, everyone dashed to action stations. A depth charge was made and it was reported that the target was surfacing. All guns were immediately trained on the likely spot, when up came a ruddy great whale, he spouted, looked at us reproachfully and leisurely swam away.
At the later 'Crossing the line' ceremony we presented the skipper with "The order of the Whale" with a tin replica to hang around his neck.
We later sank the Italian submarine Malaspia so the 'dress rehearsal' had proved useful.
A young O.D. Said he was going to start smoking a pipe. His mates connived him that he had to put in a request to the First Lieut' for permission. This he did, and everyone along the line, including the coxswain fell in with the joke. The young seaman turned up at the table with the request men and defaulters was piped. With most of the lower deck watching closely, he was told to march up to the table and produce his pipe. This was presented for Number Ones inspection who asked the coxswain if it conformed to K.R's and A.I.'s regarding bowl size and stem length. He confirmed that it was so. The seaman was told to insert it in the correct orifice. He appeared mystified at this, but it dawned upon him, and he placed it in his mouth. After being inspected at various angles, permission was granted and a pleased young O.D. Went back to his mess.
A request was put in for a 'Grudge Fight'. When asked why, the aggrieved matelot said "One of my mess mates had pinched me banger" Permission was granted. As such a heinous offence could only be expiated by the shedding of blood. The fight was held on the foc'sle during the first dog watch under the close supervision of the G.I. After a few blows had been exchanged, the G.I., that honour had been satisfied, the boxing gloves removed, hands shaken and everyone returned to their respective messes, satisfied that justice had been done.
When **Vimy** was entering Falmouth she ran aground on a sand bank. Despite going 'full astern' she wouldn't shift. The skipper was desperate, as running your vessel aground meant big trouble for a Captain. He had a 'Clear lower deck, hands lay aft' piped and all proceeded to the stern. The order was given for everyone to jump simultaneously. (together, all at one, for the uninitiated). After several jumps by all concerned and with the engines going full astern, the suction of the sand was broken and we became unstuck. It

must have been an unusual sight for the people ashore to see so many matelot's behaving in such a peculiar manner. Although on second thoughts I don't know.

We sank U-187 in a combined attack with HMS Beverley and some of the U-boat survivors were placed in the various messes two of them were placed in the E.R.A's mess, one of whom spoke perfect English, I believe he was the navigator. It seemed very strange to be living with and conversing with our bitter enemies. An amazing incident occurred one night when action stations sounded. As you can imagine everyone was dead to the world and this German went round shaking the sleepers, shouting "U-boat!, U-boat!" It was obvious that he did not want to be sunk again.

During daylight hours on convoy escort duty a torpedo attack was made on the **Vimy.** I was on deck at the time and could see this torpedo heading right for the spot where I was standing. I was petrified and thought the ship would be finished. Fortunately the ship was low on fuel and supplies and was higher in the water, the torpedo passed beneath the hull. My 'Oppo' in the engine room swore he heard the torpedo scrape the keel as it passed under us! Anyway the helm was put hard over so we could get to the position where the attack originated. The wheel was moved so quickly that the rudder jammed in the hard over position and the steering engine shaft that actuates the rudder mechanism sheared. The **Vimy** the proceeded at high speed to run ever decreasing circles and everyone knows what can happen in such circumstances, we could have disappeared forever! It took us about six hours to rectify the damage. Until then we had to steer by engines and with the rudder hard over we proceeded in a crab like manner, strange to behold.

At the end of one arduous convoy (although they were all like that) we were cheered into Liverpool docks by other escorts tied up alongside. Our skipper was so taken up by all this public admiration that he forgot that we were still underway and in full view of all the top brass and the assembled ships company's. **Vimy** rammed the lock gates and put a two foot dent in the stern of the ship. As can be imagined the cheering intensified, but the skipper refused an encore!

One of the stokers had a nice little side line. He made badges and brooches for his mates to give to their girl friends. This hobby entailed the use of a blow lamp and he used the small forward store as his workshop. The blow lamp got knocked over, the store being full of 'Bluebell' metal polish, cotton waste etc; it began to burn like mad. Being a well drilled stoker, he pulled the water tight door closed and once he was out side he raised the alarm. The smoke spread rapidly and the ships side glowed red hot. The fire was situated beneath the Hedgehog ammunition lockers and panic ensued in trying to get the projectiles removed. The ship was in the middle of Wembury Bay in the

middle of a large portion of the invasion fleet ready for 'D' day. Fire boats came from everywhere and water and foam poured down on us. Surprisingly damage was slight and did not affect the ships operations.
Finally I came off the middle watch one night and entered the mess, which was in darkness with the exception of the blue night light. I poured myself a drink from the carafe and failed to notice the glass contained a number of cockroaches which had fallen in and could not get out. I swallowed the lot and it wasn't until I felt them going down my throat that I realised what was happening. I was so tired there was no reaction, I just climbed into my hammock and slept.

'Luke' Garner

* * * * * *

In 1941 I went off to HMS Colingwood at Fareham to join the Navy. While I was there they were filming "In Which We Serve". At the end of the film they showed the new recruits marching behind the bands, that was us. We were always hungry, One Sunday an old C.P.O. Was standing by the serving hatch and said "Anybody want any more cake?" Five tables got broken in the rush. After training, and leave we ended up in Stockheath Camp, Havant. For anyone who never went there, let me explain. The builders were still in, there was a foot of mud and we had to walk on duck boards, if you fell of it took two to pull you out. At four o'clock the call went out over the tannoy, "One hand from each hut to collect coke and candle issue". No lights and just a combustion stove, we had bets on how many sheets of the roof we could get to glow!
Some of the men were going to the film studio to jump into a tank of oil and water and were getting thirty bob (shillings) a day for it, they were still filming "In Which We Serve" Those who were still only getting two shillings a day got the hump.
One weekend there was an exercise us against the Royal Marines, they were trying out new field kitchens as well, so it was going to be three or four days. After about six hours in a ditch with snow and ice, I said to my 'Oppo' " The first Marines we see, we surrender to" they were chuffed to get two prisoners and took us back to their headquarters, which was an old farmhouse. The Officer took one look and knew that he had a pair of idiots. They put us in the hay loft, twenty minutes later they sent up eggs, bacon, sausages and tea, followed by chicken for dinner, we even got a tot! When it was all over, our hut wanted to know why we were dry and not covered in mud.

I was then given a draft chit to H.M.S. **Wishart.** We caught a troop ship, the Llanstephen Castle from Greenock to Gibraltar and stayed on the 'Maidstone' Until the **Wishart** came in. Within five hours we sailed. Two hours later I was down the magazine, with guns firing, God knows what at, and for the first and only time I said "What the hell have I let myself in for?"
We did the North African landings and towed a Yankee troop transport the 'Thomas Stone' that had been torpedoed. After the war I received three guineas (Three pounds three shillings) salvage money. Christmas day 1942 we saw a crowd in Algiers and followed it thinking it was some sporting event, we ended up in Nitre Dame looking at Admiral Darlan laying in state.
Next it was the Malta convoys with runs ashore as Tunis, Oran, Tripoli and Bizerta. I went ashore to see my cousin, he was in the army at a town called Ferryville about twenty miles away and as the only pub was there and an army convoy was just leaving, it seemed natural to join it. When we got back. No **Wishart!.** Well it was not the first time I had done 14 day's 10A.
In the 1950's The Royal Naval Association mustered on Horse Guards Parade prior to marching to the Cenotaph for a Naval Service, the back to Horse Guards Parade all lined up to be inspected. That year the inspecting officer was Admiral of the Fleet Sir Andrew Cunningham. I was in the front row. The Admiral got about five men past me when he stopped and came back, looked me in the eye and said "I know you, Main street Gib' I had you off caps. HMS **Wishart**. "I didn't think you would remember" I said. "How many A.B's do you think an Admiral knock off? We will have a drink in the festival hall tonight".
This all resulted because I was with a leading seaman, a seven year man said when a car came down the main street with flag flying and everyone saluting, I happened to remark to him about saluting in reply he said "Bugger him, you only salute your own officers in Gibraltar and he's not one of ours". The car stopped the Admiral put his head out of the window and called us back and wanted to know the reason why we had not saluted. I got three days stoppage of pay and leave. I wonder how many have been 'done' by an Admiral?

Doug Lochead

HMS **Wishart**

Chapter 47

In war time the warship sheds its spit and polish. Shining brass and ivory decks are all very well in peace time when there is time for shining and scrubbing. In war there are guns to be manned and extra lookouts to be maintained in a steady, constant gaze for the enemy.

We sailed with the crew at action stations, a trying duty, and a state of immediate readiness because of special dangers. Respite come in some measure when the order is cruising stations, but actually there is scarcely a,minute of the voyage when there isn't tension.

"Aircraft on the Starboard side!" All eyes reach out in identification. A moment, then, though no word is said there is relaxation. A friendly plane.

But they were not all friendly planes. At dusk one night, there came hurtling through the sky a venomous attacker, and this time the staccato announcement "Aircraft" took on a meaning we all at once appreciated. It was a German bomber. It was all over very quickly, and no damage done, at least there was none to us, but whether the or not the raider escaped only the Nazis would know. A machine gun spat out at a dive bomber, which was less than a hundred feet above the water, and looked as if it might ram us. The pilot jerked from his level course, and the high explosive bombs dropped harmlessly into the sea and incendiaries sparkled harmlessly and beautifully for a short time on the water. A hit? Possibly but he climbed out of his dive and was away with a roar.

It was not long before another attacker came along on the same lines. I was standing amidships, my eyes and ears strained like all the others, when, like some winged nocturnal whale in appearance, the second bomber dived low to attack. There were loud explosions as the bombs came down and guns leapt out at him, I flattened out on the deck under the firm impression that the whole lot had crashed on me. I soon realised that I was quite wrong, and knew the reason. I had dropped right under the Pom-pom gun with its withering crash and blast.

Grateful indeed was I to the seaman who a few minutes earlier had pushed some cotton wool into my hands saying "Put this in your ears sir, it will help" It probably helped a great deal.

From my prone position I was able to see the bomber skim the water at terrific speed, through furious fire, his own machine gun bullets rattling at the funnels of the ship on out port side. With one accord the convoy was answering back, and the sky was alight with gun flashes, green and red tracers, darting up or down, making a fine display of pyrotechnics. Shore batteries added their full weight of flying metal and crashing explosions. In this case as in the previous one, the bombs fell harmlessly in the sea some yards from our stern, and the bombers rear gunner had caused none of us any harm. So, in a matter of minutes, danger had come and had been beaten off. All the time the convoy moved slowly on.

Nobody on board had much to say about the proceedings, which were all in a nights work. Attacks were expected, and we were ready for the next. The third when it duly came, was less exciting, the bomber shearing off as the guns struck first blow. So, it wasn't a bad night after all, other nights were quieter still except fro the stream of invaders who flew high over our mast into a hail of shells from the shore.

How was all this concerned with defeat or victory? I pondered. In its way, it was a battle won for us, and attack beaten off, on object gained. That object was keeping the seas open for traffic, which if denied would seriously embarrass the railway system. As the Prime Minister said. It would be easy to reduce losses at sea to vanishing point by the simple expedient of keeping the ships in harbour, but Britain does not fight wars by keeping her ships in harbour. She sets them on their course, and defends every inch of the way.

Every ship in that convoy, the keen eyed men on perpetual lookout, skippers who scarcely left their bridge throughout the voyage, gun crews and seamen, all that night were battling for Britain by sailing on and never flinching. Sailing on and hitting back.

There were half a dozen New Zealanders in the crew, who had come from the other side of the world to join in the great work, and were proud to do it. Over a cup of cocoa on the moonlit deck, one of them remarked that it was grand to be having a crack at Jerry, but as we sat under the cover of the gun mounting, we talked less of war but of simpler, sweeter things in life.

I was to read a day or two later the German communiqué on ship losses from attacks on coastal convoys. How fantastic they seemed in the light of what I had seen and experienced. In the claim the tonnage of the wrecked ships were set out. But, think a moment. What can a bomber pilot know of tonnages of the wrecked ships in his brief seconds of his dive in the night? Furthermore he is so swiftly harried away that he can have little opportunity to observe results. At all events, the Nazis could not rightfully claim the that night or any of the voyage a hit on the convoy.

'Number One' who is second in command found opportunities by day for pursuing his favourite sport, which was shooting at floating mines. A mine for him is something of a private 'nark' with the Nazi's or a diversion which is his own prerogative by divine right. "The Germans don't play according to rules" he told me whilst explaining how the British mines, should they break their moorings owing to, say, a rusted cable, are automatically made safe.

Firing at them with a rifle is no more than target practice, but if a prong of a German mine is hit, up she goes with a bang.
While we were having lunch one day, word was brought to the wardroom of a mine on the starboard side fairly close in. 'Number One' shot out of the room, and I, this time hoping to see one explode, followed, arriving just in time to see a pile of water shoot up into the air with a terrific explosion, a dark heavy mass of turbulent sea. Framed in the doorway, I took a great deal of the blast and was all but floored by it. I was warned to seek cover to avoid the pieces of falling mine casing. I had clear evidence of the tremendous power of the mine, and the menace that it can be. But it is a menace quite under control, cunning and ingenious though the Nazi's are.
"Another ship saved" a seaman aptly remarked.

A.M. Lee
HMS Woolston.

Chapter 48

1944

It was early January 1944, after initial training at 'Royal Arthur at Skegness and signals training at 'Scotia' at Ayr. I found myself on a draft from Chatham to HMS **Westcott** who was at the time berthed at Greenock.
I arrived at Glasgow railway station after a long and tedious journey. There were three others on the same draft. When we reported our arrival, we were told that transport down to the docks would not be available for at least an hour, so to lose ourselves., we did not need a second telling so we adjourned to the nearest watering hole where I was introduce to my first 'Black and tan'. The most I had drank until then was the occasional 'Brown Ale'. After three pints of this nectar we were called to our transport, one of the Naval trucks. By the time we arrived at Greenock I was a little worse for wear. However, somehow, I still don't know how, I managed to negotiate two gang planks and landed on the deck of HMS **Westcott.** I was directed to what was to be my mess, down a hatchway to the mess deck.
Somehow, I managed, with the help of others, to sling my hammock and actually get in it.
The next morning I was awakened to find that my hammock was swaying. We were at sea!
I was told to report to the Yeoman on the flag deck. When I eventually found my way there I met the other members of the signals branch. I was shown around the flag deck, the flag lockers, halyards and various signal lamps, two ten inch, and an aldis, and the bridge, the binnacle various brass voice pipes, the chart table which was on the port side of the bridge with its canvas cover, which was to hide any light when the navigator or officer of the watch would be plotting or checking our course during darkness, which was almost twenty four hours during the winter months in those northern climes, this was where I was to be when on watch, when not busy with signals I would be at the side of the bridge, with powerful binoculars as an extra lookout.
By this time the sea was getting a little rough and I was beginning to feel nauseated. Oh why did I leave the comfort of my home? Soon I was being violently sea sick and wishing that I could die. This was my initiation to being a matelot. I had never been on a boat before let alone go to sea. For three days I was so ill that I eventually passed out. Apparently I was rolling from one side of the flag deck to the other with the motion of the ship. When one of the other signal men said to the yeoman "What are we going to do about him Yeo? "Leave him there, he'll live" was the reply.

However the ship pulled into Iceland and I had a chance to recover. After a brief stay, riding at anchor we were off. Destination Russia! I was about to learn of the hazards and hardships of those who were being employed in the escorting of convoys to and from Murmansk and Archangel.
A few days at sea and we were out of fresh food, from then on it was dehydrated vegetables, which was always packed in square tins. Meat too became non-existent except of course Corned beef, or corned dog as we called it. The only respite from this was when things were really quiet, we would drop a depth charge, and with everyone on deck with boat hooks, buckets, anything to grab as many as we could from the hundreds of fish that had been blown to the surface, with their guts blown out of their mouths. Of course the fish was delicious.
But the memory of the intense cold (temperatures could get as low as minus 50 degrees with the wind chill factor) and the very rough seas are uppermost in my mind when I think of those trips to Murmansk.
The ship, like most of the V&Ws had been built in 1917 as a short range destroyer with a speed of some thirty knots. In 1943 she had been converted to a long range escort vessel by removing her 'Woodbine' funnel and one of her boilers to make way for extra fuel space. This conversion reduced her speed to 22-25 knots, and when she was at full speed she vibrated violently.
Conditions on board were primitive, no baths or showers, you used a bucket. This was also used for doing your dhobeying or to the uninitiated 'washing'. There was certainly no privacy.
In the mess which was about 29 feet by 25 feet about twenty-five men had to sleep, prepare food and eat it. To wash your clothes you scraped 'flakes' off a bar of 'Pussers Hard' (soap) you would then take it to the galley and if the cook was in a good mood he would let you put it on the range to heat. Then you would take it on the upper deck and get busy with the scrubber. There were time when this routine was just not possible, and you would go many days before you were able to change into clean clothes.
When in harbour, Sunday mornings would be 'Captains Rounds'. The mess had to be scrubbed out, hammocks stowed away, everything had to be neat and tidy, then you would retire from your mess whilst the Captain scrutinised the mess, everything had to be shipshape and 'Bristol Fashion'. This routine was not possible whilst at sea, being 'Watch About' ie; four hour on and four hours off (that is if you were not called to action stations).
By the time you came off watch and removed your oilskin or duffle coat and then the other sodden wet clothing and climbed into you hammock, most times near exhaustion, there was not much of your four hours off left to snatch some sleep, and if action stations sounded you could go some time before you were able to do that. There was a time when I dozed off standing

up while on watch, thank goodness it was only momentarily for if I had been caught 'napping' I would have been for the high jump, it certainly meant a very serious charge. Whilst on watch on the bridge, unless you were engaged signalling you had to keep a constant lookout with binoculars glued to your eyes watching for aircraft, U-boats and if you were close escort, keep an eye on the merchant ships, making sure they kept station and did not make too much smoke, for some of them were coal burning ships. Occasionally there would be one develop engine problems and would drop back out of line whilst the rest of the convoy carried on, then you may get detailed to stay with it for protection until it could get under way again.
Convoy work was mainly boring, on the odd occasion we would get a 'ping' from the Asdic, Action stations would be sounded and then it was all systems go. Everyone at action stations would have their ears pricked listening to the Asdic and eye scanned the ocean looking for the tell tale signs of a periscope of the wake of a torpedo.
On one occasion a U-boat had been reported on the surface ahead of the convoy, being nearest we were despatched at full speed to intercept.
We were accompanied by another V&W the **Whitehall** (I think) We were Senior Officer Escort and were ahead of the **Whitehall**.
The Yeoman (who was a very competent man) had his telescope to his eye scanning the horizon ahead. "Hook on" "Enemy in sight and the Battle ensign". We were breaking all speed records, vibrating like the devil pounding through the sea, (can you imagine what it was like for a seventeen year old to be on the bridge of a British destroyer in hot pursuit of the enemy?).
"U-boat dead ahead sir!!" Hoist enemy in sight, battle ensign to the masthead!" was the yeoman's cry. He had spotted the U-boat long before anyone else. Everyone at action stations. Gun crews, depth charge parties. All those on the bridge had their binoculars trained on the U-boat. (My first and only sight of a U-boat until VE Day plus one). The, "U-boat about to dive sir!" came the cry from the alert Yeoman Hall. How did he know?
The range and direction was given to 'B' gun's crew. The Gunnery Officer, Trevor Riches confirmed that he had it in sight, but at extreme range, so with the gun at an angle of approximate 45 degrees the order came "Open Fire!!" With the crash of the gun the peak of the Gunnery Officers cape fell off! But what a brilliant shot. Dead in line with the U-boat but just a few yards short of the target which by now making a hasty dive to the protection of the waves. There was not enough time to get off another shot before the U-boat disappeared. Then the ensuing depth charge attack, first the 'Hedgehog' - to no avail, then the depth charges, what a spectacular sight when they detonate. On this occasion there was no evidence of a kill. We continued the search,

but the conditions in those icy waters are of no assistance to the Asdic operators. We then had to resume our station in the most important duty that of protection of the convoy.
So we continued our way to Murmansk, or should I say Polyarno, for that is where we naval vessels were (If you were lucky) berthed. Whilst the merchant ships continued up the Kola inlet to Murmansk. What a God forsaken place, not the ideal place for a run ashore. I did try to go our of the dockyard area once, only to be confronted by a Russian woman dressed in a dark khaki great coat and the usual Russian fur hat with the red star in the front, armed with a rifle with fixed bayonet, Nikt you are not going walkies was the impression she gave me when brandishing the bayonet. I'm sure she would have disembowelled me had I persisted. All the Russian people looked so very sullen, tho' the children were eager to barter for anything, they looked so pitiful.
We escorted another three of these convoys before we were called to another task. 'D' Day and the Normandy landings.
We left the Clyde on the 3rd June, armed with a pamphlet from General Eisenhower telling us of the great crusade that we were about to embark upon. When we turned left instead of right on leaving the Clyde we knew that it was not to be another Russian run. We rendezvoused with the Warspite, but because of the deterioration of the weather we had to sail around the Channel Islands for a couple of days before proceeding to the French coast. Warspite's task was the bombardment of shore batteries at Caen. What a thunderous roar when she opened up with a broadside, this went on most of the day. Come dusk a signal was sent asking permission to go in close, to do our little bit. We were told to stay where you are. The next day we developed a leak in one of the boilers, on reporting this we were told to return to the Solent for repairs. No lame ducks were welcome in this environment.
As we steamed up the Solent, vessels of every conceivable type, Royal and Merchant ships cheered and blared away on their sirens etc; may be they thought that we had been wounded in battle!
After we had anchored, I was on watch when I noticed among all these hundreds of ships a light was flashing our pennant number. On answering I found that it was my brother who was serving on an MTB. Looking at him through my binoculars I could just make out his balding head. Of course there was no possibility of meeting up.
On completion of the temporary repairs we were detailed to patrol off the French and Belgian coast. This we continued to do calling in at Dover for fuel and supplies. Then it was off to Dundee to get the boiler cleaned and repaired.

On the 31st October we escorted two large personnel ships, this was a fast convoy, the two ships, the Empress of Australia and the Scythia had 11,000 Russian nationals on board who had been 'captured' in France, while serving with the Germans. When we arrived at the Kola Inlet we had to anchor in the mouth of the river. No one was allowed ashore, and the British shore establishments were not allowed near Murmansk. What happened to those unfortunate Russians?
We did two more of those convoys to Russia, On one return convoy in December I was on watch and saw in the distance a huge flash, followed by the sound of an explosion. I was soon to learn that it was the destroyer Cassandra who had been torpedoed, lost her bows and had to return to Murmansk.
Our last convoy to Russia designated JW63 sailed on the 30th December, and arrived on the 8th January. By now there was almost 24 hours of darkness, with very much cloud, snow and ice which meant that there was no interference from the enemy. The return convoy RA63 sailed from the Kola Inlet on the 11th January 1945, once again we were not intercepted by the enemy, but we encountered a far greater and fiercer enemy, that of the weather. We were about three days out from Murmansk. North East of the Faroes when the storm blew up, soon the winds were at hurricane force, forcing the ships to heave to, or take shelter where they could.
On the **Westcott,** it was horrendous, we were being tossed about like a cork I was on the bridge, soaked to the skin, hanging on for dear life, whilst those in the mess below were being thrown about to such an extent that some received injuries. 'Jock Gilmour our S.B.A had split his head open and had used his clean underwear to bandage it. Fuel oil had escaped through in to the mess deck mixed with the salt water was swilling around intermingled with various items that had not been stowed away. What a filthy stinking mess. One minute the ship was riding on the crest of a huge wave and then she would plunge down into the trough and the next wave would come right over the top of us. Everything had been battened down, no one dare move without a life line. How long the storm lasted I do not know, I do know that it seemed a lifetime. I think it was the only time that I feared for my life.
How we survived I will never know, maybe by the skill of the Captain and the helmsman, or may be by the Grace of God.
When the storm did eventually subside, it's severity was evident. Much damage had been done, anything not secured had disappeared boats had been smashed, carley rafts gone, rails were bent there was a heavy swell running and on attempting 180 degree turn, a wave caught our beam, and the old ship keeled over at an alarming angle, she stayed there for what seemed

ages, but the old girl righted herself, I'm sure quite a few hearts missed a few beats. We again resumed our voyage, but we had to go to the Faroes for an emergency repair apparently rivets had been forced out of our keel!
On out arrival in the Clyde at the end of January 1945 we had to go into dock for storm damage repairs, this was to be **Westcott's** last Russian convoy. She did other work, a few trips across to Ireland escorting the ferry from Stranraer to Larne. The war in Europe was soon to end. We were anchored in the Clyde on VE day. "Splice the Main Brace"!!
Celebration went on till late in the day we were firing Very Lights, star shells etc; the officers came forward on to the seaman's mess carrying bottles of beer and spirits. The Skipper, Lt, Cmdr Reed asked for a cigarette and a light. Who ever gave him the light singed his beard! He accused me of trying to set light to his beard and threatened to throw me overboard!
The next day we were ordered to proceed to Iceland. Apparently the marines there had gone on the rampage. We took with us some senior ranking officers to try and sort thing out. On the way we came across four U-boats which had been ordered to remain on the surface, on contact we gave them direction to proceed to Cambletown in Scotland.
On our return we were paid off. Soon the old **Westcott** was to be scrapped. She had served our country faithfully and well for 28 years, she had steamed thousands of miles without breaking down. During her very long and illustrious career she had been involved in incidents from China to Russia, from the Mediterranean to the North Atlantic. Now she was to be scrapped, a very sad end to a wonderful ship.
Her name is spoken with great pride and affection by all who served aboard her as do I. Why? Maybe it was because she was my first ship, maybe because she had most of my guts, or perhaps it was in her that I grew up.

Stormy
Ex 'Bunting Tosser'
H.M.S. **Westcott**

Chapter 49

Convoy JW 57

I joined **Wanderer** from the cruiser Shropshire at Devonport in 1943.
After coming off the Shropshire it looked like an old tin can. Then it was all action. Russian convoy, Malta, Gibraltar, Argentian, Newfoundland, 'D'day etc:
I think one of the most unhappy incidents that I remember, was when we, with the **Watchman** sailed on the 20th February to escort the Escort Carrier Chaser to join the convoy JW57 to Russia. I still see it as if it was happening now. I was working part of ship. Looking up I saw one of my friends, who was on the mid ship Oerlikon going over the side and passing the guard rail right where we were standing. We released the aft Carley float immediately, but by the time we had received permission from the Convoy Commodore to turn round and go and rescue him, and by the time we found him and got him aboard, despite the Doctor working frantically on him it was too late and alas the poor lad died.
We buried him at sea in his hammock. I was one of the burial party. He was from Scotland and nineteen years old.
After this, all life belts were half blown up That incident remains in my memory to this day. It is something that you just do not forget.
Now for an amusing incident, it occurred the day after the sinking of U523. A secret order was received by the Captain. The ship was to enter Portuguese territorial waters under the cover of darkness, proceed up the river Tagust(?) And rendezvous off Lisbon and meet an unspecified small vessel which was give two recognition letters to be flashed back. Thereafter picking up an RAF party consisting of a Squadron Leader and four other ranks which we thought would be going back to Gibraltar. Lisbon from the ship was amazing, after the blackout at home, it was just like the Blackpool illuminations.
The best of it was we had survivors of the U-boat down below and their navigator was in the Captain's day cabin with the dead lights screwed down. We had our Oerlikon and a party with Sten guns trained on the boat just in case. It was just like a scene from a film.
Then from the boat stepped a man, dressed in dinner jacket and wearing a Anthony Eden soft black hat and a Sherlock Holmes type of cape slung around his shoulders! We never heard a word or find out what it was all about.
Some years later in the Captain's Commander Whinney) book "U-boat Peril" it said that Wanderer on August 26th 1943 was an advance party to

implement the agreement signed on August 18th with our oldest Ally, Portugal to supply aircraft, spitfires, barrage balloons for use in the Azores with air bases for British aircraft protecting convoys. This agreement came into force in October 1943. The Portuguese firmly refused to allow the Americans the same privilege.
I remember when we dropped a depth charge of the coast of Newfoundland. All the fish came to the surface, we were all clinging to the scrambling nets hauling the fish aboard. The Newfoundlanders came and thanked us for the fish. As I was the only one in our mess able to clean the fish I got the biggest piece.

Cliff Armstrong.

* * * * * *

An incident in the Naval War which will take its place in the chronicles of courage was the engagement on January 26th 1944 between two British destroyers, the **Vampire** of the Royal Australian Navy and the Thanet on the one side and a Japanese cruiser and three destroyers on the other.
The conflict began after dark in the region of the Endau Peninsular, when our naval forces attacked a Japanese transport about to land troops. Our destroyers raced into action against heavy odds. After a running fight one Japanese destroyer was sunk, the second was damaged and the third retired. It is regrettable that the Thanet an 'S; class destroyer of 905 tons completed 1918 after a valiant fight was lost. These destroyers were veterans of the last war and mounted guns of only 4 inch calibre as compared with the Japanese 4.7 weapons.

* * * * *

The memories of Ordinary Telegraphist
Ken. G. Holmes.

I was on board HMS **Warwick** on Sunday 20th February 1944 at the age of twenty.
I was in my mess at about 1145 when an explosion shook the ship violently and a cloud of dust fell from the overhead pipes that ran through the mess. My first thoughts were to get my life belt and head for the upper deck. My life belt was the type that had to be blown up like a car inner tube, was rolled up and hung on a hammock hook near the door. I grabbed the life belt and made for the door. The mess was on the starboard side of the ship and the

only access to it was by a ladder that lead upwards to a hatch which opened out on the upper deck aft of the forward superstructure. This ladder also served the E,R,A's mess which was on the port side.

I was first to the doorway of my mess but was beaten to the ladder by one of the ERA's. On looking up I could see some burning wreckage across the hatch top. The ERA went ahead of me and either him or someone on the upper deck cleared the wreckage away. I proceeded on to the upper deck where I found oil, some of it burning on the deck, and seemingly spurting up somewhere near the funnel.

The wireless office was at the rear of the forward superstructure and as I came on to the upper deck. I saw the P.O. Tel' who was my boss, shouting for people to go their action stations. Mine was in the H/F, D/F office in the stern of the ship, and when I looked in that direction, I could see that the stern was no longer there. I was actually standing on the port side of the ship by the whaler, and efforts were being made to lower it. Unfortunately burning oil; had dropped into it and it was obvious that it would not float when it got into the water. I had, by this time donned my life belt and was in the process of blowing it up, and seeing that the whaler was useless, I moved to the starboard side where efforts were being made to lower the motor boat. This was also proving fruitless as it appeared that the lowering gear had jammed. I was standing next to a P.O. Who said, if I remember correctly, that this was the third time this had happened to him. As he said this the ship heeled over to port and I grabbed the wire hand rail that went round the ship. I was fortunate, as I got hold of it, but some of the others waiting by the rail didn't and they slid down the oily deck out of my sight. I climbed over the rail and on to the side of the ship which was now almost level, I slid down it and jumped off the bottom of the ship into the water. I was fully dressed in overalls and wearing boots, but my life belt was inflated and I remembered during my training told that if such an emergency happened to me, that I should hold my life belt down to prevent it striking me under the chin when I hit the water. This I did, and I arrived in the water amid a flurry of arms and legs belonging to the others who had jumped with me.

The water was icy cold and came as a bit of a shock, but my first thought was to swim away from the ship before she sank and pulled me down with her.

There was a heavy swell on the sea and I found that I would go up on one rise, and then down, but I didn't come up quick enough before the next rise, consequently that one came over my head. So, half the time I was in the water I seemed to be under water as well. The oil that covered the top of the water was a problem as well, it meant that I had to make sure it did not get into my eyes. At first I could hear men shouting, but from the time I jumped

into the water I never saw another soul. For all I knew I could have been the only survivor.
Having swam away from the ship as far as I thought safe, I turned to look behind me. The bows of the **Warwick** were still above water and I could see a man sitting on the capstan on the forecastle. Who he was I didn't know (the lad was Jamie Norburn - he could not swim, thought he might be rescued, but went down with the ship) I was treading water or doing a bit of breast stroke whilst looking round to see if any help was in view, when I saw a destroyer heading our way. I began swimming towards it and I could see some of the crew lowering scrambling nets down the side. Then just when I thought I was going to be saved the destroyer sped away. To make matters worse, a few minutes later she started dropping depth charges, although I was a good distance away, as each one exploded it was like being punched in the stomach. I swam away to increase the distance from the explosions, and, after some time (I don't know how long) still not having seen any other person in the water, or the Carley floats, which I found out later had been launched, I sighted on one of my upliftings on the swell what appeared to be three boats heading in my direction. I started to swim towards them. At first I thought that I had done too well as it appeared that I was going to be run down by one of them, but, I adjusted my direction and found myself alongside one of them. I raised myself up in the water and shouted. There seemed to be no one on deck, but as I shouted a man came out of the deck house. How he saw me I don't know as the water was covered in oil and so was I. He did see me though and threw me a rope. I grabbed it gratefully but was dismayed to find that because of the oil it was sliding out of my hands. I promptly took a turn round my wrists and hung on. My saviour must have been a very strong man because he hauled me up the side of the ship with no help from me and threw me on the deck. He said something to me in a language I did not understand and for a few minutes thought that I was going to end up in a prison camp! He realised that I did not understand, and then in English he told me to go down below. I went to a cabin with a roaring stove blazing in it, and I began stripping off my clothes. I could not do anything with my boots, which were of course wet through, then a man came down and cut them off for me. At that time there was no one else in the cabin, and I stood over the blazing stove and was unable to feel the heat. I was so exhausted that I got into a bunk. I must have passed out, because I don't remember any more until I was awakened by another survivor still in his wet and cold clothes! This was quite a shock as I was in the nude and was just started to get warm. I looked round and saw that there were a number of the **Warwick's** crew aboard, but they were unrecognisable to me as they were all covered in oil. I understood by

this time that we were on our way to Padstow, but I lost all track of time and have no idea how long it took us.
On arriving at Padstow a member of the fishing vessel's crew gave me a pair of trousers and an old blanket to go ashore in. I climbed up the ladder to dry land and the realised how lucky I had been to still be alive. I owed grateful thanks to the man who had hauled me out of the water. It seemed that most of the survivors had been landed by this time and we were directed to get into a lorry which was standing by and we were transported to the R.N.A.S (Royal Naval Air Station) at St Merryn.
We were greeted by a P.O. With a basin full of rum and given a cup full!! It was only after that I began to feel human again! We were fed, kitted out in Battle dress, and given a bed for the night before being transported to the R.N.B at Plymouth. There we went through the joining routine, issued with new kit and eventually sent on survivors leave.

Postscript;- By Shipmate J. Wood. **H.M.S Whitshed**.
Nearly half of the **Warwick's** crew were lost. Ken was rescued by a Belgian fishing trawler whose skipper was Marcel Bacquaert. At six foot two inches tall and wearing a size eleven boots, that fisherman must have been one hell of a strong fellow. When I think of him St Peter always come into my mind.
The ship that turned away was the 'Wensleydale' - six months later to the very day she sank U-613 with only one survivor, he was the engineer. In the 80's we learned from his son, that for the rest of his life he spoke nothing but praise for the men of the Wensleydale who picked him up. They could not do enough for him! Funny Old War.
There are six trees in Padstow, St Merryn Churchyard planted in memory of the six boys. They were planted in 1984 and Ken planted one of them. There is also a plaque on the harbour wall. Ken went to this big event in 1996.
At the back of the Church in St Merryn there is a plaque dedicated to H.M.S **Warwick**.

Iced up during Russian Convoy
JW 57 February 1944

Officer of the watch on the bridge of a V&W lighting up with a box of 'Swan Vestas'. Note the 'voice pipes'

Chapter 50

Hardships! Hardships!
You don't know what hardships are!
So say's Joe Beckett
H.M.S. Vimy

I'll come clean, I was born into a middle class family. My father was a bank official. My older brother and I went to Birkenhead Institute, this was a grammar school and my father paid ten guineas a year for each of us.
When WW2 broke out I was thirteen and evacuated to Oswestry in Shropshire. I left school when I was sixteen in 1942 and entered Martins Bank at their head office in Liverpool.
Very unfortunately and tragically my brother John was killed whilst serving as a Sub Lieutenant Observer in the Fleet Air Arm. Quite naturally my parents were devastated, and from then on, all their love and affection was centred upon me.
I was a corporal in the ATC (Air Training Corps) as I had always wanted to fly in the RAF. Because my brothers death whilst flying, my mother was very insistent that I did not fly. Consequently I volunteered for the Royal Navy through a system called the 'Y' scheme, which was supposed to be a short cut to obtaining a commission.
So I got my papers in June 1944 a couple of months before my eighteenth birthday. I entered the R.N. In HMS Royal Arthur 'Skeggy' (Skegness). One of the things I remembered there, was going on a run ashore and booking at a theatre to see nude females in the show. They had boa feathers and were not allowed to move!
During my interview by a RN Lieutenant I was asked why I wanted to join the Navy. In my utter stupidity, I said, "I really wanted to join the RAF and fly, but my mother wouldn't let me, so I joined the Navy as second best".
The RN Lieutenant went Puce and nearly bust a gut. He said in no uncertain terms that I'd better make the Navy "Bloody first best from now on!"
Amazingly I wasn't thrown off my course and was drafted to HMS Excaliber near Crew for my initial training, which was very demanding, both physically and mentally, but an absolutely super for a fit eighteen year old. We weren't even tired by the second dog watch, we had enough energy to play very competitive soccer and hurley in the evenings.
After twelve weeks half of Effingham Division passed out and half failed, but there were three of us about whom they could not make up their minds. We were interviewed by four officers chaired by the C.O. Capt., Figgins RN, a very formidable character.

I can' remember much about it except that the final question was;- "Did I think I had done well enough in the interview to pass?"
Of course I didn't know, but I figured if I said "No" I was bound to fail, so, I said "Yes", and they passed me!
I was the drafted to Dauntless for eight weeks sea training. We were taught everything, seamanship, navigation, how to cox a whaler, how to fire a six inch gun etc: We all had to wear an arm band with a number on it, so we were observed all the time. The only time that you felt private was when you were having a Ess Aitch One tea!
After eight weeks I was told that I was too immature to continue officer training, and was sent to sea as a matelot to see if I could mature enough to have another bite at the cherry at a later date. This was considered the "Kiss of death".
The next step was a draft to HMS **VIMY** based at Sheerness. The draft was routed via Chatham barracks and an overnight stay in the infamous tunnel. Any minute one expected to meet the artful dodger or Fagan from Oliver Twist! (I thought Chatham was full of Artful Dodgers. Ed.)
On the trot boat taking me to **Vimy**, we passed a ship with a hole in the side. This was **Wallace** that had hit a mine off Ostend.
When we arrived on **Vimy** they were piping "Hands to stations for leaving harbour" I was told we were taking a convoy to Ostend! I was shit scared. So there was this young eighteen year old in December 1944, who thought that everyone lived in a semi-detached and voted Conservative, plonked into number one mess in the forecastle of a V&W, the youngest and greenest OD imaginable. If you have never lived in number one mess of a V&W destroyer you have never lived. Talk about "See Naples and die".
When the sea was rough, the mess deck was awash. The heads (toilets) had no doors, the washing facilities were primitive beyond belief! The Captain had a bath, the officers had one between them, about 30-40 PO's had six wash basins between them (no taps) the rest of the crew had six between them. To fill them with hot water, you pumped cold water into a tank over the coal fired galley, when hot, filled a bucket and carried it to the wash place.
Like all V&Ws, number one mess contained a steam winch which was used when weighing anchor, around this was a hammock netting where we kept our hammocks when not in use. It emitted so much steam that our hammocks soon became sodden wet. No wonder that TB was rife in the pre-war Navy. So this was to be my home for the next six months, and unbelievably I enjoyed myself.
I had my first alcoholic run ashore with the two Geordies who had befriended me, taught me how to drink pints of mild, and generally looked after me.

Our job was to escort convoys half across the Atlantic and swap them with the Canadians.
I had two action stations. One was part of the depth charge party aft. This was exciting but hard work, dangerous too. The other was as telegraph man in the wheel house, a real cushy number, at times I was allowed to take the wheel and steer the ship, this was a real thrill.
VE day we were alongside Sheerness docks. Half the ships company had twenty-four hours leave, including your truly and the two Geordies, Green and Laverick. We went up the smoke (Naval slang for London) for the day. It was wonderful, it is hard to describe, it was so packed with people, it felt as though the whole of the U.K. were there, singing in the streets, pubs ran out of beer, male and female strangers were snogging each other, and more, wherever you went. I often wondered how many babies were born in the first half of February 1946. It must have been a record.
Whilst aboard **Vimy** I was a C.W. Candidate and unless you have been one you cannot imagine what it is like, not being accepted by either the lower or upper deck, it was like being a sea leper.
Nevertheless, as long as I kept my place and did my job I was tolerated. There was another C.W. Candidate aboard whose name was Jacques. He was known to the matelot's as Jack Hughes!
Before I left **Vimy** I was made A.B. And was very proud of this. Also my sea time aboard entitled me to the Atlantic Star of which I am extremely proud. On reflection, when I think of the sailors that did four or five years on Atlantic convoys covering the dark days of 1942-43, I feel very humble.
Eventually **Vimy** was paid off and I was drafted to HMS Raleigh at Torpoint, this was more pre-officer training. Quite hard work and very different to being at sea in a V&W.
I would like to make and appreciation on behalf of the H.O. Ratings and the RNVR officers to the regular RN men, both officers and ratings. I appreciate that we were often cack-handed and bloody useless but by and large you tolerated us in your typical RN way. Thank you most sincerely.
(What happened to the Hardships? Ed.)

******

Another Vimy Story

Sheerness is surely the most miserable and depressing of places for a draft to 'clew up' four C.W. candidates straight from school, and here we joined HMS **Vimy** in mid winter.

As I recollect the welcome we received could not have been bettered, the aura of the old V&Ws so apparent and sustained. Not without misgivings did we welcome the end of the German war six months on.

Those six months were full and rewarding. First as 'Hedgehog' sweeper. What an unfortunate weapon, more lethal to HM ships than U-boats.

The gunner 'T' sought me out in the mess, was I in the rattle? Not a bit of it, congratulations for my industry permitted training left and right, not previously achieved.

Then dinghy sweeper, The C.O. Lt, Comdr., Phi's RN, was a passionate sailor and I began to enjoy Sheerness and the Thames Estuary. An extension of this duty meant that I was crew member of the whaler, dropped at Deal and sailed to Sheerness.

The best fish and chips ever tasted arose out of a provisioning a ship for North Sea patrol and orders changed to escort an Atlantic convoy.

An 'Asdic Ping' resulted in depth charging a shoal of cod, so scrambling nets were rigged, and the cod was hauled aboard - big eats,

Another occasion illustrated the confidence of the British. There were Spanish fishing boats in the convoy lane, which was highly suspect, and ignoring the order to heave to 'B' gun put a shot across their bows, then the gun crews changed into number threes. We manned the whaler and boarded what we imagined to be the senior officer. The vessel was subjected to an abortive search and ordered South. Only when we returned to **Vimy** did we realise that we had carried no arms whatsoever, which was certainly not the case with the Spanish!.

Our motor boat was useless, once again 'B' gun's crew manned the whaler and this time, when slipped we fell into a trough of a wave and not the crest, shipping an enormous amount of the North Atlantic. The objective upon this occasion was to take the doctor to an American Liberty ship, as a crew member had suspected appendicitis. The doctor and the S.B.A. Did manage to grasp the climbing ladder as the whaler turned turtle, the bottom boards had split, 'B' gun's crew were in the drink but managed quite quickly to board the liberty ship in spite of the efficiency of the Americans managed to throw both ends of the line to those who were in the water! That was the first time that 'B' gun's crew had seen drink dispensing machines, they finally returned to **Vimy** with excellent warm clothing and sea boots. Not the end of that story, because we manoeuvred alongside the whaler, hooked on and manned the falls. The weight of the whaler and water caused the davits to buckle, twenty eight years had taken it's toll. A jury rig from the top of the mast enabled the whaler to be shipped - with care. The great complaint of the whaler's crew was, that the weather became calm and the motor boat was able to collect the doctor and S.B.A. When they all thought that a return to

Vimy was not possible and had been looking forward to a hero's welcome in the United States.
We were senior officer of the last Atlantic convoy of the war. As Quarter Master I was able to swipe the White Ensign flown from **Vimy** on that occasion, sadly now mislaid.
At Sheerness we de-stored and de- ammunitioned ship and thence to Immingham. Whilst the CW's were excused duty pending draft, this Quartermaster was required to take the wheel. **Vimy** well lightened, was clearly not taking kindly to the anticipated 'paying off' and showed her displeasure by bobbing around like a cork in a mill race.

Peter Scudds

* * * * * *

We had just completed two years of escort duty in the North Atlantic, and for some reason we were cruising around alone just off the south west coast of Ireland. We were serving no purpose there, and all on the lower deck were wondering why we were there.
On June the 4th the Captain called the attention of the ship's crew and said "I have a brown cnvelope here and I am supposed to open it at this time and read the contents to the ship's company. We heard the rustling of paper over the P.A. System and the Captain started to read "At 7 am, on the 6th June, the Allied armies will be landing in Normandy. We will be there. Good Luck".
On the night of the 5th we were crossing the Channel and at around midnight, a tug was towing a section of the Mulberry Harbour, and we were heading between the tug and the large section of the Mulberry Harbour. Someone on the tug must have seen what was happening and dropped the line so that it would not foul our screws. The section struck us full force on the starboard side, it split the **Vanquisher** open where the hull meets the deck for about twenty feet, causing a three foot opening at the centre to a point on each end, it caused no damage to the equipment. The hole was covered with canvas so no light would be shining from the boiler or engine room.
I was in the Asdic room when I heard the crash, I can imagine what it was like for the rating at the depth charge thrower about four feet above the water level and to see this thing coming at you which was about three story's high. He ran over to the port side and jumped overboard. Not anything to get excited about on that night. We continued on towards France. Further on we were attacked by E-boats. Their method was to attack two at a time, so that one could have you broadside target. Our idea was to head straight toward them, as a torpedo would not explode if it hit inside eleven degrees.

We arrived at the Utah beach head in the early morning and was for some time screening a R.N. Battleship who was shelling the shore line.
This is the part that is hard to believe:- At about 11 am, a liberty ship signalled the **Vanquisher**. "Send a small boat to pick up your man". No one would expect a ship to stop to pick up one man in those conditions. We sent a whaler over and he was brought back in a completely dry civvy suit. As he climbed up the scrambling net, someone said "What some guys will do to get a new suit", a lot of other things were also said that cannot be printed here, they were all joking of course.
Many things happened on that day that I will never forget. **Vanquisher** made twenty three trips between then and the end of August.

****

H.M.S. Woolston
By G. Hutchinson

On the 15th July 1944 I was posted to HMS Pembroke to await my first sea posting. I was also able to purchase a gold wire winged flash of lightning to sew on the right arm of my best Naval suit to indicate that I had now passed out as a R.A.D.A.R. Operator.
Although not permitted in peace time, the 'in' thing for the war time sailors was to be 'tiddly'. This meant, first of all to from a neat 'tiddly' bow on the cap band by sewing a small button in the centre of the bow, and instead of wearing the bow over the left ear as per regulations it would be next to the HMS on the hat band, and whilst on leave the hat would be worn on the back of the head, something that you would not dare do whilst in barracks.
Next the collar, with the three white stripes attended to, the issue collar was dark blue, so we would bleach it to attain a lighter blue, then you did not look like a 'sprog' who had just joined, and to give the impression that you had served in some warmer climes and your collar had been bleached by the sun.
The tunic issue had a distinct 'V' cut in the front which we cut to a 'U' shape, and the silk neck piece would be tied in a 'tiddly' bow at the front. The tunic was also machined in at the waist to give a tighter fit. The bell bottom trousers when issued would have 22 inch bottoms, these would have a 4 inch gusset in each leg to give a 26 inch bottom, then to finish off the trousers would be given a good press with seven horizontal creases. Those who could afford to would go to a naval tailor and have all these modifications carried out professionally, then you would keep your 'tiddly suit' for going ashore or on leave only.

Whilst in Chatham barracks we were kept busy square bashing, peeling spuds, mess cleaning, whit line washing and generally having our bodies and minds occupied. Walking across Chatham parade ground was not permitted, everything had to be done at the double, otherwise it was at your own peril and you would find yourself with stoppage of pay or stoppage of leave.
I enjoyed some weekend leave whilst there, until I was posted to HMS **Woolston** at Rosyth dockyard on the 24th September. I caught the train from Kings Cross to Waverley station Edinburgh. Struggling with my kit bag and hammock and weekend case I caught the next train to Inverkeithing, seeing, and crossing the Forth Bridge for the first time. When I finally arrived at Rosyth dockyard I had to catch a Naval tender to the **Woolston** who was anchored in mid stream. I was accompanied by another ordinary seaman Roy Cantwell.
No sooner had we been detailed to the forward port mess deck, stowed our kit bags and hammocks, when we were told that we could go ashore until 2300. Roy and myself took up the offer, even though we had been travelling all day, so back we went to Edinburgh. On our return we found that we had to kip down on the port side lockers because there was insufficient room to sling our hammocks.
Early next morning reveille was piped at about 0500 and after getting dressed we had to muster with the other seamen on the forecastle port side as equally eight men were lined up on the starboard side.
We weighed anchor or slipped the buoy. It was very calm, but I had not yet found my sea legs and found it very difficult standing still as HMS **Woolston** slowly made her way under the Forth Bridge out into the Firth of Fourth and on in to the North sea to escort a convoy going South.
For the next three days I was seasick and did not feel too good, as a matter of fact I wished that I had never joined. Some of my mess mates did not mind, because they helped themselves to my rations.
Woolston was an old V&W destroyer built in 1918 by Thornycrofts, her recognition and pennant number which was L49 was painted on her sides just forward of the break in the forecastle.
There was a steam capstan in the mess deck and for this inconvenience we were entitled to an extra 1/- a day classified as Hard Lying money. The stokers and artificers mess was just below the seamen's mess.
Just forward of the break in forecastle and between the port and starboard gangways was situated a small cooks galley, two members from each mess would prepare the food and take it to the galley for the cook to his duty.
The heads (toilets) and washrooms were situated between the bulkheads from the break of the forecastle and the mess decks. You could not afford to be shy when using the toilets, because the partition between the pans were so

low that you could pass the time of day with you 'oppo' sitting on the next pan. The officers quarters and wardroom were situated aft.
HMS **Woolston** was armed with twin four inch gun turrets fore and aft coupled with rocket launchers. On port and starboard amidships were single Bofor guns. For submarine warfare there were depth charge rollers astern and depth charge throwers on both starboard and port quarters. There was an Asdic set plus two radar sets, one amidships and one just above the bridge.
Invariably there would be three escort vessels on patrol and occasionally four. Sometimes we would have the old American four stackers which had been transferred under the Lend Lease Agreement. During theses escort duties I would spend my watch on the midship radar set. This set did not have a cathode ray tube which showed a circular sweep. Instead it depicted echo's in a straight line with blips bobbing up and down. One could distinguish between low flying aircraft and ships. I would also do a watch on the forward gun turret. In the winter, one of the crew would go down to the galley and bring back a jug of 'Kye'. It was a very thick chocolate drink which was made from scraping a solid block of this special chocolate into a 'fanny' and adding water, then brought to the boil, depending on who made it, it could be thick enough to stand a spoon up in it.
At times we would have a little quiet sing song among the gun crew, but we would get a very curt command from the bridge if we raised our voices too high.
It was different when I was on the radar set, for I would be alone for four hours, just watching the echo's bobbing up an down on the screen and only reporting if there was anything suspect occurring.
The washing of clothes or 'dhobeying' would be done in a bucket and was either hung amidships between the two smoke stacks or hung down in the engine room to dry.
At sea we were permitted to wear overalls as rig of the day, with leather sea boots which reached up to the knee and thick white sea boot stockings which were turned over the top of the sea boots, but as soon as we sailed into harbour it was back to Naval uniform.
It could be very cold on convoy and if the weather was bad, as it often was, the heavy seas would wash over the destroyers low deck line from the break in the forecastle to the stern. I was fortunate to be one of those recipients of one of the lambs wool lined leather coats donated by South Africa. Also in rough weather, life lines would be rigged from the break in the forecastle to the stern. On theses lines would be short lengths of rope with an eye splice and thimble, so that anyone walking along the deck could do so with reasonable safety.

There were times when the convoy would come to a complete standstill due to thick fog. The escort vessels had radar, but not all the merchant ships were so well equipped. I can remember one day when I was on duty on the forward gun turret, in one of the lay to situations, when a submarine conning tower just slid past our bows. I can only assume that it was one of ours. On another occasion the nearness of enemy became a reality. Action stations would be sounded and then some unfortunate merchant ship would receive the full force of an exploding torpedo and within minutes the unfortunate ship would be going down to the bottom. Sometimes action stations would not be sounded until the first torpedo had struck. On either occasion it would be full steam ahead and as soon as the depth charges had been set, they were either rolled off the stern or fired from the quarter throwers.

From the time I joined the **Woolston** to the end of the war with Germany. I think we only had one possible sinking of a U-boat. That was when we saw oil and clothing come to the surface, but as that was a ploy played by both sides to mislead the attacking surface ships, it could not be classified as a kill only a probable.

When we eventually returned to the mess deck, we would find that the enormous stresses set up by the exploding depth charges had stressed the ships riveted plates and she had let in water. Another aspect of the depth charge explosions would be that some of the hammock slinging bars would snap so some of the matelot's would have to find somewhere else to sleep. I had to wait four or five weeks before I was allocated a berth, that was when one of the other shipmates was drafted off the ship. The hammocks were so closely slung that we were virtually in one large swaying bed. To avoid breathing each others breath we used to sleep alternately head to foot.

If there happened to be action stations during the night, we would immediately come awake, grab some clothes and run like mad to our action stations. On one occasion a German E-boat sped up between the lines of the merchant ships, firing its torpedo's and guns. There was a bit of a 'ding dong', but no major hits, just shell holes in the ships funnels and side.

Sometimes the rough sea would free mines from their moorings and these floating hazards would give the gun crews some extra practice.

We were granted four free travel warrants each year, so when the **Woolston** went into Leith dockyard for a refit I used one for some home leave. The train journey from Edinburgh took some 8 to 9 hours overnight, the train was always completely crowded with service personnel going on or returning from leave. When the train pulled into Kings Cross it was an experience to see the number of service men who had no ticket, with just one or two ticket collectors on duty, they had no chance to stop the surge of passengers, some would jump over the barriers or would offer any piece of cardboard that looked like a ticket. Most of the ticket collectors could not care less, as they probably had some member of their family serving in the forces anyway. Some of the servicemen would just push their way through the barrier without offering tickets or fare.

In early May 1945 HMS **Woolston** with another six destroyers left Rosyth and headed towards Norway.

❧

June 3RD 1944

SUPREME HEADQUARTERS

ALLIED EXPEDITIONARY FORCE

Soldiers, Sailors and Airmen of the Allied Expeditionary Force!

You are about to embark upon the Great Crusade, toward which we have striven these many months. The eyes of the world are upon you. The hopes and prayers of liberty-loving people everywhere march with you. In company with our brave Allies and brothers-in-arms on other Fronts, you will bring about the destruction of the German war machine, the elimination of Nazi tyranny over the oppressed peoples of Europe, and security for ourselves in a free world.

Your task will not be an easy one. Your enemy is well trained, well equipped and battle-hardened. He will fight savagely.

But this is the year 1944! Much has happened since the Nazi triumphs of 1940-41. The United Nations have inflicted upon the Germans great defeats, in open battle, man-to-man. Our air offensive has seriously reduced their strength in the air and their capacity to wage war on the ground. Our Home Fronts have given us an overwhelming superiority in weapons and munitions of war, and placed at our disposal great reserves of trained fighting men. The tide has turned! The free men of the world are marching together to Victory!

I have full confidence in your courage, devotion to duty and skill in battle. We will accept nothing less than full Victory!

Good Luck! And let us all beseech the blessing of Almighty God upon this great and noble undertaking.

Dwight Eisenhower

Chapter 51

'TIDDLY WIV'

From the Book "Seagulls in my Belfry"

By Rear Admiral C.C. Anderson

The command was H.M.S **Wivern**. She was one of the most famous of the grand old V&Ws in which I had done my Midshipman's destroyer time, and for nearly a quarter of a century, she had been known to the Navy as Tiddly Wiv".

I had been long enough in the Atlantic Escort to have an almost unbearable envy of the destroyers which could double our speed and had no fewer than four real working guns, **Wivern** had all this, plus our outfit of torpedoes. I was moving to a infinitely better, faster, more strongly armed ship- a ship which could really take some offensive action. Having been on the helplessly on the receiving end for so long that was cause enough for jubilation.

But this wonderful ship was to be mine. I was to be in command, and in wartime, which must be the zenith of any Naval Officers ambition. Moreover this was not just any ship, which could be honour enough. This was the 'Tiddly Wiv'. Command of the **Wivern** was more than an honour, it was a trust.

The trust lay alongside the Devonport dockyard wall looking anything but 'Tiddly'. She had gone alongside a sinking Canadian Corvette to rescue survivors and the corvette had sunk during the operation with the depth charges set to twenty five feet. The resultant explosion would have finished off many new destroyers, but the V&Ws were built to last. With a vast hole in her bottom and her engines lifted clear of their seatings. **Wivern** was towed some hundreds of miles back to Gibraltar and, eventually, to Devonport dockyard where they took the old ship in hand and made her seaworthy once again. There were snags, as we were to discover later, but they were not the ships fault. In all the years I drove her we never once missed a convoy, though on occasions, we had a stokers sledge hammer knocking wooden wedges back in when the steering engine tried to rattle itself loose from the bulkhead.

Meanwhile she lay alongside the wall looking as forlorn and derelict as ships do at the en of a refit, dirty unpainted, her upper deck covered with electric cables, unmentionable dockyard intimacies and lethargically squatting dockyard maties. Only a loving and knowledgeable eye could visualise the splendid little ship that would eventually emerge from the grime and filth of it all.

'D' day came and went and the rain poured down. Apart from the Engineer Officer, the whole Wardroom were as new to their jobs as I was to command. Number one was a junior R.N. Lieutenant, Number two, the navigator, was old enough to have been a school master in peace time but had never navigated before. There were two Subs' one R.N. But both brand new, and Gunner 'T' whose thin stripe was equally virginal. Chief on the other hand, was a real old reprobate of a Lieutenant Commander R.N. A man with years of sea time behind him who found himself in the difficult position of having to yield to precedence in the Wardroom to a completely inexperienced RN First Lieutenant almost young enough to be his son. With a half stripe more than his Commanding Officer it was a classic formula for difficulties and it is said a lot for Chief that there was none.

Some weeks after I joined, the ship commissioned. The rain had stopped at last and it was a sunny summer's evening in the dockyard. I stood on deck, looking down the jetty, waiting for the main bulk of the ship's company to arrive. A couple of three ton trucks turned up, full of bags and hammocks, and then, round the corner they appeared, a long column of marching sailors. It was a small drama the dockyard had known so many times before over so many years in peace and in war. The dockyard maties did not even look round. A destroyer's ship's company joining their destroyer was no great event in Devonport.

But to every marching sailor a new chapter in his life was about to begin. Good ship or bad? Home or abroad?

Down past Drakes Island lay the open sea and the war to which they were about to return. What was this commission to hold for them? What were they taking on? I looked at the strange but familiar faces. Soon I should know everyone and the character behind it. Most were even younger than the Wardroom, but there were obviously some very good Petty Officers among them. Already by the very act of falling in and marching down to their ship together, the first fragile bond had been forged. They were no longer individuals in barracks belonging to no one in particular. Here for the first of so many times came the preparatory order, "Ship's Company". Before they halted and turned left. Now they were looking at the ship with an appraising stare, pointing out things to each other. What in particular? I realised that a lot of eyes were looking at me. Why? Good God I was the skipper of course. What this ship did or failed to do would be my responsibility and mine alone. When my boat was hailed with me in it, the Coxswain would reply, **"Wivern".** In report I should write not, "**Wivern** did this" but "I did this". The Officers stood up when I entered the wardroom. To the sailors I would be the ultimate authority but, for more than that, the man on the bridge whose touch and skill would certainly regulate their living and possibly their dying too. This was command, and command in wartime at that. This was all my past training was supposed to have trained me for. Now in **Wivern** there was no one to go to for help. This ship and these men were mine. The whole weight of the Navy and England at war was behind me but, when it came to the crunch. I would be alone. Twenty seven years old two stripes on my sleeve. I went down to my cabin and sat there while the whole realisation flooded in on me. I felt totally humble and totally proud.

The next morning I addressed the ship's company for the first time. I told them something of our ship's history, how she had always been known as 'Tiddly Wiv', about the depth charges and how she had stood up to them, what we ourselves were now going to do. She my not be the newest and glossiest destroyer in the fleet, but our predecessors who had loved and served her for twenty-five years would look to us in her last commission, to humour their trust. "Always remember" I concluded, "An old violin plat the sweetest tune". It was just what they wanted to hear, and another bond was forged.

We sailed from Devonport to Harwich, where we joined the Harwich Escort Force. Here, with sluicing tide behind us and a vicious cross wind. I had to secure to head and stern buoys. By the time I had mastered that one, ship handling held no further fears.

We went out every night to patrol the off shore convoy route against E-boats. As we passed Felixstowe dock, we could see the MTBs and MGBs (Motor gun boats) emerging, great powerful monsters compared with the old First Flotilla and the Wobbly Tenth of my day.

Times had indeed changed.

One evening we were steaming up the swept channel off Lowestoft when we heard aircraft. My hackles still rose at the sound, I looked round anxiously to see a huge group of planes coming out from over the land. As I watched the noise increased and I spotted more and more till the whole sky seemed full of them. Even in Crete I had seen nothing like this, but even more were to come. The droning became a roar till the very air above us seemed to be throbbing. Low over the sea and at all heights till they were specks above, from horizon to horizon, the whole world seemed full of aircraft. The ship's company had emerged on deck and we all stood in awe, faces turned up, looking at the limitless aerial armada the sky literally saturated with aircraft. It was a thousand bomber raid on its way to Germany and anyone who had been on the receiving end could only feel horror stricken pity for the city which was to receive this load. How far we had come from the days of Dunkirk.

After we had operated from Harwich for a bit and shaken ourselves down into an efficient fighting unit, it was decided to combine all the small Hunt class destroyers to form the Harwich Force and concentrate the bigger V&Ws to Rosyth to escort East coast convoys.
The job entailed taking some thirty or forty ships down the East Coast to the Thames and we soon learned that the bigger and better merchant ships the greater the problems, we sailed from Methil early in the morning, formed the convoy up in the middle of the night off Newcastle and the Hartlepools, and entered E-boat Alley the following evening. This was the bulge of the East Anglian coast where the southbound route went to seawards of the dangerous sand banks and shoals off Yarmouth and the North bound route passed up inside. The third night was spent in Sheerness, sailing the next morning with a north bound convoy and backing up its escort as far as the Humber, then returning the next night to Sheerness having reinforced the southbound. After this, we took we took the next day's northbound convoy the whole way back to the Forth and Rosyth.
The main problem was usually fog. The ships had to sail in two long lines and a big convoy was often ten or fifteen miles long by the time one had included the stragglers. The lead escort was essentially a bell wether showing the way because the big ships came first and thc deep sea masters coastal navigation was often primitive. The escort at the rear would be chasing up stragglers or running up and down the long line at twenty knots, keeping a general sheepdog eye open. Fog produced immediate shambles. Some ships forged hopefully on. Others hauled out of the channel and anchored Others anchored on the spot, which raised difficulties if a forge on man happened to be behind them. Close control and co-ordination was impossible.
Off the south east coast of the Wash where the two swept channels split, there was one particular narrow passage between the sand banks marked by two buoy's. Deep sea Masters were liable to take a horrified look at the closeness of the two markers, lose their nerves and pull sideways like a frightened horse refusing a jump. This left the big merchant ships beam on to the channel and with inadequate room to manoeuvre even if the Master possessed the skill to handle his ship in such confined waters. The tide moved fast, the remainder of the convoy bore inexorably down and the CO of the escort aged before his time.
The other indigenous danger was drunken merchant ship's Masters. On one occasion, the Master of a large passenger ship was so drunk in the early morning that he could not be awakened when it was time to start from Methil. His Chief Officer said that he was not paid to take responsibilities of command, and refused to sail, so the ship missed the convoy and remained at anchor.

Another worse example happened when a merchant ship suddenly veered out of our southbound convoy and crossed the vicious shoals off Yarmouth straight towards the northbound convoy in the inshore channel. It was a pitch dark night luckily, high tide. I followed horribly conscious of the big vulnerable propeller which must have been sweeping round literally inches above the sand. Morse lamp, a ten inch lighting up his bridge from almost alongside, blasts on the siren, none had any effect. Finally I opened fire with the Oerlikon just ahead of his lifeless bridge and we brought him to a halt just as he was bout to ground on the inshore banks. Fortunately the northbound convoy was running late or there would have been a veritable motorway pile up. As it was I had to put my navigator on board to take the ship into Sheerness because the Master and all his officers were too drunk to understand what was happening. It was all in days work.

All through the autumn and winter we flogged up and down the East Coast, Christmas came and went. (We sailed at 0400 on Christmas morning with loudspeakers blaring 'Silent Night, Holy Night' across the waters of the Forth. Gales and fog gave way to gales and snow. Early in the New Year we actually met a freak calm. I saw the last of my convoy safely into Newcastle and increased speed for home. It was just after midnight and the sea was glassy. I stood on the bridge and peered ahead. Out on the Starboard bow, the darkness of the night looking wrong. There seemed to be a white tinge to the blackness. "Must be snow" said someone idly and went on to wonder if we were due for leave when we got in.

The wind hit us with a sudden brutal force, made all the worse by its total unexpectedness. One minute we were gossiping peacefully in a still, quiet middle watch, the next the wind was howling and shrieking around our ears as if we had suddenly entered a typhoon.

Quickly the calm water became transformed into a mass of racing tumbling waves and still the wind increased. After half an hour, the world was a terrifying, screaming hell. The seas were now mountainous and, with the comparatively shallow depth, infinitely more dangerous than those in the Atlantic.

In the wheel house the Coxswain took over. I stood on the bridge peering over the windscreen watching the forecastle buried in water one minute, then lurching up, up, up the next as the bow lifted out of the water. The whole mad inferno had a dreadful exhilaration and I felt a crazy urge to shout back into the storm.

But after a while I began to feel that something was wrong. At first I could not identify it. Then I realised that the bows were not lifting up as they had been. Now she was putting her nose down but the forecastle no longer came surging buoyantly up, it stayed submerged and sluggish, as the great waves washed over.

Chief appeared on the bridge beside me. Putting his arm round my neck, he pulled my head down and screamed into my ear over the noise of the wind. He told me that the forward magazine was flooded. Devonport dockyard had earned speed for the speed in which they got **Wivern** back to sea but, to do it they must have skimped on the welding. Now a weak bit had gone and we had tons of water where we desperately needed buoyancy. And the leak was beyond pumping.

All night the Coxswain wrestled with the wheel, trying to keep **Wivern's** head into the sea. On the bridge I hung on grimly, working the engines to help him. Down in the engine room exhausted men clutched their wheels, trying to give us the response we needed. The rest of the ship's company, wakeful and appalled, hung on in the shambles of their mess decks. Everyone knew that, if that waterlogged bow took charge, the end would come terrifying and sudden.

I broke radio silence to send a storm warning down the coast of winds gusting force twelve, but the Commodore behind us refused to believe it. "Force twelve", he said, "I doubt it". He was quickly convinced. Even in the sheltered waters behind the sand banks, he lost four ships. One was blown into a minefield, two ran aground and one was simply never heard of again. To the North of us, another destroyer lost bridge, funnel, mast and upper works, but had the buoyancy to stay afloat. Happily we did not know this at the time.

In **Wivern** our world was our own staggering stricken ship, overburdened bows trying desperately to lift the great waves which thundered and crashed down on to the forecastle. Inside flinching to every hideous blow, feeling the sluggishness, knowing of the water compartments beneath their feet, the sailors had nothing to do but listen, think, and wait.

On the little open bridge, peering out into the ghastly night, soaked to the skin and very frightened, I remembered the Navy Prayer - "Oh Lord preserve me from the dangers of the sea and the violence of the enemy". For so long, I had thought only of the possibility of death coming from the Germans. Now, suddenly, it seemed very likely that it could be the sea which would kill me.

And so the long hours passed.

With the dawn, the wind decreased to force eight and we looked out to a tumultuous sea with thrashing, wild white waves but only with the normal gale sized strength.

Slowly I risked more speed. With dreadful reluctance she answered to the helm and we set course for the Firth of Fourth. When we got to Rosyth, there was no question about leave. The ship entered the dockyard for repairs and we returned thankfully to homes that we had thought never to see again. But one thing I knew, she was a wonderful little ship.

After our storm damage had been repaired we did another convoy during which one of our ships, SS Dalemoor, was mined in E-boat alley. I went to her as she sank. Some of the crew, unfortunately led by the Master, had already jumped overboard into the sea and the presence of these swimmers in the water made getting alongside rather difficult, but I managed it and eventually succeeded in saving everyone.

When they were all safely on board the errant Master came up on the bridge. He turned out to be one of the most famous characters who had run the Franco blockade during the Spanish civil war when, apart from more strategic cargo, he had taken crates of Scotch to the Republicans. A suitably grateful General in the Republican forces had presented him with the Spanish King's own cigarette box which the General had appropriated from the Royal desk whilst looting the Palace. Now the Master said he would like to give it to me in thanks for their safe deliverance. I rather suspected this was subtle way of asking me not to mention his unworthy conduct in my Report of Proceedings, but whether it was or not I shall never know because I didn't anyhow. There seemed no point in crucifying this sad shivering, frightened old man. He did send me the box a few weeks later.

We sailed again at 0800 on the 14th March. We were now running on familiar tram lines. North of Newcastle, no problems, Newcastle to the Humber, routine navigational and convoy stuff, Humber to Sheerness. E-boats, mines, and generally stimulating nights. We knew just what to expect. With this background in our minds, we picked up two merchant ships from Methil. As usual we would be alone with the convoy until reinforced by the escorts from the Humber for the run down E-boat Ally.

Even with a well buoyed swept channel, leading some twenty plus old merchant ships through fog and gales was quite a job. (I was still in my twenties and the ship's company were mostly even younger) and it was made no easier by E-boats, U boats (we sank one) and recalcitrant old masters in little pre-war one funnel tramp steamers who didn't like being in convoy anyhow and tended to go their own way. It was one of these, in a convoy code named "Pug Dog", who must have provoked me into verse during the long night watches.

Anyhow I found it in the back of the Night Order Book and, as a view from the Bridge, it may serve to amuse, so, with apologies to Lewis Carol, here it is:

"You are straggling my Pugdog' the young escort said,
The merchantman close by his side
'And you passed twenty-one buoy some five miles to port.

"Why don't you allow for the tide?"
"In my youth said the ancient, we didn't have buoys
But we got to the Thames just the same
And the tide in six hours will be sweeping me back,
This police persecution's a shame".
You are straggling my Pugdog the young Escort said,
In fact you are ten miles behind
You are making us late for our rendezvous time
Don't you think you are being rather unkind/".
"I am doing my utmost" the ancient replied
And I don't care when we pass Tyne,
I'm doing six knots and the convoy's speed is six,
Tell the Commodore not to go nine"
"You are straggling my Pugdog" The young Escort said
Trying bravely to still be polite,
And in spite of my signals by R/T and lamp
You are still showing a very bright light".
Said the ancient "I've shown it for forty five years,
And,although I'm not saying it's right
It's been that way now during nine years of war,
What the hell is the difference tonight?"
"You are romping my Pugdog" the young Escort said
As the merchantman shot down the deep,
"After straggling like that you have 48 hours.
Your behaviour is really too steep".
Not a word said the ancient's. Hull down in smoke,
He was lost out of sight far ahead.
But a senile old chuckle came back on the wind,
It was all that the old-timer said.

It was Sunday and one of those rare, sunny, early spring days that make one think, quite unjustifiably, that winter had gone at last. I wanted to get some sleep in the afternoon so that I would be reasonably fresh when around midnight. I had to start assembling the darkened shapes of the unpredictable individuals who would come milling out of Newcastle, I had an early lunch, looked at the two merchant ships steaming placidly along behind and left the bridge for my sea cabin. The Officer of the Watch took over and the Asdic operator sat in his little office, listening with boredom to the ping, ping, ping in his headphones as we swept through the sea ahead. We had never heard a U-boats echo and indeed, we had never even had the opportunity to exercise with one of our own submarines. U-boats did not operate off the East Coast and, though we had the set and operators, it had never occurred to anyone on the board or to the staff ashore that we should ever need to use them seriously. The set had not been modernised during our refit and the operators were out of practice and needed experience.

To seawards as I drifted off to sleep.

Kapianleutnant Hans Joachim Schwebke watched the scene through his periscope. He too had reason to be proud of his command U417 was a brand new 770-ton, type V11 U-boat which had just arrived for its first patrol between the Firth of Forth and Flamborough Head.

This, and the thinking behind his orders, became clear from post war studies of captured German Naval records. Doenitz, suffering from heavy losses in the Atlantic, had reverted to his old trick of trying to find weak or unguarded points to attack and had guessed correctly, that there might be easy pickings down our East Coast. Schwebke was therefore a guinea pig. If he was successful, his friends would all come over for the easy kills. If our defences proved too strong - well, nothing had been lost except one U-boat and Doenitz would try somewhere else.

Schwebke fired at 1400 on the Sunday afternoon and the old, familiar thump of the exploding torpedo shattered my sleep. Within seconds I was on the bridge looking back unbelievingly at the Norwegian Magne, the last ship in the line, already sinking fast.

Wivern turned into a beautiful circle of foaming water, white against the blue sea, and raced back to the sinking ship to use her for a datum point for the search. Luckily experience in the Atlantic had made correct action almost second nature. One did not even think before automatically starting the requisite search. As I did so the lookout reported another ship approaching up the swept channel from the Southward. It was the South African 'Loch' class frigate, Natal.

Never had I been so thankful to see another ship. Not only did the hunt require a minimum of two A/S vessels, but I had a feeling in my bones that I knew where the U-boat was, that it was in the other half of the search area, which by the book, I should not reach for some time. And here, au moment critique, was a beautiful brand new anti submarine frigate with all the latest Asdic's and even better the new wonder weapon - an A/S mortar known as Squid which was supposed to be really lethal. I told Natal what had happened and gave her the position to start her search.

Natal altered her course and sure enough, gained almost immediate contact. A few minutes later we saw the Squid missiles arch through the sky and the sea reared up through the heavy explosions.

There followed the short anxious wait to see what, if anything, came up. A large amount of wreckage, or best of all, bodies live or dead were what we hoped for. A little oil, or only some wreckage, was no good. We had learned that such misleading debris could be ejected from a U-boat as it escaped. More was required to be sure of a kill.

In fact a little did appear but certainly not enough to prove success. The sea resumed its calm, untroubled blue and I prepared for a long hunt. There were two of us, one a superbly equipped ship, and I had no need to run after the convoy. We might well get him.

However the South African had other ideas. He was only on his way to Scapa Flow to work up, but apparently, he thought it more important to keep to his schedule than to help sink a U-boat. Explaining his unusual idea of priorities, he wished me luck and left **Wivern** to it.

Rosyth in the meantime, was humming like a disturbed bee hive. Every conceivable ship was ordered to sea forthwith to join the hunt for the intruder. This was one U-boat which, on our very doorstep, must be destroyed. I continued the search without much hope. If we had both lost him after our first attack. **Wivern** alone was not likely to find him again and it would be hours before we got the support so urgently needed.

The long afternoon and evening passed and the light began to fade. We were ten miles away from the position of Natal's attack and still searching. Then as dark crept over the sea we saw it - a long slick of diesel oil staining the calm water.

Steaming up I investigated all round the source, but never an echo could **Wivern's** elderly Asdic pick up. However, the U-boat must be there and its position was clearly marked. I hauled of and came back, steaming right to the centre of the slick. Getting to the end I plastered the position with depth charges. Then I did it again and again.

When we had spent all of our twenty-five depth charges, we had still brought up no wreckage, but the oil was coming up thick, sluggish and hard. It was obvious that the U-boat would not be leaving. By now all available ships from Rosyth were just over the horizon and, with no depth charges left, it was time to think of rejoining the convoy. Fixing the position exactly to Berwick Lighthouse, which had been clearly visible all day, I reported the situation and left.

On arrival at Sheerness I got down to the detailed analysis of the action. A specialist Officer from C-in- C Nore's staff kindly came and helped and, between us a few hours work produced a text book Report of Proceedings, complete with sketch maps and narrative of the operation of both ships. It was obvious that Natal's initial attack had damaged the U-boat, but it still had managed to withdraw at about three knots and, left in peace. Schebke would presumably surfaced after dark and withdrawn to seawards and safety. However the damage, though it produced no visible oil at the time, had eventually resulted in the tell tale slick which had given away its hiding place, ten miles from the original attack and thus offered us the chanced which our primitive ping would have otherwise denied us. Although Natal's sense of priorities may have seemed odd, his Squid had certainly handed the U-boat on a plate.

We carried out the usual convoy cycle via the Humber, had an extremely successful brush with some E-boats, and returned to Rosyth to find ourselves heroes. It turned out that none of the ships that turned out from the Forth had found anything. Darkness had fallen by the time they arrived on the scene and the oils slick had disappeared in the night. With equally old and useless Asdic's, they had picked up no contact and, after searching all night, they returned to harbour. With the lack of hard evidence, this left an obvious doubt in the minds of the Admiralty as to whether the U-boat had been destroyed.

The experts in London were only too aware of how important it was to make sure that Doenitz was discouraged in this particular gambit. They guessed that success would produce a plague of U-boat attacks o the East Coast which was simply not geared up to meet. A hunter killer group had therefore been sent to Scapa Flow to investigate. These highly skilled specialist had no difficulty in finding the U-boat in the exact position I had reported and, three days after **Wivern** had left, they blasted the wreck open and gained all the evidence needed to prove destruction. Because no living U-boat could remain submerged for three days. Wivern had been credited with the kill.

Messages of congratulations poured in. Our gin bills quintupled overnight. Nobody, ourselves included, could get over the fact that an old V&W from Rosyth had sunk a U-boat. It was if a pedestrian had run over a car.

We sailed for another convoy, came back - and found that we had been sold down the river. It appeared unbelievably, that the First Sea Lord didn't like South African's and his staff thought it would only be Politically desirable but useful with their master if the story could read that a South African frigate unworked up, had casually destroyed the U-boat in passing. Natal had put in no proper records because she lacked the bridge organisation to do so. Mine, so comprehensively and carefully produced had been suppressed and replaced by an imaginative if inaccurate 'narrative concocted in Rosyth. All the signals and letters of congratulations from C in C downwards were forgotten and Natal was given the sole credit for the kill.

As a result, Roskill's 'War at Sea', based on Admiralty records, and the Confidential Book listing U-boat actions and the ships that were present at

the scene, show U-714 as being sunk by Natal alone with no other ship's in company.
Under the circumstances, it is not remarkable that Natal collected two DSC's two DSM's and five Mention in Despatches. What is surprising is that **Wivern** actually earned three Mention in Despatches for her success in an action in which, officially, she never took part!
It was very demoralising to find the Admiralty behaving like this but, by now, events in the war were moving so fast that the vast canvas of Germany's defeat began to fill our minds to the exclusion of all else.
Then came 'V.E' day and our role changed. With the East Coast convoys no longer necessary, the Rosyth Escort Force was redeployed to run a shuttle service to liberated Norway.
Wivern was one of the first to cross the North Sea to Stavanger, Kristiansand, and Oslo run and, as a result, we had the privilege of taking back to their country two members of the Central Leadership of the Milorg (Underground Resistance) who had been forced to escape to London, via Sweden, with the Gestapo hot on their heels. Through them I was introduced to the Milorg leaders in each of the ports that we visited, so that a close and fascinating liaison developed between **Wivern** and the Norwegian Underground movement.
Apart from this we quickly found that wherever we went, children came up smiling shyly, took our hands and walked beside us. I explored the town with two kids each side of me and met all my sailors, hands equally gripped by enchanting little blonde boys and girls of five or six years old. A Norwegian friend explained, "Ever since they can remember, they have heard of Father Christmas, who will bring them presents, and the British who will bring them freedom. You just happened to turn up first. Now you know what would happen to Father Christmas if he ever came to town. It was greatly humbling and very moving. Our nutty (chocolate) ration soon disappeared.
We sailed for Kristiansand which was being run entirely by the Milorg under one of the most famous of underground leaders, a huge man called Robstadt, and here the **Wivern** and Milorg friendship really blossomed. Robstadt had taken over the old Gestapo headquarters, a pretty little villa in a pinewood on the outskirts of the town. In the cells below, the entire Gestapo team were locked up. A Milorg man showed me his wrists, the scars plainly visible where a device had been clamped on it which tightened a turn every few hours producing excruciating agony, and the Gestapo men who had done this to him were locked up below, but the Norwegian had never gone down and as much as kicked his backsides. Would we have had such decency and discipline under the same circumstances? I was shown their Gestapo

captives. Blonde, blue eyed, good looking Aryans and dark, sulky young men sitting in a cell with their dhobeying strung up on a line. Germans are very clean. As the door opened, the Gestapo men sprang up rigidly to attention. They considered themselves to be soldiers and this was the correct military way to behave. The Norwegians closed the doors and smiled ruefully. "It is most interesting for us", said one, "to see now how professionals should behave in defeat. We were only amateurs and disappointed our visitors dreadfully."

I was invited to sit in on the Gestapo chief's interrogation by a government representative from Oslo. The Gestapo chief, Koener, he was a short, squat, ape like man whose muscles bulged obscenely through his tightly fitting uniform. He came into the room, handcuffed, and bowed to me correctly on his way to face his interrogator. Sitting on a stool, words spilt from his mouth denunciating his ex- colleagues. Nothing had ever been his fault. He was only a soldier obeying orders. He had never known of torture. Everyone else was to blame. The Norwegian interrogator listened and encouraged the damaging confidences (amongst other things, the German Naval Liaison officer was denounced as a Gestapo agent. I had him arrested the next day). At the end I was given the little leather thronged cat 'o nine tails he had used on the faces of his victims when he was the interrogator. He had christened it "Wotan" and carved the name on the wooden handle. It is beside me as I write. We went on to Oslo where we finally landed our Milorg leaders, and then we spent the next few weeks on the Rosyth, Stavanger, Kristiansand, Oslo run, but time for **Wivern** was running out. The end of the European war meant a concentration in the Pacific, but there was no call for elderly V&Ws in that area.

On our last trip I discovered that the army mails were taking three weeks to reach home, so I offered to take the lot, letters and parcels, and have them in the U.K. mails in forty-eight hours. This offer was rapturously received and a convoy of three ton trucks turned up loaded with mail army were ecstatic. What could they do for me? I suggested that they might loose some of the champagne they had "liberated" from the Germans, who had stolen it from the French.

As a result, at a time when champagne had been unavailable in the UK for years, every one of my sailors was able to take a free bottle in his kit bag to celebrate his homecoming.

But even with this and the end of the war, there was a remarkable atmosphere of subdued sadness on board because, on our return to Rosyth we must turn over our much loved ship to the knackers yard. It had been a wonderfully successful and happy last commission and it really hurt to think that the end had come - and particularly such an end like this.

Our thoughts and feelings must have been obvious to the Norwegians. We were due to leave Kristiansand for the last time, early in the morning, just before we sailed a deputation of the Milorg marched down the jetty carrying huge garland was presented to the ship with the words “Good Bye, Good Luck **Wivern**”.
On arrival back at Rosyth the customs were duly notified about the champagne, (which listed as sparkling wine after having a share). Every member of the crew received a bottle, the remainder went to the wardroom for the departure celebrations, for sadly, Wivern had finished her active life and the crew and officers were to be sent on leave and then had to report back to their respective depots after the expiry of their leave.
The ship had been de-stored and stripped of her bell, name plates and badges. With them went her personality and the ‘Tiddly’ from ‘Wiv’.
I said goodbye to my ship’s company and my thoughts were with that opening talk by the wall in Devonport Dockyard which now seemed so long ago. I looked round at the faces around me, the familiar, well known characters.
They had been a splendid ship’ company and they had maintained our trust. We all knew it and we all knew that, with the death of this small stricken hull on which we stood for the last time, something precious and a corner of our hearts would have left our lives forever.
She was towed away from the grey waters of the Firth like a tired old dog, collar removed going slowly off to be put down. But on her final journey, where my commissioning pendant had flown, she wore at her mast head our own honour - ‘Goodbye, Good Luck, **Wivern’**

Chapter 52

H.M.S. Viceroy

I joined the ship in Rosyth on the 19th November 1944 as O/S Sidey RC.3. Not yet eighteen years old I stood in awe at this mighty warship, (Until then I had never seen a ship that close). Once aboard I was soon made to feel at home by my mess mates. Quire a few of the crew were Scots, which made it difficult for me at first, for me a s a cockney to understand what they were saying, no doubt they had the same problem with me, but in no time at all we were all pals together.
Soon I was in the routine of watch keeping on those East Coast convoys. When not manning the Radar set I was starboard lookout on the bridge, and will remember those bitterly cold night watches to my dying day.
It was on such a patrol on the 16th April 1945, we were abreast of Newcastle, when the merchant ship SS "Arthurduke" was struck by torpedoes and we were called to action stations. Our Asdic soon located the U-boat and we prepared to attack. I was on the bridge as starboard lookout, when our Captain John Manners gave the order to fire. I pressed the button which gave the signal to the men on the quarter deck to the depth charges.
With the engines at full speed we dropped pattern after pattern of depth charges, bringing to the surface patches of oil and debris, until our supply of depth charges had depleted. Unable to continue the attack we rejoined the convoy.
Some days later we were in the same area again and after relocated the spot, we once again dropped depth charges. This time, in addition to oil and debris a large cylinder popped up to the surface. This was duly hoisted aboard. On opening it up, we discovered several crates of brandy, all undamaged.
Later one of those bottles was put in a presentation case and sent to Winston Churchill who acknowledged the gift in a Prime Ministers personal minute.

*****

The submarine **U-1274** was the last U-boat to be sunk by a surface ship of the war.
Soon after VE day **Viceroy** was despatched to Trondheim in Norway, there we saw for ourselves the huge concrete pens with the German U-boats still in them.
The Norwegians made quite a fuss of us. Prince Olav himself inspecting us on the quay side. WE then sailed along the Norwegian coast calling at other

towns, Christiansand, Alesund, Christiansund etc; doing a victory march in each town we visited. We were hailed like conquering heroes.
On our return to Rosyth, all crew members subsequently received an illuminated scroll from Prince Olav thanking us for the liberation of Norway. I still posses my copy along with those happy memories to this day

Eric Sidey
Ordinary Seaman RC3
HMS **Viceroy**

PRIME MINISTER'S
10, Downing Street.
PERSONAL MINUTE

SERIAL No. M. 468/5

FIRST SEA LORD

Thank you so much for sending me the presentation case of brandy from the U-Boat which I shall keep as an interesting souvenir.

Will you please convey my thanks to Captain 'D', Rosyth Escort Force and the Commanding Officer and Ship's Company of H.M.S. VICEROY for all the trouble they took in producing the very handsome casket and offer them my congratulations on the successful attack.

Winston S. Churchill

12 May. 1945.

Chapter 53

though the war was coming to its conclusion, the convoys however continued HMS **Whitehall** was the last of the V&Ws to escort a Russian convoy, when convoy RA64 sailed from the Kola Inlet on the 17th February, this convoy was notorious because of the violent weather. The U-boats too had some success torpedoing two of our ships, the sloop Lark, who's captain was Hebworth Lampton, who had been in command of the **Westcott** 1943-44. The other was the Flower Class corvette Bluebell from which there was only one survivor.
Those old V&Ws that had originally been built mainly for the protection of our shores in the English Channel and the North Sea, had stood up to the fiercest of weather conditions in probably the worst area of the oceans.

* * * * * *

Wiggy Bennet & Prince Philip

When Prince Philip was in the Rosyth Escort Force in the **Wallace,** he had a full set of whiskers then, and Princess Elizabeth thought he looked good.
Then I was aboard HMS Kent in Colombo when he joined us from the Ramillies. There was a bit of a flap at first as to hoe we should address him being a Greek Prince. However the at problem was soon solved.
At sea he was in my watch of lookouts in the ADP, three each side, and during that period he was not backward in borrowing the odd fag or the makings.
We were patrolling around the Islands mainly, but then went down to Freemantle to collect a convoy of Australian troops for the Middle East and North Africa.
That lull was soon shattered when we received orders to go to the Med'. Prince Philip then left in a hurry and went to the Shropshire, The Admiralty didn't want any Royal blood shed.
!947 I was at Corsham, Wiltshire at a National Service training camp. The P.O's leadership school was not open then. Prince Philip arrived at Corsham and at times was Divisional Officer in the Captains office, among his duties was Officer of the Day and as such would do the 2100 and 0400 rounds of the three camps on bicycles with the P.O. Of the guard. As P.O. Barracks guard I did several jaunts with him around the Corsham countryside. He was still there when I left.

Prince Philip coming aboard HMS Centaur from Britannia by jackstay transfer

"You put your left foot out and shake it all about"
Prince Philip in the galley of HMS Centaur 24/3/55

My last encounter with Prince Philip was in the Med' when I was on the Centaur, he came aboard from the Britannia had to rig the Jackstay gear, then, later on as President of the P.O's mess I had to show him around the mess which housed about 150 P.O's and was the width of the flight deck.
He was impressed with the colour scheme. We were the first RN Ship to be allowed to repaint the messes and dining room with other than white.
'Wiggy' Bennett served on many ships in his long naval career, his favourite was HMS **Wolsey**. He retired to Cromer and was a great friend of the Cromer lifeboat crew. Not long after relating the above story to me, he sadly died, leaving so many stories untold.

"V.E" DAY

We were at anchor in the Clyde off Greenock. We had been expecting the news for a few days, we finally heard it over our wireless sets. Everyone was in high spirits, not least because the end of the war meant that we could expect 48 hours shore leave, being sailors we were all looking forward to a chance to celebrate with a good drink and a good time for all.
But then, at the very last minute, there was some problem with the duty boat which was supposed to go to Iceland, (I was given to understand that the captain was the son of the local Admiral) We were therefore detailed to take over as duty boat.
So on VE night, just as the lights were coming on for the first time in nearly five years, with fireworks going off, we instead of going ashore and enjoying ourselves, had to put to sea.
At least we got to celebrate the end of the war in Europe. The Skipper, half cut, came down to the seaman's mess deck with two big fannies of rum and let us all splice the 'main brace'. But there was still this tremendous feeling of being cheated.
Quite apart from that the next few days at sea were bizarre. On the way to Iceland, who had spent the whole war hunting down submarines hoping to destroy them, was now searching them out for quite a different purpose. Because Germany had surrendered the subs had orders to come to the surface and signal their position. We had to find them and signal their commanders how to navigate through the minefields into the nearest British ports. We must have located three or four during the time it took us to reach Iceland.
It was about two weeks before we were back in Gourock. Of course, we finally got our shore leave and went out on the razzle then. But it was not the same, it felt as though all the excitement was over, as if there had never been a war, the place was pretty quiet.

In June the ship was paid off, we were all sent back to our respective depots, most of us to await drafts to the Far East and the Japanese conflict.

Chapter 54

Norway

Nine old destroyers left Rosyth, slipped beneath the Forth Bridge at two minute intervals formed in line ahead. This was to be their swan song, their last operation.

Throughout the war, they and others like them had been the back bone of the Rosyth Escort Force taking daily convoys between Methil and the Thames, latterly a humdrum hard work task, more concerned with mines and wrecks, isolated attacks by E-boats and submarines.

Northwards they turned at May Island, steaming in two columns at 15 knots, then East off Montrose, zig zagging 400 miles between minefields to the coast of Norway. Their wardrooms and mess decks crowded.

Norwegian intelligence officers, big, grim, with rucksacks, shoulder holster hidden beneath their battle dress. Men who had been in and out of their country at the risk of their lives. Planning sabotage, were going home for the first time in uniform.

In every man's stomach was mounting excitement.

We joined a fleet of small minesweepers wallowing towards Lister Light in the south west tip of Norway. Mines popped up on all sides. Some of the destroyers turned South for Kristiansand and Oslo. We headed North for Stavanger, Bergen and Trondheim.

The Norwegians stood in rain and spray for hours waiting for the clouds to part on the mountains around Flekkefiord and Egersund.

Off Stavanger, a pilot, who had been warned secretly had been tossed for ten hours in an open boat. In **Wolfhound**'s wardroom he reeled off first news of home to his countrymen.

Although it was nearly midnight, folk left every house along the fjord, ran shouting towards the town. The low quay's were thronged with cheering, singing people as we anchored in mid harbour. Remember that night Shipmates? The first pungent whiff of herring canneries?

German merchantmen, E-boats and armed trawlers lay within a cable length. Around the docks that night, patrolled like grey ghosts with rifle and bandolier, the bold eyed disciplined youths of the resistance, hunted no longer, in the open at last.

For three glorious weeks we ran a 'Mail Boat Service' day and night through the narrow leads 400 miles to Bergen and Trondheim, scarcely ever seeing open sea. Fishermen stopped hauling their lines and rowed to greet us, every coaster and herring carrier dipped their ensign as we swept at twenty knots through the narrow Fjords with a big Norwegian flag at the masthead. With

service, V.I.P's mail and stores we sped across to Rosyth overnight each week.
For three more weeks the **Wolfhound** lay at Stavanger as base ship, Our lads vied with each other to be jetty sentries, turned themselves out like guardsmen.
Already some of the ships had been ordered home to be paid off. Wolfhound had celebrated her 27th birthday on VE day.
The last thing the friendly people did was to find us enough white bunting to make a magnificent paying-off pennant.
The whole town turned out as we cast off.
I like to think that they will never see these lovely old ships lying rusting on the mud at Grangemouth. The children we gave chocolate to will tell their grand children of the trim grey ships, **Wolfhound, Wolsey, Wallace....**

* * * * * *

On May 7th 1945 **HMS Vanity** returned to Rosyth having once again completed another North Sea, East Coast convoy duty. We were fully expecting to have a short break before setting sail escorting another convoy down the East Coast, calling at Immingham and the down to Sheerness.
Our Captain informed us that we would be flashing up and setting off at 0500 the very next morning. We were not too chuffed about this, but orders being orders, sure enough we were out of the pens, steaming under the Forth Bridge and out into the North Sea dead on time.
I closed up on my radar set (Type 271 - 5 inch screen- hand operated aerial). Other than marker buoys found nothing, no ships, no convoy! At 1100 on the 8th May The Captain came over the Tannoy. "Splice the main Brace!! The war in Europe is over. We naturally followed the order to a man! However we were not to return to Rosyth until early on the 9th May. **HMS Vanity** had been kept out to sea so the ship's company could not indulge in the end of the war celebrations taking place in Edinburgh on the night of the 8th May 1945. There were already enough rough sailors in the city that night!
As soon as we did return to Rosyth we were ordered to take aboard and stow in the engine room as many large cardboard boxes as possible. These we very soon found out, contained small tins of "Iron Rations or "Hard Tack". A couple of very thick, very hard chocolate etc: Needless to say that we were not very interested in our cargo or the contents. We were to Flash Up and deliver our cargo to the paratroops and service personnel in Norway immediately.
What a nightmare, when not closed up on the radar I was one of the night lookouts. I swear that some of the waves broke just below the bridge! It was

oxo and toast all the way there. (So easy to heave up when calling for your old friend 'Bert'.) However after completing the morning watch, I came out of the radar cabin and found a lot of the ship's company hanging over the starboard side guard-rails. Looking over the guard rail myself I saw that my shipmates were very busy pushing a floating mine off the ship's side with broom handles! Someone mentioned in typical matelot terms that no one should strike the the mines horns! Obviously no one did, otherwise I would not be relating this experience. When the mine was far enough away from us. The officers on the bridge believed that they could blow it up by using revolvers and small arms fire. They failed and the last I saw of it was floating away in the morning mist. I believe we must have sailed through, or very near an enemy minefield.

On arrival at Stavanger, we had to proceed slowly and wait for a German E-boat to come out and pilot us into the harbour. The German officer in charge of the E-boat made her 'turn on a tanner' (sixpence). Impressive.

The first thing I noticed on tying up alongside the harbour was that the sea was full of jelly fish. Fifty years ago the harbour was surrounded by small sardine canning factories. The heads and tails of the sardines were washed down wooden troughs into the harbour sea water. The jelly fish were thriving on this waste.

We unloaded some of our 'Iron Rations' and met some army personnel whilst at Stavanger and within twenty four hours we were on our way to Kristiansand, then on to Oslo. We sailed through beautiful fjords with wooden houses dotted among the pine forests, each small house proudly flying a Norwegian flag from it's own flagpole. Our ships loud speakers were turned on full playing 'Land of Hope and Glory' and 'There'll Always be and England'.

Whilst in Kristiansand we took over an empty German wooden hall. We practically empty Jack Dusty's store in order to lay on a buffet and entertain the Norwegian teenagers. The cooks (singe 'em and burn 'em) baked as much bread as they could. We really had a great afternoon, and after six years of occupation our hospitality was really appreciated.

Most of the Norwegians spoke good English, and I met one girl who's father had been a ship owner. I've often wondered what happened to her and her family.

Our next port of call was Oslo. The passage from Kristiansand was very rough, a life line was rigged along the iron deck in order to get to the radar cabin. One of my shipmates, coming off watch was very nearly washed overboard. A wave actually threw him at the starboard door leading to the mess deck and broke his collar bone. For the first time ever, our ship had a Doctor onboard. He was I believe a Norwegian Doctor taking passage from

Kristiansand to Oslo and he was able to look after my shipmate. On arrival at Oslo he was transferred to a hospital where, I found out later, he had a wonderful time, the Doctors and nurses looked after him very well indeed.
We were berthed stern to and we were not very far from the main shopping centre and King Haakon's Palace. A shipmate and I went ashore for the afternoon and evening on the first day that we arrived. We noticed that some of the girls wore head scarves because they had had their heads shaved because they had been fraternising with the Germans. During the afternoon we met a Norwegian sailor who was serving with the Royal Navy. He had been based in Scotland for most of the war and had just returned home. He was very anxious to show us what a beautiful country Norway was and how the people had existed since Quisling had taken over the country.
We boarded a train at Oslo station and travelled to the small town of Skien (a forest area where ski's were made). We became quite apprehensive walking around the small town, as there were a lot of Germans still there. Some were queuing up at the local picture house with their girl friends. The scenery was beautiful and before returning to Oslo our Norwegian shipmate invited us in to a small cafe.
We sat down while he spoke to two men, who produced sheet of newspaper containing coupons. The lady cafe proprietor cut about a quarter of the paper out and then produced half a dozen rock cakes, which we enjoyed. He then advised us not to eat too many as they were made out of wood pith. Similarly when we arrived back in Oslo were invited to have a cup of coffee, which turned out to be made of oak leaves. Cigarettes at the time were made out of grass!
We said our goodbye's to Oslo and Norway and set sail for Rosyth quite early in the morning, but were amazed to see small motor boats and other craft sailing out with us, with the tops of fir trees in the bottom of their boats. Later we learnt that King Haarkon of Norway was returning that very day to Oslo from England where he had been in exile for six years, the small boats were going out to meet and greet him.

Geoffrey Barwell
Ex AB/RP3 R.N. (HO)
HMS **Vanity**

* * * * * *

I was aboard **Venomous** as a Stoker Mechanic and remember a German Naval Pilot coming aboard to help navigate through the very large minefield, which covered much of the northern approaches to Norway.
A flotilla of minesweepers swept ahead of us and I remember seeing some cut mines bobbing about. I had a feeling of apprehension for my previous ship HMS Quail had been badly damaged outside Bari harbour Eastern Italy by a mine in which we lost all the quarter deck and sadly a party of seamen who had "fell in" on entering harbour. Plus the men drawing grog for the pre dinner tot. About thirty men all told.
I also remember landing in Kristiansand and seeing German marines, still armed and whilst another shipmate and myself were disobeying in the stokers bathroom perched starkers on the edge of one of those big round shallow bath tubs. We heard giggling,, my mate said "look Yorkie" and looking round saw some Norwegian female visitors by the bathroom companion way, enjoying the view.

******

Wolsey was on a North Bound convoy to Methil when a flight of Lancasters came down to mast head level and waggled their wings. We all felt that, that was a signal that the war was all but over.
On our return to Rosyth, I applied for weekend leave to be at the christening of number two daughter, which was granted. Just as I was about to leave the ship, I was told that I had to return to the ship as soon as the ceremony was over. I did and as I went aboard I witnessed a lot of activity as all sorts of material was being taken aboard.
Next day we assembled at Methil and with the rest of the escort force, we sailed for Norway. On the way across I was chief of the watch in No 1 boiler room and as we raced across the North Sea in formation at high speed it was obvious that some of the old rust buckets were in trouble and dropped back. In the boiler room I was having trouble keeping everything going as spray was coming down the fan chutes and completely obliterating the gauges.
We did everything we could muster to keep up with the engine room I was informed later that we did reach 32 knots!
On reaching the Norwegian coast we were met and escorted into the fjord by a German warship. (E-boat) It showed off a bit as it danced around us. (I was off watch at the time)
Some of our group had gone North, whilst others had gone South. We were in company with **Wolfhound**.
Units of the first Airborne Division had preceded us into Stavanger and had taken over the Luftwaffe barracks. One day several jeeps drew up alongside and took all the chiefs and P.O.'s to their barracks where they indulged in a lot of French wine. So bad were we all that the duty driver brought a truck to

take us back to the ship. On arrival at the ship's side, they all went aboard except me. I had decided to do a bit of exploring and was made a welcome guest in the home of a Norwegian family. Later I did get back on board and apparently singing the Red Beret song. "We are a bunch of B****! Are we, we would rather **** than fight for victory!!
Looking back on that I find there was a sense of letting ones hair down after over six years of war. I hasten to add that heavy drinking was never my forte.
During our stay in Stavanger the wine store of the submarine crew's was found by someone, and for some days the best red and white wine was being consumed. In the end it was discovered by the officers and a sentry was put on the wine store. One day we went out to sea and sped down the coast to Egersund. On the way back we dropped a depth charge, and as far as the eye could see there were fish of all sizes floating on the surface. The ship smelt like a fishing trawler, there was sufficient fish for us and everybody else including the local hospital.
We left for Rosyth and on the way dumped our depth charges off the coast of Scotland.
As we entered Rosyth we could see all the other destroyers devoid of all upper deck equipment and looking like the scrap that they were about to become. It was very sad to see those ships like that.

Alf Floyd

Wolfhound at Stavanger

By F.D. Bugg

I was on the **Wolfhound** as we pulled into Rosyth the buzz was going round that we were waiting for a seaplane to land on the Forth, carrying some top brass Germans to discuss going into Norway. The eventually took place, but no one was sure if the take over would be completely peaceful, or whether some units would resist.
Lorry loads of stores were put aboard, there were boxes stowed everywhere. Then some soldiers and brass came aboard. There were quite a few of the V&Ws assembled, and it was a rough crossing.
After dark the **Wolsey** and **Wolfhound** split from the rest, but we did not go rushing in.
The Airborne Division had gone into Stavanger airfield and we waited for the signal from them. At the same time we took on a pilot, who took us into Stavanger Fjord. We received the correct signal and proceeded in, it was about midnight and as we entered the fjord the whole place was lit up. There

was a massive bonfire at the end of the jetty and literally hundreds of small boats with lights on all around us. The pilot had to call out over the loud hailer for them to back off long enough for us to drop anchor, I think the whole town must have been cheering us in. None of them seemed to want to go home and many were there when we turned to in the morning. The only dissent came at 'Hoisting Colours' when a German freighter ran up the Swastika. Both destroyers trained their guns on her, she soon hauled it down. Later we went alongside the jetty and began unloading the stores, and that was not easy, every man and his dog were there to greet us.

What happened to the **Wolsey,** I don't know. I understood that we were R/T boats and one of us went through the fjords to Bergen and Trondheim keeping R/T communication with the one at Stavanger. We did that trip two or three times, it was the most beautiful journey that I had ever taken, the people in Stavanger were wonderful and could not do enough for us.

We were given the first day's newspapers with photo's of our ships on the front page, and the people on the jetty, plus a record of the nights events.

The war was coming to a close and after a few skirmishes with E-boats and U-boats. The Skipper informed us, that as we had been good boys, we had been given a special assignment.

We were in Rosyth dockyard when loads of trunks, cases etc; began to land on board, some were stowed below, the large cases had to stay on the upper deck. When we were ready to sail, all types of men came aboard and were ushered to the wardroom. Norway was our destination, preceded by minesweepers, there were plenty of mine bobbing about. I had the forenoon watch on lookout on the starboard side of the bridge and had many a scare.

When we reached Kristiansand, the rocks and islands were amass with people cheering and waving, boats with children shouting, chocolata, sukker. Being off watch I was standing near the Mediterranean ladder leaning over the handrails, when this large cabin cruiser came alongside and an officer came aboard and went down to the wardroom, leaving a pretty girl in the cabin having a drink,. Somehow I attracted her attention and gave her the sign that drink was no good. She smiled. When Grego Gregson (This being his name). Kari the girl must have told him what I had done. He waved me over on to his boat and plied myself and another shipmate who had followed, with drink out of a secret compartment, where he kept butter, bacon etc.

We found out that Grego was a leader in the 'Milorg', the underground resistance. He was actually a Scotsman with just one hand. He always carried a revolver, and would use it especially against the Germans. The girl Kari was his secretary. Early in the war she had been at university and her parents who owned merchant ships had left to come to England, leaving Kari behind. Later I found out that she was living in a flat with a nurse.

Before leaving in the cruiser Grego gave me an address to visit when ashore. Little did I know that I was to follow him ashore with two other shipmates to take over a large building from the Stappo, (Norwegian police working for the Germans), we were told that they were worse than the Germans.
The large building, was made up of several flats, with telephone exchange, teleprinter, armoury, laundry etc in the basement. On arrival the building was almost empty of inhabitants, but there was plenty of crockery, utensils and other equipment, even Luger pistols.
Instead of taking a flat each, the three of us chose a flat and moved in together, combing the other flats for the best equipment. We settled in and took a watch each on the telephone exchange which had been defunk for some time. We soon began to get plenty of calls, not knowing if they were Norwegian, German or whatever. After a day we were pleased to see three army lads of the Welsh Regiment. Then came the S.A.S with Paddy Maine and other officers living in the upper flats. They were dropping empty beer bottles down on to the jeeps parked below and down the central staircase. The building also had a lift.
After a few days the army lads came in with bottles of German rum, Schnapps and red wine which we made into a punch by putting a large bowl on the stove filling it with red wine, well sugared, with rum and schnapps then heated it up. We then invited girl friend who had befriended us, some of which I found out later had been Quislings. One of the Welsh lads had a girl in his flat and kept her locked in, she did get out one day and went round the building looking for this guy with a Luger in her hand. She was confronted by an officer. He was put on a charge and was never seen again.
Soon the people of Kristiansand learned of the cache of booze and we were pestered into selling them a bottle or two, only to be invited to a party and help them to drink it! I remember that at one party the Norge started play acting, some of the plays were rather crude.
After a week or two of walking around the town, I somehow met a chap, who, after talking about football, took me behind the counter of a bank, where we organised the first football match to be played in Norway since the war. It was HMS **Valorous** versus the Milorg. It was England versus Norway. As the captains exchanged flowers, and even though we won 2-1 we were all treated to what was available, there was very little available in those days.
On May 17th which was a main celebration in Norway, I was sitting on watch with steel safety doors and grid open to footpath level, it was a nice night, when a beautiful girl put her head in and asked if she could come in, no doubt she had been in before, for when a Milorg sentry, who had been

watching from across the street came across, she ran off holding her head in her hands. They used to cut off their hair if they fraternised.
The building across the road was the headquarters of the underground movement, this was the address that Grego had given me on that first day.
Finding a gramophone in the basement and borrowing records from the ship, we organised the first dance in the Soldatenheim (soldiers home) which was not more than forty yards away.
I must say that I was being well victualled from the ship and also by the army. While sitting there having a meal, two of our army friends brought in a German SS Captain dressed up as a corporal, he came in so humble, took off his cap and put it on the table, which was instantly thrown to the floor saying "You don't put caps on tables" then gave him the job of scrubbing the tables and removing crumbs from the groves with a toothbrush.
Sitting in the dining room playing records people began coming in and started dancing, when in walked Grego with two women, one of them was Kari the other was his wife. I immediately asked Kari to dance and asked if she remembered me, she did, we danced all night. When it was all over, Grego took us to the back of the soldiers home where the big launch was moored. We were soon under way going up the fjords taking it in turns at the helm, drinking and firing very lights into the sky. I do not recollect if I returned to my place of work that night!!
Soon after visiting Kari and her nurse friend at their flat and being plied with Danish bacon, butter etc; it was time to leave Kristiansand and come down to earth, or should I say water? Back to **Valorous** and back to England.

J. Garforth

Operation Apostle
13th May 1945

HMS **Woolston** pennant number L49 was on a buoy in Sheerness waiting to escort a convoy up the East Coast to our home base at Rosyth. As a young signalman, I was on watch when I received the following signal from the tower at Sheerness.
To, **Woolston** from CinC Norc;- "Congratulations on your half stripe" thus elevating our very popular skipper, Lt, J.B. Cox to Lt, Commander. Thereby making us a more senior ship. All the ship's company that this promotion was well deserved and long overdue. It also meant that we would be senior ship in our section of "Operation Conan" which in turn was part of "Operation Apostle" which was the dismantling of the German high command in Norway.

A short while later, on or about the 12th May we took aboard a large contingent of military and Naval personnel whose duties would be administration for the Allies in the city of Bergen in West Norway, which had been a big U-boat base.
We sailed on the 13th in company with **Vivacious**, the Norwegian Corvette Acanthus, British and Norwegian minesweepers and some M.T.Bs also manned by Norwegians.
The trip across was quiet and uneventful with good weather conditions, and apart from a heavy swell as we neared the Norwegian coast it had been quite pleasant. The swell became more pronounced because we had to steam at slow speed. As we entered the fjord we began to be accompanied by a score of small fishing and other boats, we were almost surrounded by the time we came alongside, giving us a taste of the welcome that awaited us as we berthed on the fish quay.
The quay was absolutely packed with our Norwegian friends and allies, who gave us an unforgettable welcome with cheers, waving, laughter, and here and there a few tears.
As soon as the gangway was cleared the skipper and our party of V.I.Ps disembarked and eventually we were able to welcome aboard as many of our new friends as we could cope with. The first few hours after we arrived are just jumbled, a vague memory to me, but I do know that it was a truly wonderful experience for all on board.
Being a watch keeper it was some little while before I was able to go ashore, but, I remember seeing many German servicemen still around and apparently going about unmolested. We also saw many Russian ex-prisoners. Everywhere we went there were shouts of “Welcome to Norway” or “Welcome to Bergen”. One instance I recall particularly was of a beautiful little girl of about two or three, with her grandfather saying to me, “Welcome to Bergen”. I was never so pleased to have a bar of ‘nutty’ in my pocket that I could give to her. I will always remember her.
We had a constant flow of visitors for quite a while, this meant that we soon ran out of supplies of ‘Nutty’ fags, bread etc: We had to await the arrival of the cruiser Norfolk for replenishment of stores, especially bread. I became friendly with a resistant fighter who had a very disconcerting habit of flashing his hand gun about. Luckily it never went off on board ship. He took me to his home where I met some of his family. His mother gave me half a dozen eggs, which were very welcome in our mess. It is a matter of great regret to me that I cannot remember his name, as I would like to have contacted him later in life.
After a memorable and enjoyable stay in Bergen, Kristiansand and Oslo, we again sailed for Rosyth and the reserve fleet. Our ship’s company went

various ways after our brief spell in Norway. The little girl that I remember so well is now probably a grand mother herself, the resistant fighter too, he will be a grand father perhaps many times over. Who knows? Good luck to them all.

P.S. The day I took the signal informing the skipper of his promotion, he sent for me. Wondering what it was that I had done wrong, I went to his cabin. I was relieved and pleased when he gave me a tot. Which is apparently a tradition.

Harry (Spider) Kelly
Ex Signalman
HMS **Woolston**

HMS Woolston approaching Bergen May 13th 1945

Being greeted and escorted by small Norwegian boats

Heaving lines. The first contact

Anxious moments

The final few feet

The first contact

Waiting for the gangway

The bridge to freedom after so long under Nazi rule

The cheering crowd

The playing of the national anthems

The Captain goes ashore

Norwegian Officers going ashore

Thanks for the gift

Welcome to Bergen

The crew of HMS Valorious marching through the Norwegian town of Kristiansand

Chapter 55

So ended yet another bloody war, the end of an era, another passage in history. The end too of a class of warship that was the pride of the British Fleet. Yes the old V&Ws made us proud, and the men of Fairfields, Alex Stephens, Yarrow, John Brown's, Wm, Denny's, Beardmore's, Thornycroft's, Cammell Laird's, J.S. White's Swan Hunter, Doxford, Scotts, who built them, should also be proud of their part in producing the finest ocean going destroyer ever to be built.
Scrap iron was at a premium, it seemed that the breakers could not get hold of them quick enough. Soon they were all dismantled and broken up. The last to survive was the **Valentine** who had been beached in 1940 off the coast of Belgium. She was broken up in 1953.

The last farewell

There she lay, so still and cold
Of her many a story could be told.
Now she was naked as she was born,
All alone and looking so forlorn.
Throughout her life she had many men
Some went back to her again and again

Only a few she did not please
Most men took her with ease.
At times she was not so loving,
But her men were all forgiving
Throwing herself about, left to right,
They still loved her as well the might
She was quiet as I stroked her

Feeling her body, so cold and bare,
Lovingly my hands did caress,
With feeling and tenderness
As touching her I sensed vibrations,
Bringing back old sensation,
They came from deep inside
As if she were a young bride.

I recalled the last time we met
She was the one you could not forget

She still looked good though not so young
And her praises were still being sung.
It was sad to see her now, broken and bent,
As to the graveyard she slowly went.
I was glad I was able to make this trip,
To bid farewell to my very first ship

A SEQUEL

This is an account of the unveiling of a memorial to the British Forces contribution to the Norwegian campaign of 1940 A campaign made famous by two battles on the ninth and thirteenth of April in which a posthumous V.C. was won and the Germans suffered the loss of ten destroyers. Rather less is known of the war of attrition that continued for another two months until the evacuation on the tenth of June.
German air superiority coupled with twenyfour hours of daylight, the close proximity of newly acquired airfields, negated the supremacy of the Royal Navy, and precipitated round the clock bombing.
Ships with antiaircraft capability, notably the recent converted 'C' class cruisers were subjected to unprecedented attack, their guns being fired to destruction by exhausted crews.
Nevertheless Narvik was captured if only briefly until evacuation became necessary when the low countries were overrun. Two thousand five hundred, mainly British sailors remain forever within the Arctic Circle.
Our first visit to the magnificent North Norway fjords was April 1940. Sixty-three years later Narvik was revisited when the Mayor, Olaf Sigurd Alstad (successor to the renowned Theodor Brock) and the Royal Norwegian Navy, invited British veterans to attend the unveiling.
We had an interesting meeting with the Press, and while answering questions from the reporters accidentally rediscovered where our ships had met. During the first attempt to take Narvik on the twenty-fourth of April, Colin Orton of HMS Warspite, rangefinder recall helping to send over one hundred and fifty fifteen inch projectiles; Peter Taylor HMS **Vindictive**, from his silent pom pom watched them pass overhead, but was not counting them. Dan Jones HMS Effingham was also in the cavalcade. **Vindictive** then detached, went into Bogen to pick up waiting Irish Guards from an armada of

commandeered Puffers (one cylinder fishing boats) bobbing around like corks in a rising gale, who came aboard via scrambling nets? All six foot six of Cecil, Roy Hughes (Irish Guards) A blizzard intervened, and the bombardment was abandoned. Cecil Roy is the last remaining survivor of the bombed troopship Chroby. He became a prisoner of war and was sent to Auschwitz.
Off Bjerkvik on the 13th May in Hewrjangs fjord, HMS Effingham carried the new military Commander General Auchinleck and the French Commander-in-Chief Bethouart. **Vindictive** carried Colonel Magrin Vernere commanding the Foreign Legion and his staff, also Piere Lapie, scribe and author of 'With the Foreign Legion in Norway' disembarking cut throat Legionnaires in the first opposed landing of the war. The Squadron was lying very close to the land and Dan remembers recalls seeing a little girl being held by a man with a white flag, a sight he has never forgotten. The interviewing reporter then made enquiries and we learned that the little girl whose name is Oddney Melby is now sixty seven and is touched by Dan's memories. At the time she was a little over three years old. Fifteen days later Narvik was retaken by Norwegian, British, French, and Polish forces. On the 17th May, with the South Wales Borderers embarked HMS Effingham struck rocks at twenty knots and had to be sunk. At Harstad, Allied base in the335 Lofoten Islands, **Vindictive**, after towing the crippled Tribal class destroyer HMS Eskimo, from Skelfiord, (Cripple Creek) to Baroy, both ships to continuous bombing, became A.A guard ships for some sixteen days and notched up a total of ninety-nine direct high, low, and dive bombing attacks, sustaining one minor shrapnel casualty and damage to funnel, crane, mainmast shrouds and motor cutter. When the campaign ended on the 6th June all six HA gun barrels had to be replaced on their return to Greenock.

P.J. Taylor

HMS **Vindictive**

The Fate of the V&Ws

Valentine By Air attack. 1940
Valorous *
Vanessa *
Vanity *
Vanoc *
Vanquisher *
Vansittart *
Vega *
Velox *
Vendetta *
Venitia Mined 1940
Venomous *
Verdun *
Verity *
Versatile *
Vesper *
Veteran Torpedoed 1942
Viceroy *
Vidette *
Vimiera Mined 1942
Vimy *
Viscount *
Vivacious *
Vivien *
Volunteer *
Vortigern Torpedoed 1942
Voyager Air Attack 1942

Wakeful Torpedoed 1940
Walker *
Walpole Mined 1945
Wallace *
Wanderer *
Warwick Torpedoed 1944
Watchman *
Waterhen Air Attack 1941
Westcott *
Wessex Air Attack 1940
Westminster *
Whirlwind Torpedoed 1940
Whitehall *
Whitley Air Attack 1940
Whitshed *
Wild Swan Air Attack 1942
Winchelsea *
Winchester *
Windsor *
Wishart *
Witch *
Witherington *
Wivern *
Wolsey *
Wolfhound *
Wolverine *
Woolston *
Worcester Mined 1943
Wren Air Attack 1942
Wrestler Mined 1942
Wryneck Air Attack 1941

All marked thus * were scrapped.

Lord Louis Mountbatten
giving his farewell speech to the crew of HMS Centaur on his retirement Malta 1955

Chapter 56

During October 2001 a commemoration ceremony was held at the Royal Naval College Greenwich.
After a service In the Royal Naval Chapel, those present proceeded to the beautiful Painted Hall where tablets were unveiled to the memory of twenty one American Citizens who had come over to this country between 1939 and until the United States entered the war and volunteered for the RNVR and lost their live whilst serving on British ships, Members of their families and many dignitaries from the USA and this country were in attendance.
Two years later it was discovered that there were two more American citizens who lost their lives whilst serving as officers aboard the ill fated HMS Veteran that was torpedoed and sunk on 26th September 1942 whilst escorting convoy "Maniac" R.B.1, with a total loss of life.
On 22nd June 2004 another ceremony was held at the Royal Naval College Greenwich to add their names to those already there.
The Brother of Surgeon Lieutenant Francis Mason Hayes, the Veteran's Doctor, travelled with his family to be at the ceremony.
After the service and dedication, a copy of the book "Convoy Maniac" was presented to the members of the family of Lieutenant's Haye's Brother, by the Chairman of The V&W Destroyer Association on behalf of the author Jim Reed, who was unable to attend due to poor health.

This book is dedicated to all those who served on the V&W destroyers of 1917-1945 particularly my shipmates of H.M.S Westcott with whom I had the honour to serve.

Appreciations

My Sincere thanks to:-

The Imperial War Museum.
for the use of photographs.

Capt.; B. de Courcey-Ireland & Family
For allowing me to use copy from his book "A Naval Life"

Rear Admiral C.C. Anderson for use of copy from his book
"Seagulls in my Belfry"

Jim Reed for copy from his book "Convoy Maniac" RB!

Dr David Jackson for copy from his book "One Ship One Company"

To the three survivors from the SS Induna for their stories of survival in the Arctic against all odds

To all those V&W shipmates who have contributed to this book.

To my wife Viv for her patience.

And to Carl Shilleto who encouraged me to write it in the first place.

C.W. Fairweather